Holdi

"I Sued the Mafia and Lived to Tell About It"

(THE STORY OF SUNDANCE DANE & KERRI JAMES)

To Our friends
Andy & Karen

who have treated us
to so many wonderful

Holiday get togethers
& feasts!

Hope you enjoy —
With Love   — Doug
*   & Kerri too*

A True Story
By

Doug Dane Fenske

Strategic Book Group

Strategic Book Group
P.O. Box 333
Durham CT 06422
www.StrategicBookClub.com

ISBN: 978-1-60911-328-5

Typography and page composition by J. K. Eckert & Company, Inc.

Printed in the United States of America

I dedicate this book to my best friend, and the love of my life, my wife Kerri.

Contents

Acknowledgments

This is a true account of my life story. Many of the names of individuals and companies have been changed to protect the innocent (myself included), and to avoid possible repercussions (legal and life-threatening) from (purportedly) mafia organizations.

I thank all of my family, and all of my friends who have contributed to the writing of this book, by being part of my life story (in addition to personal assistance at times), but most of all, I thank my best friend, my life partner, and the love of my life, my wife Kerri.

Author Doug Dane Fenske resides in Santa Barbara, CA, with his wife, Kerri James-Fenske.

Doug and Kerri in high school.

Introduction

Holding On is a true story, a love story, including an internal voice, which haunted me from young adulthood, taking me down a long and winding path, with my greatest journey finally leading me back "home," to a first love. It begins in a time that no longer exists, when life was slower and simpler, something I think many people unknowingly long for today. It contains the struggles of building a family business from scratch, and the battle against an ever growing metropolis, and the unscrupulous actions of a county government, so threatened by private enterprise that it must eliminate its competition (to guarantee success of it's $100 million project), in concert with the state regulatory agency, and two ruthlessly competitive mega (purportedly mafia) corporations. Our story began in a time when who you were, your word, and what you stood for were important, and meant something, and they can't stop being important today! Any society is only as good as the actions of its people! It's just that we've learned to ignore it!

I was born (named Howard Douglas Dane Fenske, always called Doug) and raised on a dairy and beef cattle farm in the mid-west, the only son of an ex-professional heavyweight boxer (with a nearly perfect record), whose shoes I tried to fill, and whose admiration I always strived to gain. I began my education in a one-room country school, separated from the encroaching city, only by the Grand River, which surrounded our farm, and the uniquely rural "Riverbend" area we lived in. "Sugarbabe," a sturdy Welsh with saddle, was my transportation to and from school, until my younger sisters came along, and then she pulled us to school on a sulky in the fall and spring, and a sleigh in the winter.

It wasn't a perfect childhood, but it was a good childhood. The Riverbend boys and I freely roamed those thousands of acres between us, living lives of the "Huck Fin" adventures we had read about, which in our minds could not have been more ideal. My parents were decent, honest, hard-working people, who loved my four sisters and me, and did the best they could. Whatever mistakes they made parenting us were small. I respect them for the wonderful life they provided us, and I will always love them with all my heart!

My parents stopped farming, and started excavating, and selling aggregates from our farm while I was still in grade school. My first endeavor at making money was raising chickens for eggs, which I sold mostly to relatives, neighbors, and passers-by, who saw my hand-painted sign at the end of our gravel road. Before I reached my teens, I started into the farming business, raising crops and beef cattle, first on our farm, then later on leased ground as well, but always I continued to work for my parents, helping in the family business.

There was a horrific fire on our farm, during the winter of my senior year in high school, which changed our lives. Following the fire, which destroyed our farm shop building, and nearly all the equipment we owned, uninsured, my parents and I started from almost nothing, to build a successful recycling and solid waste landfill business (Fenske Enterprises), which won state and local awards. I started boxing in high school, then attended Michigan State University, where I continued to box, while coming home every weekend, staying intricately involved in the family business.

While in pursuit of my MSU Civil Engineering degree, in 1968 (boxing under the name Doug "Sundance" Dane), I won the coveted "Golden Glove Award," in West Michigan titled, "Boxing's Heisman Trophy." However, a year later, during spring break 1969, just prior to heading out to Daytona Beach, Florida with some buddies, I suffered a devastating accident at home on the farm. As I was hurriedly packing, my father convinced me to take one quick look at a design change he had made, on a heavy equipment invention we had been working on. That decision cost me the end of my right foot. I missed that spring term, lost my "2S" student deferment from the draft, and was given a "1A" (first draft eligible) classification, in spite of my injury. Though doctors told me that I would always walk with a limp, and I would never run or box again, I faced draft induction, and going to Viet Nam.

After graduating from Michigan State, while working as "Operations Manager" for Fenske Enterprises, I became restless. Young, driven, and naive enough to be fearless, I wasn't satisfied just running the family business. I ventured out developing enterprises of my own, including the organics land application business, and the (known to be) mafia controlled, dangerously competitive, hazardous waste land-fill business. One of the largest solid and hazardous waste disposal companies in the world then took actions against my business, for which I sued them. My life was threatened. The ensuing litigation, which lasted four and a half years, left me in continual fear for my life, and was undoubtedly the cause of unforeseen repercussions in years to come.

Lifelong sibling rivalry and family jealousies then came into play, and things became personal. When my parents refused to meet my older sister's unreasonable demands for more control in the family business, my sister resigned and started her own business, in competition with ours. She then went on the attack, with a lawsuit of allegations against my parents, my father specifically. My father's health soon began to decline, from which he never recovered. Curiously, not long after my politically connected sister quit, Fenske Enterprises started having environmental permitting problems. My parents retired while Fenske Enterprises was in the middle of the permitting difficulties, and believing that I could turn things around, I purchased the business from them, and incorporated as FEI. I could not begin to imagine the hurdles that lie ahead.

However, a rainbow will often emerge, through some of the most severe storms. While Fenske Enterprises was going through its permitting struggles, my ten-year marriage, which had been failing for a number of years, came to end. Simultaneously, the same internal "voice thought," which had told me (ever since I was a young man), "You already met who you're was supposed to be with," started again. Less than a year later, I became reacquainted with a lost love, whom I hadn't seen in twenty years!

Feeling inspired, shortly after we re-met, I started to make a comeback in boxing. I refused to heed the doctors' words regarding my foot injury, as I strongly believe most any handicap, including age, has only as much power over us as we give it. In Grand Rapids, Michigan, in 1989, at forty years of age, twenty-one years after the first one, I won the "Golden Glove Award" again, and became the only boxer in history to win it twice! I now have won the Southern California Golden Gloves championship several times, and at age sixty-one, I continue to box, with a permanent "Age-Discrimination Court Order" (the only one in the nation), which allows me to do so. Through all of life's pain and struggles, boxing has helped somehow, to keep me sane.

As a result of politics, our business was forcibly closed. We continued to battle for over ten years, trying to right the wrong we had suffered, and reestablish FEI. With the assistance of the Governor's office, I was able to obtain a signed document from the state regulatory agency, admitting that the Fenske Enterprises facility should not have been closed, and "could reopen, if consistent with the County Plan." This became our "Catch 22." Contrary to state law, which requires counties to include "existing facilities," the County removed our "existing facility" from the "County Solid Waste Plan." When I attempted to have our "existing facility" put back into the plan, I was thrown in jail!

In 2001, I started to write this book, telling our story, just now complete, December 2010.

1

Humble Beginnings

I was born (named Howard Douglas Dane Fenske, *always called Doug*) December 16, 1948, on a cold wintry day in Grand Rapids, Michigan, the second child of five (and only boy) of Howard Dane Fenske, and Leona Marie Schulz. I came along two weeks late, and my dad had to rush my mother to the hospital while Christmas shopping.

My mother had convinced my father to quit his professional boxing career, leave Detroit, where they had met, and move to the Grand Rapids area, where my father was born and raised. My mother didn't like boxing from the time they met, but agreed to stand behind my father, provided my father agreed to quit the profession, once he suffered a loss. Even though he had an impressive record, and his first and only loss was only one fight short of a shot at the world heavyweight title (then held by Joe Louis), my father made good on his promise.

My father was born (the 2nd of three boys), and raised on a small dairy farm, just west of Grand Rapids, with a tough father (Reinhart Fenske), who didn't believe in "sparing the rod," and mother Anna Dane. When my father decided to box professionally, he moved to Detroit, which he and his chosen trainer, Julius Piazza, thought would provide better opportunities. My father had an outstanding, undefeated record as an amateur boxer, and held two consecutive "Golden Gloves" state heavy-weight titles, when he was matched up against "Diamond Belt" heavy-weight boxing champion Julius Piazza.

Detroit had formed the Diamond Belt tournament some years earlier, after Detroit had been kicked out of the Michigan Golden Gloves. Reputedly, in previous years, there had been continual fights in the crowd (including some knifings), whenever a Detroit boxer was in the ring, and eventually Detroit was out. Julius Piazza had held the Diamond Belt heavyweight title for a couple of years, when he and my father met. After my father defeated him, Julius professed that my father was the best boxer he had ever encountered, and proposed that my father turn professional, and Julius would manage him. Both men were young (early twenties), and the match was made.

My father was a good professional boxer (tagged "The Grand Rapids Plow Boy"), and Julius was a good manager. Of Italian decent, Julius had many connections in the pugilist world, and my father's professional boxing career took off. By the time my father suffered his first and only loss as a pro, in a match with Lou Nova (in Madison Square Garden), he was ranked with the top ten heavyweights in the world. The winner of his match with Lou Nova was scheduled to take on Joe Louis in a World Heavy-Weight Championship bout.

My father was a small heavyweight (5′ 11″, 184 pounds), and would have been better matched in the light heavyweight division, but in the nineteen forties, the only significant money was in the heavyweight division. Nova was a big man for heavyweights in those days (6′ 2″, 225 pounds), and my father, who won most of his fights by knockout, was unable to put Nova down. My father was fighting a case of strep throat at the time he met with Nova, which undoubtedly hurt him, but regardless, Piazza was unable to convince my father to postpone his bout, and my father's loss put him in the position of making a decision between boxing, and a relationship with my mother. Fortunately for my sisters and I, he chose my mother.

My mother was born and raised on a vegetable and crop farm near Pigeon, Michigan, the fourth of seven children. Pigeon was a tiny rural town (still is), near the top of the thumb of Michigan, and when my mother graduated from high school (class of six), she moved to Detroit, and began to pursue a career working for the Dodge (automobile) estate. She and her sister (my Aunt Louise), and a friend rented a room in the same apartment complex as my father, and before long she and my father met, and started dating. My mother professes to everyone that she has continuously hated boxing (although I could always tell that she *secretly* admired my father for doing so), and not long after their relationship began, she started to pressure my father to quit boxing. At the time of his loss to Nova, my father was undefeated, with over thirty victories, the vast majority by knockout, and I'm sure that it was a tough decision; however he kept his word, and retired from boxing.

A short time later, my parents were wed in Pigeon, moved to Grand Rapids, and soon (with money my father had saved from boxing) bought the 160-acre dairy and beef cattle farm, that I and my four sisters were born and raised on, just five miles from my father's homestead farm, where my grandmother still resided. Our farm was at the south end of Kenowa Ave, a gravel road, which is the boundary line between Kent and Ottawa counties (hence the name), and there were no nearby neighbors with children for us to play with. It was beautiful farm, with a large white house (featuring a pillared front porch), and a large two story white barn, on a magnificent setting, at the "dead-end" of tree-lined Kenowa, which a friend years later dubbed, "The Avenue Of Trees." Kenowa with its huge oaks, and maples on either side of

Mom and Dad's wedding in Pigeon, Michigan.

The farmhouse.

the road, with branches that nearly touched at the middle, formed the appearance of a tree-leaf tunnel, as you drove down the road.

Before long, my father, who loved machinery, purchased a hay baler (one of the first in the area), along with a combine, and expanded to custom hay and straw baling, and grain-combining for other farms. With some of the extra money from custom farm work, my parents increased the farm size to 262 acres a few years later, when they bought the "Morry" farm, at the South end of Kenowa, right across from ours, and some adjacent vacant acreage on the north side of our farm. They bought the entire Morry farm (which had a small barn on it), with the exception of the Morry house, and two acres. The Morry's were older, and their children were grown and had left home, by the time Karen and I were born, or old enough to play with neighbor kids.

When my parents bought our farm, there was a second house on the property, which they eventually rented to a family with two small boys, Jacky and Paul, who became playmates for my sister Karen, and I. I was very sad when they moved out, and my parents sold the house, which was moved to a new location, 1 1/2 miles up Kenowa Ave. Not long after Jacky and Paul moved out, my sister Karen (18 months older than I) started school, and I was very upset. When we dropped Karen off for her first day, I cried and begged my mother to let me stay at Riverbend, a one-room school (grades k–12) on Kenowa Ave, two miles north of our farm. It was actually two years later before I could start school (because of my birth date). My mother always told me, if I hadn't come into the world two weeks late, I could have started school a year sooner. The rule at the time was that children could start school at 4 years of age, provided they turned 5 by December 2. It wasn't that I knew I would love school, in fact once I did start school, I found that I would far rather be home on the farm. It just wasn't fair that my older sister got to do something that I didn't, and the days were pretty long and lonely, until she came home. I had a puppy to play with, and lots of room to romp, but I learned to watch the kitchen clock for Karen's return.

One day when I was bored (that first September) I decided to walk to Grandma Fenske's house. I told Mother (hanging clothes out to dry in the back yard) where I was going, but she didn't take me seriously, and she didn't have a clue that I knew how to get there. Grandma lived about five miles from our farm, and even though it was fairly safe on all country roads, it was a big challenge for short 3 1/2 year

Karen and Doug.

Doug, as a toddler, playing with Sparky.

Doug, Karen, Jacky and Paul Scott.

old legs. I actually made it about 3/4 of the way there, and I had made two correct left turns before being discovered. I was on the home stretch, only a mile or so from Grandma's house, when a family friend who was driving by spotted me, and with the promise of a cold soda, talked me (and my beet-red cheeks, *it was near 90 degrees that day*), into riding back home with him.

Mother was getting quite worried by the time we arrived back at the farm, but this was 1952, and times were different. Child abduction was almost unheard of. In fact, on one previous occasion, Mother had asked a grocery store parking lot attendant to keep an eye on Karen and I, while she dashed into the store and picked up a couple of items. The attendant responded, "Lady, **nobody** wants your **kids**; everybody's got too many of their **own!**" Mother laughingly repeated the attendant's words numerous times, and there was probably truth in his statement, however, Mother did keep a closer eye on me, after my adventurous, attempted hike to Grandma's house.

Karen and I played well together, at least from my perspective, considering my alternatives, and I always had plenty of things planned, for when she did return from school. My father placed a 20 ft. by 30 ft. log building (moved from another location), on the same site on the farm where the second house had been, not too long after it had been removed. This gave Karen and I a place to play out of my mother's hair. My father stretched a cable from the peak of the log building (referred to as the "playhouse," *years later the "bunkhouse"*), at a gradual angle down, 200 ft. laterally over to a tree, next to the farmhouse we lived in. He hung a tire, attached by chain, to a pulley on this cable, which provided Karen and I (and any visiting playmates, or cousins) with hours of entertainment, whenever we wanted to take a fast ride.

My aunt Louise, and later my uncle Hank (both siblings of my mother) each lived with us for a few years, and seemed like older siblings to me. I tagged along behind my uncle Hank (twenty years my senior) like a big brother. I'm sure it drove him somewhat nuts (he would frequently state, "Douglas, you're a **bum**"), but he didn't seem to mind, and it was easy for him to get away if he wanted to. Uncle Hank eventually started a dairy route, and in my preschool years, I sometimes accompanied him in his panel truck delivering milk, which was bottled by hand right on our farm.

I was afraid of my father early on. I would hold on to my mother's skirt when he came home from the fields. Having been a professional

Mom, Dad, Karen, and Doug in Florida.

boxer, he was a rugged looking guy, and he had some rough habits. From my first haircut on (in my early years), I was scared to death of the barbershop, and I cried whenever it was time to get a haircut. Mother thought it was because I was a "sissy" about having my hair cut, but actually it was because Elmer Neinhite, who had been a high school classmate (and football teammate) of my father, owned the barbershop. Each time my father and I paid a visit to the barbershop, the two of them would immediately take to wrestling each other, sometimes tumbling out of the door into the snow bank, while all others cheered them on. This was very traumatic to a young child, who had no idea that something, which seemed like a genuine fight, was all in fun.

Even though I know he loved me, some of my father's habits were harsh, like banging his forehead into mine, or smacking his hand down hard on my thigh, if I fell asleep next to him. Many times (as a toddler or small boy) I was startled awake by such a smack, when I would fall asleep on the seat of a truck, while riding with my father. Mother could not understand why I was always so resistant to going with him, and labeled me to others as a "mama's-boy."

Actually, from my first memories on, I felt that I was **too** tender for this world. I'm not sure that I'm any different today (*just more proficient at masking my feelings*). I vividly recall coming home from kindergarten sobbing, because a classmate had told me that I was ugly, and after studying my reflection in a mirror, I believed him. When I was a young boy, my entire evening at a fair in Grandville was ruined once, when a Ferris wheel rides keeper yelled at me.

Mother often told me that I was *too sensitive,* and advised me to repeat to myself, whenever I could not fight back the tears, "Sticks and stones can break my bones, but words will never hurt me." I memorized that statement, and I repeated it to myself continually, but it didn't seem to help much.

In the early 1950's while digging fence post-holes, my father discovered that there was gravel on our farm. My parents soon began another business of excavating, trucking, and selling gravel (crushed on shares), along with sand (discovered elsewhere on the farm), and topsoil, which was plentiful (as much as 15 ft. deep) on the banks of the Grand River, which bordered the entire south side of our farm, for over a mile. Michigan is a glacial state, and in the last "Ice Age" the entire state was covered with massive (1 mile thick) glaciers, which traversed from North to South across the entire state, mixing soil types immensely. Clay, sand, gravel, and topsoil were all plentiful on the farm, and my father initially purchased a heavily used, single axle '49 Ford dump-truck, to truck soils with. I passed many hours bouncing along with him, on the worn-out, stiff spring seat of that old truck, delivering aggregates.

My father was very mechanical, and quite inventive. Although he had little money to purchase equipment etc., he did well. He built our first two front-end loaders (which he used for excavating, and loading soil into trucks) out of old truck frames, truck rear drive axles, combine engines, and steel buckets (which he fabricated entirely out of flat steel) activated by hydraulic cylinders. My uncle Hank, and a couple of neighboring farm boys (Ed and Glenn Cass) were some of my parent's first employees. Oh the memories I have of some **fast, wild** rides on those homemade loaders, with those young guys (in their late teens, or early twenties) at the wheel!

I'm sure that my mother (much more in tune with caution than my father) voiced numerous objections, to no avail. When Mother wasn't present, such as when Dad and I picked up Karen from school in a dump truck, anything was possible. I can remember my father raising the dump box to full height (with my sister Karen and I in it, begging him to), as he brought us home from Riverbend School, down bumpy gravel Kenowa Ave. As he did, Karen and I would cling by our fingertips to the dump box apron (which protected the truck cab), and squeal with pleasure or fright, depending on how long we were hanging on (with legs and feet dangling). I recall being very scared, and screaming that I couldn't hold on any longer. I shudder to think what could have happened, if one of us had lost our grip. It not only was a long fall to the hard gravel road, which was moving fairly fast under us, but the several hundred pound steel tailgate below us, was banging shut from the rough road. There was plenty of motivation to maintain your grip, long after what seemed humanly possible for a little kid. In part it was the era, so I don't want to make my father out to be senseless or foolish, and I know that we begged to ride in the box of the dump truck, but he did sometimes use poor judgment, creating dangerous situations, as later on in my teens I **learned** all too well.

My father's industriousness, and my mother's thriftiness (she did all the bookkeeping, invoicing, payroll, etc.) helped them to do quite well, and in 1953 they purchased a brand new Kaiser Manhattan automobile. That winter we made a trip to visit my mother's Aunt Mary, on her ranch in northern California, that I will never forget. I hadn't started school yet, and my sister Karen was in the first grade (six years old), so my parents requested time off for her. I was **so** excited to go to **California**! We had our first television by this time, which resembled a tall nightstand, with an oval screen. There were only three stations, which ran from about 8 or 9 AM, until 9 or 10 PM. The rest of the time the TV screen displayed a test pattern (resembling a target, with a steady hum in the background), which Karen and I watched a lot, waiting for something to come on. I had seen enough TV to fall in love with cowboys (westerns were prevalent in those days), and I had been told that California was the place where all the cowboys on TV were located, so there was **no** place I wanted to be more than **that**!

California was a long way to travel in those days, and constantly on our trip (which took about 10 to 12 days), I wore a cowboy outfit, which Santa Claus had given me that Christmas. My mother's parents made the trip with us, and 8 hours per day (including meal stops) was about the maximum, in a 1953 Kaiser (top speed 55 mph), with four adults, and two little kids. State after state, California never seemed to happen. Each time we crossed a state line, the six of us would sing in unison, good-by to one state, and hello to the next, such as "Good-by Arkansas, Hello Oklahoma." Since we left in early January, we took a southern route to avoid snowstorms.

Time seemed to drag, especially for an anxious five year old, plus I was **positive** I'd see Roy Rogers, and the Lone Ranger, as soon as we crossed the California state line. We traveled west on old "Route 66," which a few years later became the theme for a popular TV show (by

California trip in the 1953 Kaiser. Doug in cowboy outfit.

the same name), which I never missed. We also made stops to site see (Grand Canyon, etc.), and take pictures.

I clearly recall the adults excitement, at a couple of impressed pedestrians pointing out our license plate, as they crossed in front of us at a stop light, in a small town, shortly after we had arrived in California. We crossed into California near Needles, and I was excruciatingly *shocked,* at seeing nothing but the same desert terrain that we had been traveling through in Arizona, with **no cowboys**! I staunchly protested the absence of cowboys, *immediately* when we crossed the state line! I **just** wanted to be with the **cowboys**! I **knew** that **I** was a **cowboy**, and that love never left me, directing my life in years to come.

California was **beautiful**! I loved the palms, and the beaches. We drove through Hollywood, and a place called "China Town," and eventually arrived at my Great Aunt Mary's ranch, bordering the Sierra Nevada Mountains, north of San Francisco. It was a cattle ranch with **coyotes** always present, whose yipping and howling we listened to every night! The ranch was pretty wild, and they lost some cattle to mountain lions every year. I **loved** it there, and I cried when we had to leave, but I held on to the memories, and the love of California.

2

The Family Grows

When I was five and a half, shortly before I was to start school (August 1, 1954), my second sister (Janice) was born. My sister Karen and I weren't allowed to visit her or my mother in the hospital, but we accompanied my father to pick them up and bring them home. I had never seen a little newborn baby so closely, or at least I had never paid so much attention to one before. I studied her intently as we traveled home, and I marveled at how much the little specs on her nose resembled those on a pear. I reached over to her (resting peacefully in my mother's arms), and gave her nose a little squeeze, to see if it felt like a pear. Jan immediately began to **wail**, at a volume of which I had no idea that newborn babies were capable.

Needless to say, I was promptly accused of pinching her, and instantly the recipient of a smack in penance. This was the first of a number of well-learned (and *sometimes* deserved) lessons, on the repercussions of being the cause of tears, shed by my younger sisters.

Fifteen months after Janice, my sister Patty came into the world, and twenty months after her, my sister Linda was born. As the years went by, this became quite a load for my father to carry up the two flights of stairs to bed each night, but he was strong, and at our coaxing he often made the trip with all five of us on board. Mom and Dad loved us all dearly, and did the very best they could, devoting their lives to their family.

Mom, Dad, Karen, and Doug, with newborn Janice.

Karen, Janice, Granma Fenske, and Doug. 1953 Kaiser in background.

I loved all of my sisters very much, but we clearly had different interests, and on numerous occasions, I begged my mother to have a brother for me. Years later, my mother admitted to losing a baby, in the five-and-a-half year gap, between my sister Jan and myself, which could have been my brother. Mother explained that she had chased our cattle out of a cornfield next to the farmhouse while pregnant, and a fall resulted in a miscarriage. It was too early to determine the sex of the fetus, but Mother claimed that the miscarriage had disrupted her plan of having six children, which was a somewhat ambitious aim, for one who had not experienced maternity until 30 years of age, especially unusual in the 1940's.

From time to time, I would get into trouble (actually quite frequently) for teasing my younger sisters, whom I christened the "Three Little Pigs." My antics prompted my four sisters to form a "We Hate Boys" club (sponsored by Karen), which in my parent's absence (fortunately a relatively rare occurrence), often resulted in me being locked out of the house. Needless to say, I was the "odd man out," not offered a membership, and I endured a number of rainy afternoons, and evenings in the barn (staying dry), at the **discretion** of that club!

My sisters stuck together, and I learned the meaning of, "Yours Is The **Broken One**," which I heard the four of them sing out in unison

Janice, Karen, Mom, baby Patty, and Doug.

The "Three Little Pigs"—Patty, Linda, and Janice. Also, Karen and Doug.

numerous times. On an Easter morning, if five paddles with a ball on a rubber string were passed out, I knew enough to reach for the one with the snapped line. When five apples were set out in a dish, I just saved time and reached for the one with the bruise, knowing that I was up against a stacked deck, and that is the one I would wind up with anyway. Most of the time I didn't care, and I learned how to eat around rotten spots, and tie a knot in a rubber band, no problem. The little ones usually left part of their apple, and grew tired and left their paddle lay in a short time anyway.

I admittedly would tease my little sisters to tears at times, however they quickly learned that tears brought about abrupt retaliation, and they became quite proficient at turning on howls of anguish, coercing my mother, or my older sister (my own **tormentor**, *who was all to willing to assist*), to intervene. I myself became quite adept at pleading with my younger sisters not to cry (expressing to them the value in "being tough"), whenever I realized that I had pushed the teasing envelop a bit too far. As time went by unfortunately, the "Three Little Pigs" tolerance level for my teasing, diminished to the point of non-existence, and they would turn on shrieks of distress instantly when I entered a room, which left me walking on eggshells. Luckily, after I had suffered various unwarranted chastisements, my mother saw through their antics, and the situation mediated itself.

At one point in time, sick of my pleading that she have one more child (a boy), my mother suggested that I make a brother out of one of my younger sisters, and start doing things together with her. I took Mother's suggestion seriously, and determined that my next younger sister (Janice), would from that day on, be my younger brother. Jan (scarcely five at the time) went along with the plan, and I announced such, as Jan and I rode Sugarbabe (a Welsh pony that I received as a 10th birthday present) into the farmyard of the Tanner boys. The Tanner boys (Dan and his younger brother Ken), friends from school, lived on an apple/dairy farm on Burton St., a gravel road that crossed Kenowa Ave, a mile and a half north of our farm. Dan Tanner, only two weeks younger than I, over time became my lifelong best friend.

The plan was short lived however, because Jan had little interest in snaps and snails, and puppy dog tails (as the saying goes), and had this unacceptable fascination with dolls and such, which was completely boring to the Tanner boys and myself. After not much more than one attempted afternoon at converting Jan into a younger brother to befriend me, Jan was back to playing house, with the other members of the "Little Pig Threesome," and I was back to matters of **substance**, like catching frogs, and snapping turtles!

Doug (left). Dan Tanner (right).

3

Sugarbabe

The Wills farm, which bordered Kenowa about midway between Riverbend School and the Tanner farm, had a mean black German shepherd named "Master," whose big teeth often left their mark on the butt of the slowest runner, on our trudge home from school. Master (who had a clock in his head) would lie patiently waiting for us (Dan, Ken Tanner and me) to pass each day when school let out, with his head on his paws, on top of the bank between the Will's front yard and Kenowa Ave. He was never there in the morning (probably in the barn with Mr. Wills, for chores), however he rarely was absent in the afternoon. When we reached the top of the hill on Kenowa (near the Will's driveway), which dropped gently for a hundred yards toward home, we would see Master slowly rise to his feet, in preparation for the chase. We would all tense up, fill our lungs, and take off when one of us yelled **GO**! The slowest runner frequently received the painful nip, but Master was an "equal opportunity pursuer," and from time to time, each of us was the recipient, regardless of our status in the race.

When I turned nine, I received a bicycle for my birthday. I had learned to ride, practicing with the Tanner boys on their bikes, and I rode my new Schwinn to school (and to the Tanner farm), whenever weather permitted. The Tanner boys (whose worn bikes were not reliable enough to make the trip to Riverbend) and I decided that my new Schwinn would help us all to avoid Master. Dan rode up on the handlebars, and Ken on a metal bracket we mounted over the rear wheel, and I peddled with all my might, as we reached the crest of the Will's hill.

Doug with his new bicycle.

We all cheered with glee, when we realized that Master could no longer catch us, as we watched him eat our dust on our first trip home.

However, we soon became a little too jubilant to pay attention to details. After enjoying our newfound route of escape for little more than a week, on a fast trip down the Will's hill, we suddenly found ourselves flying through the air, and sliding and rolling painfully on the gravel roadbed. When we came to a stop, after surveying our numerous scrapes and bruises (through tears), we discovered a whole fist full of broken spokes on the front wheel. Dan's foot had become entwined in the front spokes, and had locked up the front wheel, which had immediately catapulted us.

As the dust settled and our pains eased, we became aware of the fact that Master had become disinterested, and left. We learned that day, that it was the chase he was interested in, and if we were just brave enough to face his barks and snarls (as we learned to be) and not run, he would quickly become bored and leave. We pushed my bike to the Tanner farm, and hammered out some dents, to the best of our ability. We found some used spokes in the Tanner workshop, and even though short a few, after spacing out the missing spokes, my bike was useable.

I did not dare tell my parents what had happened, and I explained away the skinned knees and arms, as a school playground accident. I'm sure they noticed the bike dings, and had probably heard what happened, although they never said anything. I continued to ride my bike to school the rest of that year, whenever I could, which unfortunately in Michigan, because of precipitation (rain or snow), often is not possible, but I longed for something more.

For as long as I can recall, I have had a love of horses. Being a Sagittarius (sign, half-man/half-horse), maybe I was born with it. Prior to my 10th birthday, for what seemed like years, I had campaigned for a horse. I taped notes on doors and walls throughout our house, describing how well I would care for and love a horse, if I had one. The entreatment was fruitful, and for my tenth birthday, I received Sugarbabe.

Sugerbabe was a Welsh mare. Welsh are technically a breed of pony, but can be as large as a small horse. Sugarbabe (brown & white) was a large Welsh, and very strong. She had previously been paired with a Welsh stud, on a two-horse pulling team, and when the stud broke a leg in a pulling contest, Sugarbabe (also broke to saddle) was sold off as a pleasure horse.

I was **thrilled** with her, and **so** proud to own her! Sugarbabe gave me a mobility I had not yet known. She made the mile and a half trudge (or laborious bike ride on bumpy gravel) to the Tanner farm, or two miles to school (which included a couple of big hills), a breeze. When school was in session, I saddled her every morning, and rode her to Riverbend Elementary. I was **King Tutt**! I made certain that I trotted Sugarbabe through the schoolyard (for all to see) a number of times, when I first started riding her to school. I would then put her out to graze, or to be stalled, at a farm next door to the school, where my father had arranged for me to keep her. I was in the fourth grade by this time, and Riverbend had expanded from the one-room (k–12) schoolhouse that Karen and I had started in, to a three-room (grades k–6) elementary. The Riverbend school district had been annexed by the small adjoining town to the South, named Grandville, and grades seven and up were bussed into that community. Grandville was separated from the Riverbend area by the Grand River, which started its "bend" where it bordered the south side of our farm.

That was a **great** school year. I **loved** riding Sugarbabe to and from school every day. Sugarbabe helped us boys with a little mischief too, at times. On Halloween, the Tanner boys and I, and some friends, came up with the idea of putting a wagon up on the school roof, as a prank. Six of us snagged an old wooden-wheel wagon from a nearby farm, late on Halloween night, and Sugarbabe helped us tow it back to the school. We climbed a ladder we brought from the Tanner farm, attached a rope-pulley to the school chimney, and with planks for wheel runners, a heavy hay rope, and Sugarbabe's strong legs, we hoisted the wagon up onto the school roof. It was hard to stay tight-lipped the next school day, as everyone gawked, and pondered how anyone got that **heavy** wagon up on the **roof**! It took a **crane** to get it down!

Even though I had to get up early to get Sugarbabe ready, and leave early enough to make the ride to school, I **loved** it. I was always up at the crack of dawn anyway, to help my father milk cows. There were always one or two cows that would not accept a milk machine (a stainless steel vacuum container device, hung by a sling from a cows back), and therefore needed to be milked by hand. It was my job to clean manure from the gutters, and hand milk those couple of cows, while my father milked the others with the milk machines, all before breakfast.

I can remember Mrs. Neinhite, and Mr. Mac (teachers at Riverbend) requiring me to leave my "Little Abner" work-boots (a cartoon hillbilly with huge bubble-toe shoes), outside on the school steps during school hours, because they "smelled like a barn." My father always insisted on that particular brand, and style boots (bought from "Ol' Man Stanton," at Stanton's Shoe Store, in Standale, *a small neighboring town to the North*), because they "didn't wear out." The fact is, they didn't wear out as fast as my feet grew, and even though I pleaded for tennis shoes (to be like other "*popular*" kids), those boots that "never wore out," I believe, are the cause of some crooked toes that I have to this day.

Our family didn't have a lot of money to spare, we "had a lot of mouths to feed" (which I heard frequently), and shoes cost a lot in those days. I do know that my parents could have afforded shoes for me when I needed them. I just don't think that my mother or father paid enough attention, to realize when my feet had outgrown my shoes. It did later bother me that none of my sisters has crooked toes, but then none of them wore "Little Abner" work boots.

I recall trying to straighten my toes, some years later, when I was old enough to realize that my toes were crooked, and self-conscious enough to care what they looked like. When one of my teenage friends asked, "*What happened to your toes,*" as we were walking barefoot near a Lake Michigan beach one summer day, and I replied,

"Nothing, I don't know," he responded with "*Those are **hideous!***"
This was the first time I was aware that my toes were any different
from anyone else, and I was embarrassed. The next day, I tightly taped
Popsicle sticks to either side of each crooked toe, and **vowed** that I
was going to leave them there until my toes grew straight. That plan
ended abruptly that first afternoon, after toes on each foot were bran-
dishing numerous raw blisters. I stated to myself on that day, and
many times to come, "I wish I didn't have these crooked toes," which
thoughts, and words came back to haunt me a few years later.

Whenever I questioned my mother about what happened to my
toes, she replied, "Oh, when you were a little boy, you always insisted
on wearing cowboy boots." This never rang as truth to me though.
First off, even though I remember begging for them, I don't recall
ever having cowboy boots. I remember being told that cowboy boots
wear out too quickly, and "Stanton's Shoe Store" didn't carry them. I
even recall at times, as a young boy, wearing winter rubber boots (in
the heat of the summer), and pretending that they were cowboy boots.
Secondly, cowboy boots have pointed toes, and would not have
affected my toes in the same way. I am certain those "Little Abner"
work boots that never wore out, are the cause of my crooked toes.

Traveling to and from Riverbend school the following two years
wasn't as much fun for me, because my next two younger sisters (Janice and Patty) started school. This required me to hitch up the sulky (a

Patty and Janice on Riverbend Schools steps, 1961.

single-bench, 2-wheel cart), for Sugarbabe to cart us to and from school. When the winter season (usually Dec.–Mar.) began, and Kenowa Avenue was snow and ice-covered, each morning I harnessed Sugarbabe to an open wood-plank sleigh, with wooden steel-lined runners. I usually sat on a bale of straw on the front of the sleigh, and scattered loose straw on the flat wood planks behind, to cushion the ride for my little sisters, and others like the Tanner boys, who often hitched a ride home after school.

There were times, on less bitter cold days, when we had so many freeload riders after school, that there wasn't enough plank space on the sleigh for everyone, and one or two wound up on Sugarbabe's back. The sleigh was not very large though, and other than the Tanner boys and us, most of the kids lived within a quarter mile of the school, so Sugarbabe's load lightened quickly. Fortunately for Sugarbabe, winters in Michigan are very harsh, and most often my sisters and I had few, if any passengers.

Sugarbabe made the two-mile trudge to Riverbend every morning, and home again each afternoon, sometimes through foot (or more) deep snow. She was very strong, and pulling the sleigh was a breeze for her. Sugarbabe also became our first "snowmobile," and some-times, with one of us on her back, she tugged several of us around the

Sugarbabe pulling sulky, with Janice, Doug, and Patty on the way to Riverbend School.

snow-covered fields, on large inner tubes, pulled by ropes tied to the saddle horn, giving us hours of fun (discussed ahead).

Westerly winds blow across eighty-mile wide Lake Michigan, continually dumping lake effect moisture on the Grand Rapids area, and snow drifts to the eves of buildings, during winters back then were common. With little else to occupy us, most every school recess and lunch hour, nearly all the boys at Riverbend were engaged in snowball fights. The Tanner boys and I made sure that we were always on the same team, and we really watched each other's back, like brothers.

Most often, the older boys in school would team up together against us younger boys, but we learned a system to defend ourselves, when our snow fort was under attack. Dan Tanner, with his long arms that reached halfway to his knees, could really throw well, so we put Dan, "Motorcycle Ikel," "Turd," "Bored Man," and "McGoofin" (all with the best throwing arms), in the front row. Everyone in school, whether they liked it or not (and most did not), had "nicknames," given to them by Dan Tanner, which were either descriptive of the individual, or some variation of their real name. The rest of us, "Fats," "Mildew," "Gitch," "Smoffius," "K-Tan," and myself, "Ouser DuBensky" (I have no idea where Dan came up with that one), would make snowballs, and keep a supply to the front-line. With this battle plan (never running out of snowballs), we were able to fend off most any attack.

The older boys in school were led by a mean "Bully" named "Joe Baldego" who once kept charging, after all on his team had turned back. When our team saw him continue his charge, most everyone ran, because all were afraid of him. That is, everybody except the Tanner boys and myself. Just as he was leaping the snow wall into our fort, Dan Tanner hit him square in the kisser, with a hard packed snowball (supplied by Ken Tanner and I), and Dan yelled out, "How's that one taste, '**Bald Eagle**'?!" "Bald Eagle" (who was older and larger than anyone else at school) was **furious**, and tackled Dan, pounced on him, and started to wash his face in the snow. Ken and I, whom he had expected would run, immediately tackled him, and the three of us overpowered him, and gave him a face washing he will never forget. He waited the rest of the school year, and most of the following year (until he moved away), for an opportunity to retaliate, but he never caught one of us apart from the others, and never again dared to attack us as a group.

Sugarbabe was a strong mare, but she had a little problem first thing each morning, with raising her tail, and gassing me and my two little passengers, whom Mother had so tightly bundled in snowsuits and thick wool garments, that they could barely move. The temperature would frequently dip to below zero degrees Fahrenheit, and if my little sisters fell over while walking, I had to help them to their feet again, because they could not get up on their own. The first elevation of Sugarbabe's tail would bring a volume of complaints from Janice and Patty, because they knew what to expect, and they would immediately exclaim, "Pew Dougie, make her **stop**, it **stinks**!" To this I would reply, as Mother had taught me when I described the problem, "Oh, the only good horse is a fartin' horse, just plug your nose."

The only problem with that suggestion was that Janice and Patty (sandwiched with layers of clothing), could not bend their arms adequately, to reach their own noses, and they often asked me to pinch their nostrils closed for them, until Sugarbabe was done relieving herself. Since it usually took the first quarter mile or more for Sugarbabe to complete this task, it was next to impossible for me to handle the reins, and pinch their noses as well, so I taught them to sit facing one another, and pinch each other's nostrils closed. This worked well, and solved the problem.

When Sugarbabe wasn't consumed with the chore of lugging my sisters and I to and from school, we had great fun with her in the snow. She was so powerful, that she could easily pull several inner tubes at a time, so the Tanner boys and I developed the fun sport of trying to unseat one another. Sugarbabe was so trained at pulling, having been on a contest pulling team, that you had to be careful not to catch a wheel or ski runner, because she would just squat down and pull, until whatever was holding her broke free, or she broke her harnesses. There was **no** stopping her! I once made the mistake of cutting it too tight, as I entered the barn with the sulky, caught a wheel, and Sugarbabe dug in, and brought the barn door in with us. That was the first time, but not the only time, I wound up rebuilding that same barn door.

I got so much enjoyment from Sugarbabe. Before her, the only horse available to the Tanner boys and me was a big old Belgian workhorse named "Babe," on the Tanner farm. Babe was gentle enough, but so tall that we needed a step ladder, or fence to get on her. We didn't have a saddle, and Babe's back was so wide, that our short legs extended nearly horizontal. We must have been a funny sight, facing the challenge of trying to stay on-board. Needless to say, Babe frequently enjoyed watching Dan, Ken, and I (all three of us could fit on her back at once) pick ourselves up out of the dirt, after rounding a corner a bit too fast. I'm not sure that it was all that unintentional on Babe's part, as I could swear that I caught a twinkle in her eye from time to time.

After I owned Sugarbabe for a year or two, some business associates of my father (the Dermonys, of Dermony Truck, located in the Grand Rapids suburb city Wyoming) requested that my father allow them to board two Shetland ponies ("Dusty" and "Smokey") on our farm. Since the Dermonys rarely came around at all, and we boys had free use of the ponies, this was **perfect**! Dan, and Ken, and I devised all kinds of mischief, which involved Sugarbabe, Dusty, and Smokey. We developed a contest in which we would joust, in an attempt to unsaddle one another. Two riders would ride at one another, at a moderate speed. The riders would lock arms as the horses passed each other, and the rider who remained seated was the winner. Frequently of course, this resulted in both riders hitting the ground, and plenty of bumps and bruises, but it was great fun!

Each summer, Dan, Ken and I, who really lived "Tom Sawyer/ Huckleberry Finn" lifestyles, would pack some burlap grain sacks with food (sweet corn, tomatoes, and cucumbers *from the garden,* canned beans, and hot dogs), along with our sleeping bags, onto the three ponies, and head down to camp and fish on the banks of the Grand River, which was 300 ft. wide, and 10 ft. deep, bordering the south side of our farm for 1.6 miles. The camping trips, because of mosquitoes or rain, or both, usually didn't last more than a couple of days, but were **heaven** to nine and ten year olds.

Summers were fabulous in those years. Michigan, often referred to as, "Nine months winter, and three months poor sledding," always left us very anxious for winter to break. Though summers were short, or maybe because they were short, we packed as much fun as we could into those few months. We idled away innumerable hours jumping off high ledges, into stacks of loose hay, and building hay bale forts, in the haymows of the barns on both of our farms.

The forts were useful, and necessary, when we became engaged in rotten egg fights. Both farms had "Banty" chickens, which roamed freely, and nests of spoiled eggs, scattered throughout the barns, were plentiful. We were often required to shed our clothes, and hose off, before being allowed to enter the house, following one of our "egg fights." The smell of eggs, that had decayed in the 85 to 95 degree humid Michigan summer heat is putrid, and our Mothers could always tell what we had been up to, before we got anywhere near the door.

I passed a lot of time at the Tanners. It was my home away from home. There were five boys and two girls in the Tanner family; at times I must have seemed like a sixth son, and I was treated as one. The Tanners were not wealthy people by any means, but they were **good** people, who knew a lot about what matters in life. Dan and Ken's older brother Dave opened a package one Christmas, of heavily used bike peddles, when he had asked for a new set, for his worn-out bike. Through his tears, he read a note in the bottom of the box, which directed him to the apple storage building, where to his *delight,* he found a new "slightly used" bike.

We enjoyed many summer nights camping out in the barn, either on the Tanner farm, or our farm. If it happened to be a chilly or cold night, we would stack up bales of hay and straw, building a fort with a roof, which we could crawl into with our sleeping bags and blankets. The bales provided excellent insulation, and our body heat quickly warmed our cozy shelter to a comfortable temperature.

Both haymows were home to pigeons, and we learned how to catch them at night, by holding a flashlight beam on them, and scaring them from their roost with a tossed corncob. A pigeon will follow the light beam right to you (not being able to see in the dark), and we became quite proficient at pigeon catching.

On one particular occasion, we fashioned a crude cage out of old warped boards and chicken wire. After catching 15–20 birds, and housing them, we set about the business of raising pigeons. We were convinced that after these birds were caged long enough, with food and water, the cage would become "home" to them. We felt that we could then devise a method of making a profit with our "homing pigeons," by taping notes to their legs, as we heard had been done in World War I & II, and elsewhere.

Following a couple of weeks of diligently feeding, watering, and cleaning up after our exceedingly hungry, and messy "captives," we decided that they were well enough trained to "return home." One afternoon we opened the cage door, and scooted them all out. After several wide looping circles through the farmyard skyline, our "homing pigeons" returned "home," straight back to the **haymow** that we had captured them from! Perhaps our "unwilling participants" weren't the "homing pigeon" type, or preferred their "*chosen*" home to the one we had decided upon for them. Either way, that was the end of our enterprise in the "homing pigeon" business.

4

Critters and Varmints

In addition to pigeons, the Tanner boys and I loved to catch and cage all types of varmints and critters. One summer my father excavated a pond (about a half acre in size) for my sisters and I and our friends to fish and swim in. The pond was fed by a fresh water stream, emptying into a 40-acre swamp on our farm, which bordered the Grand River, and was home to all sorts of critters. The pond was predominately home to bluegill, sunfish, bass, and bullheads, which my father had stocked it with, and we kids (the Tanner boys and I, in particular) enjoyed endless hours of fun catching fish. We learned to clean, fillet, and grill them, and we savored many wonderful meals from that pond. We also developed a love for frog legs, of which the pond seemed to have an ample supply.

Whenever relatives would come to visit, the pond was a focal point for my cousins and I, providing plentiful hours of fishing and swimming. One year, when Mom's older sister Hilda, and my Uncle Chris and family came down from Pigeon to visit, my cousin Marvin and I went to the pond to fish. A requirement however, was that we bring Marv's three-year-old brother Roger with us.

We had fun and caught a lot of fish, but Marv continually had to warn Roger, as he nervously pranced around, with the impatience of most any three-year-old, "**Roger**, don't *step* on the **worms**!" We kept the worms in a tuna can, and Roger's young memory was short, resulting in numerous accidents, and a new warning every few min-

At the pond. Cousin Julie, Karen, and Doug in the foreground.

utes, "**Roger**, don't step on the **worms**!" Roger (whose antsy feet kicked the can over continually) became very frustrated with the ordeal, and we wound up using a few damaged fishing worms, which though slightly flattened, still worked okay. When we returned to the farmhouse, at the end of our afternoon of fishing, Aunt Hilda asked Roger if he had fun and caught any fish. All Roger said (scowling as he did) was, "Don't-**step**-on-a-**woorms**!"

While fishing in the pond one summer, the Tanner boys and I started to have problems with something very big and heavy taking our bait (usually earth worms, night crawlers, catalpa leaf worms, or corn bores from the garden). Whatever it was, it always broke the fishhook or the catgut fishing line, before we could get it reeled in, no matter how strong the pound-test line was that we used. Finally in desperation, we made a durable fishing rig out of a thick willow branch, stout chalk line, and the most oversized, heavy-duty fishhook we could find. We used a whole frog for bait, and before long we hooked, and after much struggle, dragged in our bait robber, the **most humungous** snapping turtle I had *ever* seen!

The snapper was **far** too heavy for us young boys to pick up, so we carefully tied baler twine to his tail, and set about dragging him home. This all had to be done with much caution, because this snapper, with a head the size of our fist, was large enough to take off a finger (or toe from our bare feet), as we had been warned many times, and had a neck long enough to nearly reach his tail. The snapper, which weighed as much as any one of us, dragged all four clawed feet the entire 1/4 mile distance back to the farmyard, and us boys were three **whipped** pups, when we finally got there. We put the snapper in a large old wash tub in the playhouse, and he became another "caged critter" of ours for a month or so, until he tired of the "good life" he was living, feeding on a continual supply of frogs, us boys were burdened with supplying to him. One day (when we probably skipped feeding him), he was just gone. He probably could have left anytime at will, but had opted to enjoy the feast while it lasted. The tracks from his clawed feet and heavy tail, left in the dirt farm road, lead straight back to his home in the pond, and our problem of occasionally losing bait, hook, line, and sinker resumed.

I've heard that snapping turtles haven't evolved much since prehistoric times, and can live to be 80–100 years old or more. With a few missing toes and other grizzly battle scars, this huge snapper was undoubtedly an old one. He had probably migrated into the pond from the swamp, and made it his private sanctuary. We boys just learned to live with the problem of losing a little tackle occasionally, and chalked it up as the cost of good fishing, in the home of "Ol Griz." My mother (93) still lives on the farm, where the pond remains, untouched by time, and I wouldn't be surprised if that ancient reptile continues to reside there as well.

The swamp on our farm was a source of many opportunities, both adventurous, and prosperous. It would freeze over in the winter, and in years to come, my older sister Karen and I had some marvelous ice-skating parties, with bonfires on the ice, and many friends in attendance. When I was about ten years old, I became acquainted with a teenage neighbor boy (Les Posler), who asked and obtained permission from my parents to trap the swamp for muskrat, mink, and raccoon pelts. Les Posler, who lived a mile north of our farm on Burton St., 1/4 mile east of Kenowa, was very experienced at trapping, and skinning pelts from varmints. I was fascinated with learning the trade, and I tagged along each night as he traveled his trap-line.

The trapping season in Michigan, at the time, was open for about three months each year; I learned a lot from Les, and gradually I became skillful at trapping myself. After collecting some "hand-me-down" discard traps from Les, I eventually started my own trap route. Santa Claus helped me out with some more traps, and as the seasons went by, I always had a trap line to check each night, with thirty or more trap sets. Trapping is tough cold work, through the ice in many places (trapping season was Dec.–Feb.), and 1–2 catches per night was good (many nights I would be "skunked"). More often than I care to remember, I came home freezing-cold, wet to my waist from falling through thin ice (some of the best sets for muskrats and mink are where water is moving, and ice is thin).

As a young boy (and *as it still does*), it always bothered me to kill an animal for it's "pelt," but whenever I expressed my concerns, my dad told me, "The swamp and farm would be overrun with rats and varmints, if they weren't kept in check," and I let myself be convinced that the trapped animals didn't suffer. I could never stand to see an animal endure pain. As I stepped out of the back door of our farm-house, one morning as a young boy, I heard a distant, barely audible, yet shrill, distressed, screeching noise, coming from our side yard. Upon tracing down the shrieks, I found a small toad, hanging onto a handful of growing grass with each front hand, crying out for help, with **all** his might!

He had been captured by a large "Blue Racer" snake, which was attempting to consume him, and had already swallowed the little toad to his chest. Blue Racers, like many snakes have no teeth, swallow their prey whole, and alive, and then secret stomach acids to digest them. I could tell by a lump in the mid-section of the Blue Racer, that this small toad was not the first to suffer this same fate. I determined that **this** small toad's desire to live, and his cries for help, were strong enough to warrant intrusion. The Blue Racer was either too *invested* in his *prize,* or not intimidated enough by a small boy to take flight. I grabbed him by the neck, and pulled the toad from his mouth, with the words, "Oh **no** you don't! You're **not** going to eat **this** toad, on **this** day!" I threw the snake over the page wire fence bordering the yard, and let the toad hop off in the grass. Maybe it was just my youthful imagination, but I could swear I saw the little toad pause after a few hops, and look up at me as if to say thanks, before he continued on.

On another occasion, one late afternoon, I heard some high-pitched screams coming from outside the barn. When I traced the shrill cries, I found that a barn cat had captured a small cottontail rab-bit, and was in the process of eating him **alive**! The barn cat had already consumed the little bunny's cottontail by the time I got there, but except for that, the bunny was unharmed. The cat ran off when I charged him, and after inspecting the little rabbit, I decided that other than short one cottontail, he would be fine. I applied some "Bag Balm" salve, from the milk-house in the barn (which we always had on hand for the dairy cow's sore utters), to his wound, which had already stopped bleeding, and I turned the little rabbit loose in the hayfield next to the barn, where he had probably been captured. Even though a few years later, I learned to hunt rabbits during small game season, they didn't suffer from that, our family used them as food, and it felt humane.

Although I know that early man depended on animal pelts for survival, modern man didn't need them. It felt completely different to me, to kill an animal for food, maybe just because I loved the flavor of wild game. Regardless, I was motivated enough to make money, to keep the trapping enterprise up throughout my mid-teen years, long after Les had stopped, and I averaged 60–80 pelts per season. Back then muskrat pelts would bring 75 cents to $1.25 each, raccoon $2.00–$4.00, and mink $5.00–$10.00 each, if I was cautious not to nick the pelts while skinning them, so I was happy to make $80–$100 per season. If one figured out the hours that went into that commerce, the hourly rate of return would be very discouraging. However $80–$100 was a lot of money for a kid my age in the early 60's, and even though I had plenty of other chores, such as cutting and splitting wood, to keep the ravenous wood burning furnace fed (which heated our old farm house), most weren't money making endeavors.

I was always motivated to make money. By the time I was ten years old, I began raising chickens for eggs. My parents purchased 30 white leghorns for me, under the condition that I keep the family supplied with all the eggs we needed. I kept the chickens in an old chicken coop on the farm, with a small fenced yard, and I sold the excess eggs for 25 cents a dozen. We had enough relatives in the area to purchase many of the eggs, and I made a sign (a chicken painted white, with a red comb and feet), which read "Farm Fresh Eggs, 25 cents per doz." I posted the sign at the tip of our front yard, on the edge of the Kenowa Avenue turn around, and with that, I was able to sell all additional eggs to neighbors and passers-by.

The chicken business wasn't without tribulation, however. The farm was home to plenty of raccoons, weasels, and fox. I wasn't ever able to construct a fence that would keep out a raccoon (which would eat eggs), or a weasel (which would gnaw a tiny hole in an egg shell, and suck out the raw egg), or a fox (fond of a chicken dinner), and I routinely needed to put my trapping skills to work. I had also become quite skilled with a shotgun (a single shot hammer-action 20 gauge), which I had acquired on my 9th birthday. More than once I used my shotgun to fend off a chicken hawk, looking to score a meal.

After I had been in the chicken business a couple of years, I returned home with my family from a visit with some relatives one evening, to a scene that looked like it was straight from a horror film. The entire farmyard was strewn with chicken feathers, such that it looked like we had a snow dusting in July, with massacred chicken carcasses **everywhere**! Whatever had killed them was still around, because I could hear a few remaining chickens squawking, out near the barn. I ran into the house, grabbed my shotgun, a fistful shells, and ran for the barn as fast as I could! There in the chicken yard, through a gate which they had broken down, were two "Malamute Husky" dogs, trying to get a couple survivors, perched on the roof of the chicken coop. Wasting no time, I crammed a shell into the chamber of my shotgun, and cocked the hammer.

As I did, the Huskies ran over to me, tails wagging, and sat down in front of me, all excited, as though they expected to be rewarded for what they had done. Needless to say, my heart melted. I love dogs. I couldn't even raise the gun to my shoulder! This wasn't a *weasel* or a *chicken hawk*. These two were licking me in the face, as I bent down to read the tags on their collars. They had escaped from their fenced yard, in the small town of Marne, **15 miles** west of our farm! Their owner was happy to get them back, but was not willing to pay any restitution. My parents had farm owners insurance, which paid a little, but after the deductible, there wasn't enough left to put me back into the chicken business. Anyway, by the time this occurred, I was starting into the cattle business, and my interest in "fowl for finance" was waning.

Ring-neck pheasants were plentiful in the 50's and 60's in Michigan, and hunting them was a very popular sport, and one that I loved. My father had received the 20-gauge shotgun, which he gave me for my 9th birthday, as payment for some topsoil that he had sold to a customer (who was a little short on cash). I was ecstatic with the shotgun, but when I first received it, I was so small, that I didn't have enough power in my thumb to cock the hammer. My father sawed off the stock (for my short arms), and rigged the hammer with an extension, which gave me more leverage, and solved the problem. My mother was concerned about my young age, so I was required to attend a gun safety class before I started using the shotgun.

My father was locally well known, and he was a friendly guy, who had lived in the area most of his life. Our farm was close to town, full of game, and was therefore a popular hunting spot. My father was also a very generous man, who would let anyone who asked (and many who didn't), come on our farm for most any reason, such as to hunt, or dig for earthworms on the banks of the Grand River. A person could make a living selling fishing worms during the milder months, and Dad always said to me, "Son, those folks gotta eat too!" At one point he allowed a band of traveling gypsy families to camp and live on our farm, down near the Grand River.

The Tanner boys and I had long heard tales of the traveling gypsies, and their exotic life style. The idea that they were now so nearby, that we could observe them for ourselves, peaked our interest and excitement. On our ventures to the riverbanks we spied on them from afar, secretly using my dad's binoculars. On one of our early missions, the gypsies, who I suspect always knew we were there, invited us to join them. We enjoyed our visits with them. They taught us the art of basket weaving, from willow branches my father had allowed them to harvest, which grew plentifully on the riverbank. Some months later as fall began to approach, in appreciation for their stay, the gypsies gave my parents a large hand crafted basket, which still remains on the farm today.

Our farm was so loaded with pheasants and close to town, that on opening day of pheasant hunting season each year, cars would be parked out the farm driveway, and for a hundred yards up Kenowa Avenue. In spite of the hunting pressure, if you were a good shot, it was easy to limit out by noon (four rooster pheasants), and I frequently did. Since my first shotgun was a single shot, which didn't give me a second chance, like the double barrels, pumps, and automatics brandished by my competition, I did a lot of practicing (with tin cans, clay pigeons, etc.), and I rarely missed.

My father taught me how to clean pheasants; Mother was a good cook, and my sisters and I savored pheasant dinners. I would scurry home from school, rush through my chores, and try to get in an hour of hunting before dark, each evening during the two-week season. Pheasant hunting was fabulous throughout the 50's and 60's, but the pheasant population started to dwindle by the late 60's, because of pesticides/herbicides, predators, harsh winters, or the combination, and eventually became almost non-existent. Dan and Ken Tanner and I bought a bunch of pheasant chicks, and tried raising them one year to replenish the supply, but it didn't help to bring them back. Whatever had caused the natural population of pheasants to diminish, eventually took its toll on the birds we turned loose, and after a few months of hearing the longed for sounds of a distant rooster pheasant cackling, they too were all but gone.

Duck hunting (in the swamp) on our farm was also very good, and the season lasted much longer. I didn't enjoy the taste of ducks or hunting ducks, nearly as much as pheasants, however it did supply endless hours of pleasure. It was a good backup, and it was something that my father occasionally did together with me, which was rare and very *meaningful* to me. I always made it a point (by opening day) to have a blind in the swamp prepared for Dad and I, and to have a special self-camouflaged hat and jacket ready for each of us to wear. Since the swamp on our farm was so large, and just off the Grand River (which ducks continually traveled), we saw a lot of action, and had plenty of success.

There was an abundance of whitetail deer in the Riverbend area as well, and when opening day of deer hunting season (Nov. 15) rolled around, the Tanner boys and I hit the woods. Each year I bought some slugs and some buckshot for my 20-gauge, and I did plenty of hunting for deer, but with little success. I got a shot off from time to time, but with my numerous chores, and sports practice, and *mostly* lack of patience to sit in a deer stand (*which was the best way to get a deer*), I rarely brought one home.

The first buck deer I ever got (as a young teen) was so important to me that I wrote a short story titled "The Legacy of Fenske's Deer" (on a paper plate), stuck it in my closet, where I found it years later. I was in top physical condition at the time, training for wrestling and boxing, and I literally ran the deer down. There had been a light snow the morning I kicked up a buck, and I got off a quick shot, but missed. I took out after him at a slow but steady pace, reloading on the run. I was able to stay on his track in the snow all afternoon, getting close enough for a shot several times, finally bagging him (a nine-point buck, and my first deer), just before dark.

Dad and Doug with a string of ducks.

5

Chores

I slept in a tiny little room, at one end of the upstairs hall, and since our farmhouse only had four bedrooms, my four sisters doubled up in two of the other rooms. Jan, being the oldest of the "Three Little Pigs," was elected to double up with Karen. Unfortunately, as a young girl, Jan had a little "bed wetting problem," and numerous nights I woke up to the angry sounds of Karen's voice scolding Jan, as she drug her by one arm to the bathroom, after Jan had peed the bed. Jan was only about three or four at the time, and her bladder wouldn't always cooperate, especially if we had watermelon right before bed (which we often did on summer nights, *fresh from the garden*). Jan finally outgrew the problem, but Mother blamed Karen's numerous one-armed drags to the bathroom, as being the cause of a cyst under her arm, which Jan needed to have removed a few years later. The cyst was non-malignant, but may have foretold of problems to come, years down the road.

Winters in Michigan get frigged for long spells. There were times, when the mercury would remain below zero degrees Fahrenheit for thirty days at a stretch, and because of cloud cover, we wouldn't see the sun during the entire time. Our farmhouse wasn't insulated or sealed very well, and I would often wake up to skiffs of snow on my bed covers (which fortunately I always had plenty of). Drafty as it was, it was a cozy old farmhouse, and I loved to snuggle up under my piles of covers, and listen to the iced "cottonwood" branches ticking my bedroom windows, as the howling winter winds drifted me off to sleep. When it was time to milk the cows on early winter mornings, and my father would bellow out, "Come-on son, let those soft warm feet, hit that hard cold floor," he wasn't kidding! The farmhouse had hardwood floors throughout, and it felt as *hard* and *cold* as ice, on winter mornings!

Being the only boy, I felt a little overburdened with chores, like cleaning the cow gutters, helping milk the cows twice a day, seven days a week, and the never-ending job of keeping the wood-bin full. Our farmhouse was heated by a large old cast-iron, wood/coal-burning furnace. My mother was from the old school, and cutting trees, chopping wood, shoveling snow, pitching manure, milking cows, virtually anything outside the house, was "men's work." Mother really seemed to believe (as she probably had been taught) that women were the brains, and men were the workhorses, and I understood at an early age, my place and responsibilities in the family. Even though in years to come (late 60's, early 70's), my sisters became "liberated women," they were not "liberated" enough to tackle splitting wood, pitching manure, or milking cows (except Linda, who by choice, eventually did it *all,* and *more*).

The farm had an endless supply of firewood. There is so much rainfall in Michigan that trees would soon sprout and thrive, on any area of the farm that wasn't continually tilled or mowed. Dry, dead wood makes the best firewood, and was always my first choice. Since the "Dutch Elm Disease" had traversed the area some years earlier, killing virtually all the elm trees (which are hardwood and very good firewood), dead elm was abundant. Whenever I ran out of dead elm (not obstructed by other live trees), there was usually plenty of dead oak or maple, most often killed by lightening strikes (thunderstorms are prevalent in Michigan). Periodically I would cut down some live trees, to create a path for the tractor (with buss-saw) and dump truck, to get through to some dead trees. I would drag these live-cut trees out of the way with the farm tractor, and leave them to dry out; then after a season or two, they too would be good firewood. With all of the rainfall in Michigan, we couldn't burn enough wood, to keep up with the continual growth of trees on the farm.

Occasionally (about once per winter), my parents would surprise me, and buy a truckload of coal. What a **treat** it was, to come home and see that black pile of coal, outside the woodbin window! Even though it was tough shoveling, coal burned *hot,* and *slow,* and it was black **gold** to me! It gave me a several week break from cutting down trees, cutting them into logs, buzzing the logs into blocks with the buzz saw (mounted on the back of a Model A, International farm tractor), throwing the blocks up into the dump-truck, hauling them home, dumping them outside the woodbin, splitting the blocks with an axe (anything over 8 inch diameter), throwing the split firewood through an open window down into the woodbin in the basement, and stacking it into cords, only to see it *rapidly consumed,* by that **firewood devouring monster** furnace!

I learned to keep bundled up warm, and I would sneak around closing registers, and skulk down into the basement, and close down the air intake flue a little, in an attempt to slow down that ravenous dragon, only to have my sisters squawk, "Mom, Doug's been closing registers again," when the temperature in the farmhouse started to drop. Interestingly enough, in 1967 (the fall I started college), my parents replaced the wood-burning furnace, with a fuel-oil furnace. As a friend of mine rationalized to me, their "firewood-producing machine" was gone. Even though keeping us supplied with firewood seemed like an enormous burden at the time, in retrospect, it helped keep me fit, and gave me a sense of responsibility and purpose, something I think many young people lack today. I have no complaints about any of my responsibilities as a boy. They helped make me strong, and I am thankful that my parents gave me the obligations they did.

When I reached the age of twelve, I became increasingly more interested in motorized vehicles, which would get me from place to place, at a much faster rate than Sugarbabe. Although we had numerous tractors on the farm, all of which I was adept at operating, tractors are work related implements, and somewhat awkward, and I wasn't yet allowed to drive a truck off the farm. I envisioned something closer to the ground, and faster. I had seen go-karts, and had even driven one once or twice. I was interested in something more on this order, only larger, so I set about trying to build one. Since I had no idea how to do so, I put most of my energy into coaxing my dad to help, with statements of how useful such a contraption would be, for things like hauling firewood home.

6

The Puddle Jumper

Since Dad was such a naturally adept mechanic, and loved building mechanical devices, it didn't take a lot of finagling to acquire his assistance in building a power-driven contraption. We started in the corner of the old wood-shop next to the barn, which we called the "Tool Shed," where he had built our first two front-end loaders. Dad and I fashioned a frame (about 4ft. by 6ft.) out of channel iron, and mounted the (shortened) axles and differential, out of an old '49 Ford Coup, from the "Bone-yard" (an area on the farm where all discarded vehicles, farm equipment, and implements were stored). We next mounted a four-cylinder combine engine over the rear axle, and an old double-width truck seat over the front axle. We mounted a four-speed floor-shift transmission between the driver's legs, and a steering wheel and column, which held the driver in place. Passengers had to fend for themselves, because the only other thing in front of the truck seat was an old cone style single headlight, scavenged from a front fender of the '49 Ford Coup.

We christened the vehicle with the name "Puddle Jumper," and the Tanner boys and I had many years, and many miles of enjoyment with her. I hand fashioned front fenders out of flat 1/8 in. aluminum, and mounted them over the front wheels, to turn with the front tires, and to keep water and mud off the driver and passengers. The Puddle Jumper topped out at about 40–45 mph, which was plenty fast for those bumpy old farm roads, and plenty fast for the gravel on Kenowa

Ave., which became washboard rough between the infrequent visits of the county road grader (other than the coil-spring seat, the Puddle Jumper had no springs). I spray-painted her candy apple red, and have many fond memories of those "Puddle Jumper" escapades.

We used the Puddle Jumper for chores, as well as play. We used her to rake hay, and pull wagons full of baled hay back to the barn. At one point we used her for pulling a long old hay-rope, tied to the rear pipe bumper, through a pulley secured to a branch, high in a cypress tree, to hoist lumber up to a tree house we were building. We even used the Puddle Jumper one early spring, as the work horse, to drag a heavy 50′ length of chain-link fence down to a flooded area on the west end of the Tanner farm, also bordered by the Grand River. The Grand River floods every spring, usually trapping fish in sloughs, when the floodwaters recede rapidly. The fish trapped in the ponds of floodwater provided hours of spear fishing adventure to the Tanner boys and I, and we anxiously awaited the floods each spring.

The Tanners kept many (crate sized) hives of honey bees, which were scattered all through the apple orchards, before the apple trees flowered each spring, to help with the pollination of the apple blossoms. The bees carry the pollen (which sticks to their bodies) from flower to flower, as they travel throughout the orchard in search of nectar, which they ingest, and from which they miraculously manufacture delicious honey. As we often did, we popped a lid, and grabbed a chunk of honeycomb, from one of the sleepy (still dormant) beehives, which were stored each winter, next to a shack by the barn, in which Ol' "Crazy-Horse Charlie" lived.

Crazy-Horse was one of a number of migrant workers on the Tanner farm, who "rode-the-rails," sleeping in boxcars as they traveled back and forth, working the orange orchards of the South each winter, and northern apple orchards each summer and fall. We loved to chew on the honey comb, suck out the honey, and spit out the wax, as a treat on our adventures, or while sitting on a crate back at the farm in the evening, listening to drunken "Crazy-Horse Charlie" tell us about one of his.

Even though it was very early in the year for a flood, and there was still snow on the ground, there had been a warm snap, and we were hopeful. With a handful of honeycomb, we hopped on the puddle jumper, and headed down to the river, to see if it had flooded yet. Sure enough, that particular year there was an unusually early March flood. The annual floods normally don't happen until late April/early May. Coming so early that year, the receding floodwaters had trapped hundreds of pike, and pickerel, which travel from Lake Michigan, up the Grand each spring, in search of quiet backwaters to spawn.

The Tanner boys and I were very enthused when we found the river already flooded, and upon exploring around, we were ecstatic to discover a bayou filled with **northern pike**, and **pickerel**, which spawn much earlier than carp and suckers, and other non-desirable fish like we usually found. The find was so **rare**, that Dan, Ken, and I, were able to attract the interest of some adults, including Mr. Tanner.

Even though the pike were very resistant, their fate at the end of our spears was much more humane, than the inevitable slow death they were facing, as the pool of floodwater slowly dried up. At first, we speared fish at will, however as the number of pike thinned out, the remaining trapped survivors became more wary, and spearing them became much more challenging. This prompted the idea of the chain link (screen) fence, to crowd the fish to one end of the bayou.

We all stood in a line, holding the screen in front of us, as we worked the flooded bayou back and forth, from end to end. The screen worked well, and we eventually speared almost all of the trapped fish. It was necessary for us to traverse the bayou from end to end, time and time again, because our screen was not quite as long as the bayou width, and each time a few would get around the ends, or through a gap under the screen. The bayou bottom was not perfectly flat, allowing escape routes, and it had sunken tree branches, and logs in places, which provided the most guarded survivors an opportunity to escape.

As we worked the screen through the bayou, on one of the last runs, a **monster** northern pike, which had been escaping us all day, **slammed** into the screen **right** in front of me! The shock stunned him momentarily, and he stopped suspended near the surface of the 3 ft. deep water. I froze for a second, astonished at his **massive** size! As I came to my senses, I quickly raised my spear, and trust straight down at him with **all** my **might**! At the last split second, the northern came to, and darted to freedom. I felt an immediate excruciating pain, and I released a **blood-curdling** wail, as I realized that I had just speared my right **foot**!

To make matters worse, when I tried to hop on one foot to the bayou bank, I could not, because unfortunately, I had run the spear through the bottom of the screen before it hit my foot, and as a result of the barbs, the spear prongs would not extract. We had to get my foot out of the murky water, so that I could see what I was doing. All of us had to work together to drag the heavy screen to the bank, as I painfully hobbled along on one foot.

Mr. Tanner cut my rubber boot away, to give us a clear view of my injury. The spear had hit some bones, which stopped it from going clear through my foot, however the tendon to my big toe was hooked on one of the barbs, and each time we tried to extract the spear, my big toe would curl up in protest. Eventually, we were able to wiggle the spear barbs free, extract the spear, and at least the first part of this painful incident was over (I awoke in a cold sweat from nightmares, *reliving the ordeal* for months). I watched from the bank, as the others made the last couple of sweeps. Other than an excruciatingly painful, follow-up tetanus shot, and a slight limp for a short time, I was fine.

We made our way back to the Tanner farm, with a couple pickup loads of fish, and endless stories, and memories. After cleaning, and filleting the fish, we froze them in the giant coolers in the Tanner apple storage building, and both of our families and many neighbors had delicious, frozen fish, all through the following year.

In future years, by the time we turned fourteen, Dan Tanner and I started "illegally" taking the Puddle Jumper into Grandville, for things like football practice, which started in August, a couple of weeks before school started. Grandville was a small town, with only one red light, and one cop, named "Skip." Most everybody knew "Skip-The-Cop," and Skip knew most everybody. Dan and I didn't know him though, only *of* him, and that was mostly from stories our

Doug with speared pike.

parents had told us, I'm sure to keep us "on the right path." We knew we were taking a risk running the Puddle Jumper into Grandville, but it sure beat bicycles. We always figured we could get away if we were spotted, until one day we **were**, and Skip took chase, **"Gumballs" on**, and **all**! Dan and I did a quick u-turn, and made it back across the Grand River Bridge and onto the "River-Road" on our farm, with Skip in hot pursuit, siren blaring.

We couldn't see how far Skip was behind us, but we knew he couldn't travel at our speed, because of all the dust we kicked up. When I rounded the last turn on the farm "River-Road," I took it a little too fast, and the Puddle Jumper flipped, **upside-down**! Somehow, Dan and I were thrown clear, uninjured. We jumped up quickly, scrambled into a nearby cornfield, and laid down flat in the waist-high corn. Skip arrived shortly, looked around a little, and finally left, after I'm sure he was convinced that we were all right.

After we were certain that Skip was gone, Dan and I flipped the Puddle Jumper back upright. The only damage was a flattened exhaust pipe, and a bent steering wheel, and after a couple cranks with the hand crank (it had no electric starter), the Puddle Jumper fired up, and we drove home. A day or two later my father asked me casually, as we walked past the Puddle Jumper, "What happened to your steering wheel, son?" I just muttered, "Oh, a low tree branch," to which he responded with a simple, "Umm, you better be more **careful** where you drive it!" Not until years later, did I find out that Skip had told Dad all about the incident in the Grandville coffee shop, and in fact, the chase was a plan they had schemed up together, to put a little scare into us, and to keep us out of town with the Puddle Jumper.

The Zonstras

Around 1961, the Zonstra family purchased and moved into the Morry farmhouse. They had four children, Sharon, Rich, Andy, and "Eddie Won Woonyer Wonstra." Eddie John Junior (five years old) had a speech impediment, which he later outgrew. Over time I became closest with Andy, who was only one year older than me, and rode around on the Puddle Jumper with me a lot (as well as legal, "licensable" vehicles in years to come), but I liked them all.

The Zonstras had decided to move from town (where they all had lived their entire lives), out to the country, and the Zonstra kids were not too hip on farm life, similar to a televised sitcom that came out a few years later titled "Green Acres" (1965–1971). My sister Karen and I (the "Three Little Pigs" were still too young), and the Tanner boys, soon realized that the Zonstra's had many hard lessons to learn about country life, and we were **all too willing** to assist. I must admit that on numerous occasions we were not only uncooperative in advising them, when they were facing the repercussions of a misguided decision that one of them had made, but in fact we were instrumental in setting up the scenario.

Opportunities arose, such as one of us posing the question, "I wonder if that water is cold," as we all were walking on the banks of the Grand River, one early spring day. We expected that this would inspire one of them to go find out, and it **did**. The trip down the steep riverbank immediately propelled Andy (most often the "**eager beaver**"), feet-first, full-body, into the icy cold river, as the rest of us stood on the high, flat part of the bank, **roaring** in laughter. The frigid river water always kept the frost in the ground, on the slippery clay banks, long after all surrounding ground had thawed, and even though the surface appeared dry, the riverbanks remained treacherously slippery for weeks after the last of the snow was gone. Any attempt to approach the water's edge, resulted in an instant bath, an **extremely uncomfortable** lesson, which each of us had previously well learned. After emptying our bellies of laughter, and watching Andy struggle with the impossible task of trying to climb the slick, icy bank, I finally extended a tree branch down to help him out.

We had many laughs at the expense of the Zonstra kids, but they were likable, and before long the "City Kids" (as we referred to them) became an integral part of the Riverbend neighborhood.

7

The Boat

The Grand River was a source of income/pleasure and pain for our family. Organic debris, deposited by the floodwaters over centuries, had created extreme amounts of topsoil on the banks of the river, which was very fertile, and grew abundant crops, but it was risky. Every spring, when the winter's accumulation of snow and ice would melt, the Grand would flood the entire south side of our farm, and sometimes (with late floods), entire crops were lost. The unpredictability of the river floods, and the abundance of fertile soils on the banks of the river, along with the discovery of gravel on the farm, helped to eventually lead my parents to the profitable enterprise of selling, topsoil, aggregates, and other soils from the farm.

For many years my father had a dream, which he often talked about, of building a "Stern Wheeler" boat to travel on the Grand River. In the summer of my 12th year, Dad decided to make his dream into a reality. Our neighbors who lived 1/4 mile north on Kenowa (Harry, *always known as Junior,* and Dorothy Wellet) were in the auto & truck parts/scrap steel business, and had purchased a 40 ft. steel boat hull to scrap out. The hull had been a US Navy LCM ("Landing Craft Medium"), designed for bringing troops, armored tanks, and other equipment ashore off ocean vessels, during WWII. The Sea Scouts had previously purchased the boat from the Navy, and modified it for their own use. The boat had a crude cabin, with sleeping bunks, a galley, a head, and a captain's bridge. My dad bought the boat from the Wellets, and with one front-end loader ahead, and one behind, dragged and pushed the boat, on wood skids, the 1/4 mile distance down Kenowa Avenue to our farm shop.

My dad worked on the boat, on and off for a year or so, and I helped to the best of my ability. We refurbished the cabin, flying bridge, and engine room. Dad also completely constructed and mounted a 10 ft. diameter stern (rear) paddlewheel on the boat, powered by a GMC diesel engine, which he installed in the engine room, along with a "Whitti" diesel generator, for offshore electric power. The boat was painted baby blue and white, was christened the "Fenske 7" (with a sign on her stern), and brought our family many years of pleasure.

The day we launched the "Fenske 7" in the Grand River was an outstanding day. My "Uncle Ken" Fenske, my dad's younger brother, who owned a successful gravel/redi-mix business, near his home (not far off the Grand), a few miles downstream from our farm, brought over one of his front-end loaders to help. They cut down two tall trees, trimmed off the branches, and used them as skids to drag the boat on. With Uncle Ken's loader pulling, and Dad's dozer pushing, they slid the boat about a half-mile down the river-road on our farm, to the chosen launch site on the Grand. A crowd was present to witness the event, even a local newspaper reporter and photographer, and the story made the front page of "The Grandville Star" newspaper.

"Fenske 7" towing to the Grand River for launching.

"Fenske 7" launching in the Grand River.

"Fenske 7" on the Grand River.

It was the spring of 1960, times were slow, stories were scarce, and this was **big** news for the little town of Grandville. The steel flat bottom boat weighed about twenty tons, drew about 18 inches of water, and we enjoyed short trips up and down the Grand, as far as we could easily travel (a couple miles either direction), for a few weeks. Then my dad made a decision to try, with my assistance, to make it to Lake Michigan with the Fenske 7 (thirty-miles downstream).

What an expedition that turned out to be, lasting a month or more. It was mid-summer by this time, the water level was low, and sand bars, rows of piling (placed in the river years earlier, to maintain a channel for barges), stumps, and many other obstructions were prevalent. On one occasion, we became trapped on a windrow of piling (trying to ram thru), nearly sank when water entered through the Fenske 7 exhaust ports, and for a week we could not break free, ahead or back. My dad finally brought one of his dump-trucks with a winch (known as the A-car, *short for Army-car, a retired army truck*), to the downstream far bank of the Grand, anchored it to two oak trees, and with 200 ft. of cable, began to winch the "Fenske 7," off the row of piling.

My "Uncle Ken," who was standing on the extreme bow of the boat, raised his hands victoriously, shouting, "**Hurray**," when the Fenske 7 finally broke free. The bow of the boat had a single chain railing, which came about to one's waistline. Almost immediately, after the "Fenske 7" broke free, while Uncle Ken still had his hands raised in celebration (and not on the railing), the boat hit another impediment, and came to an abrupt stop. Uncle Ken was instantly propelled forward, up over the railing, and somersaulted into a swift distasteful swim. He surfaced succinctly, with his celebratory cigar **still** in his mouth. This all happened so quickly, that no one had time to react, but the sight of Uncle Ken, dog-paddling below the bow of the boat, **cigar-in-tact**, brought **pangs** of laughter from all on board.

Fortunately, only a small sandbar had caused the stop, and we were soon moving again. However, shortly after this episode, we had a breakdown. The GMC diesel engine powering the paddle wheel was connected by long drive shafts, to a truck differential, mounted on the side of the frame supporting the stern paddle wheel. Undoubtedly the stress put on the differential, while trying to free the boat, had caused it to fail. A couple of days later, Dad unbolted the differential, while I waited below the paddle wheel frame, in our "dingy" (a 4 ft. by 8 ft. wooden lifeboat). As Dad attempted to lower the differential down to me it slipped, fell, and hit the flat plywood bottom of the dingy with such force, that it went nearly all the way through, and down went **myself**, the **dingy**, and the **differential**, straight to the **bottom**, about 10 feet below!

When I popped up, covered with the oil film on the water surface (from the gear lube oil that had spilled out of the differential), without thinking, Dad asked, "Did ya **lose** it?" I responded, "Dad, I had to let **go**! I needed **air**!" After several dives, I was able to fasten a line to both the differential, and the dingy, and we were able to retrieve, and repair them both. I did suffer for several weeks to follow however, as a result of an ear infection, from the dirty, silt imbued river water, and I experienced a very painful broken eardrum, caused by the infection (the first of many broken eardrums, in future years).

We finally made it out to Lake Michigan, through Grand Haven, where the Grand empties into the Great Lakes. The Lake Michigan water was so **clear**, and **blue**! The lake was so **big however**, eighty miles wide, and several hundred miles long, that we soon wanted more speed. Dad decided to install another engine, a P&H diesel, and a couple of propellers, to run along with the paddle wheel, and help the "Fenske 7" attain more speed. I assisted him, and have marvelous memories of working shoulder to shoulder with him doing so. We docked at a marina on Spring Lake (adjacent to Grand Haven), and we traveled there night after night in our old Chevy pickup, to accomplish the task.

After we had the engine in, as I was working alone one evening on my knees, drilling bolt-holes in the steel support beams on the engine-room floor (to mount floor boards), I awoke (as though asleep) to an annoying sound. I was laying flat on my side, and slowly I realized that the irritating sound was coming from the hand-drill I had been holding, which was lying on the engine-room floor next to me, vibrating. I was lucky to be **alive**! I had been knocked unconscious for a short while, from an electrical shock, and we found out the importance of using properly grounded tools, when working on a steel boat *in the water!* My thrill for the night was always an ice cream bar, which I would talk Dad into splitting with me, purchased at a gas station on our way home. On this particular night I got my **own**, with the agreement that Mother would not hear about this incident.

Every summer, when all five Fenske kids were out of school, we took a two-week boat trip up the Lake Michigan coast, traveling from port to port, only spending the night in-port, weather permitting. We often awoke to the voices of tourists walking the docks of various ports we had spent the previous night in. The Fenske 7 was very unusual looking, and one morning I recall the voice of one of the tourists, with an extreme "Southern Drawl" (they were obviously some out-of-state visitors), stating, "Paw, look at this **here** boat! It looks like it just came off the **Mississippi River!**"

Actually my father had always wanted to make a trip down the Mississippi River, which connects to the bottom of Lake Michigan, through some locks near Chicago, but we never made that trip. Usually we traveled north. A couple times we even traveled out to Beaver Island (on the northwest corner of Lake Michigan). The water was **so** clear there, that you could see fish swimming on the bottom, **twenty plus** feet down! One year we even traveled up as far as the Mackinaw Bridge, which links the upper and lower peninsulas of Michigan. All of our family **loved** our trips, and they were the **highlight** of our year! Sometimes one of us was allowed to bring a friend on our vacation with us, and Dan Tanner accompanied me one summer.

Dan was always a prankster! There were bunks on either side of the cabin, and up in the bow of the boat, which is where Dan and I slept. I slowly awoke to some muffled giggling early one morning, when I was trying to sleep in. As I wearily cracked my eyes barely open, I found myself gazing at a broomstick, resting on the edge of my bed, on the port side of the bow, stretching horizontally across to the edge of Dan's bunk, on the starboard side of the bow. As I became more conscious, and as my eyes began to focus, I saw something moving on the broomstick. Slowly I realized it was a single file, marching trail of black **ants**! When I became awake, and conscious enough to understand what was happening, I saw Dan, quietly diverting the trail of ants with his finger, from their chosen path of migration on the rail of his bunk, onto the broomstick, and across to **my bunk**, where they were already getting into my sheets, and **crawling** on my **legs**, which tickling I'm *sure* had a part in my waking!

The ants had migrated from their shore home, at the port we docked in the prior night, and crossed over to the "Fenske 7" on one of the mooring lines (securing our boat to the dock), in search of food. Dan roared in laughter, when I became awake enough to jump out of bed, with both hands smacking and sweeping the large black ants from my legs, suffering some piercing ant bites in the process. Naturally I attacked him in retaliation, and the ordeal wound up in a wrestling match. Dan was a good wrestler, larger and stronger than I, but his laughter interfered enough for me to prevail in this particular contest.

My father was not a nautical man (Dad used road maps, as we traveled in the Fenske 7 up and down the Lake Michigan coast), and we didn't have any "maritime" equipment, such as radar or a depth gauge. Often in thick fog, I laid on my stomach on the deck of the bow, continually checking the depth of the water, and feeling for obstructions ahead of us with a cane pole. Our boat steering wheel was an old steel wheel, from a hand corn grinder on our farm, on which Dad had drilled, tapped, and mounted wooden file handles, at one-foot intervals. We never really quite "fit in," with all the other "Chris Craft" boaters, and I was sometimes a little embarrassed, but we sure had a lot of **fun**, and I was **proud** of our unique boat!

Once we got caught in a severe storm, which generated such massive waves that the Fenske 7 literally surfed, as Dad and I struggled to make it to shore, and into a port. I saw the fear in my Dad's eyes, each time a new wave would pick us up, and the stern paddle wheel would spin in free air momentarily, as the wave rolled under us. Mom and my sisters were down in the cabin, and had little idea what we were going through up on the "Bridge." I held onto the steering wheel with Dad, with all my strength, as we struggled to stay in line with the waves, full well knowing that a wave would roll us, if it caught us sideways. Over the years, we had a number of scary thrill rides, in **twenty-plus** foot surf, with "small craft warnings" out, and no ship-to-shore radio, but somehow we survived it all, and created **fabulous** memories.

8

Grandville School

I always hated to see summers end, school to start, and to have to leave the farm, or the boat behind. Because Riverbend was by now annexed, and part of the Grandville school system (only teaching to grade six), starting in 1961, I had to leave Sugarbabe and my three younger sisters behind. My sister Karen (who had already been attending Grandville for a couple of years) and I, and other "River-benders," were required to catch a bus, and commute into Grandville. With me gone, the "Three Little Pigs" (Linda had started school by this time) needed a ride to Riverbend each morning. I could have harnessed Sugarbabe up to the sulky for them, before I headed out to catch the Grandville school bus, but Mother didn't think they could handle her, and they would have needed help to de-harness and stall Sugarbabe, once they got to Riverbend School anyway.

The bus picked Karen and I up each morning, and dropped us off each afternoon, over a mile north of the farm, at the Kenowa/Burton intersection. That first fall, there was an incident that could have ended tragically, had it not been for my father. As Karen (14) and I (12) walked home, we noticed that we were being followed numerous afternoons by a slow moving older white Ford pickup truck. One afternoon, the truck pulled up next to Karen, walking a short distance ahead of me, and the driver asked her if she wanted a ride. Karen, seeming embarrassed, said "No thank you." When I caught up to her, the driver became nervous, and quickly drove off, but not before I had a chance to look through the passenger truck window, and see what he was **doing**! He was **exposed** and touching himself, as he talked to my *sister!*

When we got home, we told my mother what had happened, giggling (not realizing the severity). When Karen described that the man had his "ah-hem" in his hand, my mother turned very serious and said "Oh–Oh!" She ordered us to stay in the house, and drove off, searching the farm for my father. When Dad got home, he immediately called Grandville's cop "Skip," and after explaining the situation, and arguing with Skip, who apparently claimed he could do nothing, because the guy hadn't "done anything," Dad said, "Either you **lock him up**, or I'll **kill him**!" When my father hung up the phone, he explained to my mother, that Skip had told him, "Howard, don't do anything *stupid.* You'll go to **prison**!"

My dad was waiting for us at the bus stop the next afternoon, and every afternoon for about a week, but no white pickup. Then one afternoon, just as we were getting into my dad's truck, *there he was,* driving by. My dad hollered, "**Get in**!" The guy sped off, with us in **hot pursuit**, sliding side to side, at high speeds on the gravel road. My dad caught up to him, and cut him off, just before he reached the paved road, Wilson. Ordering us to, "**Stay in the truck**," as he jumped out, Dad ran to the stranger's truck, grabbed him by the shirt collar, and jerked him from his vehicle. Karen and I couldn't hear everything said, but we did hear Dad say, if he ever saw him on our street again, he'd **kill him**! My dad loved us dearly, was *very* protective, and gave the guy the *scare of his life!* Dad gave the guy's license number to Skip, and he turned out to be a middle aged man, married, with five children, who lived in Grand Rapids, only a few miles away. He had committed no crime (other than exposing himself), and no charges were filed, but that was the last we ever saw of him. I greatly respected my father, and the actions he always took to protect us.

Grandville school was new to us all, with lots of unfamiliar faces, and kind of scary, but kind of exciting too. I had a previous taste of the Grandville school system, for a short time in the fifth grade, when we were bussed into the old Grandville high school building for a few months, while Riverbend did some remodeling. We were schooled during that time, in a building with some "special-ed kids" (emotionally and mentally handicapped students), some of whom were known to be violent, and my experience had not been very good.

On one occasion, a Riverbend classmate, nicknamed "Pay-dork" (instigated by Dan Tanner, because he was the habitual loser in our coin tossing games), came to me begging for help. Pay-dork was actually a year ahead of me in school, a year older than me, and (at this time in our lives) a little larger than me, but he was somewhat lacking in the courage department. An older, larger "special-ed" student had been constantly following him everywhere he went, terrorizing him, and scarring him to death. I wasn't an experienced fighter, and I didn't like conflict, but I **was** brave. At Pay-dork's pleading I intervened. When an opportunity arose, with fists doubled, I jumped out in front of his "intimidator," warning him that if he didn't stop following Pay-dork around, "He was going to answer to **me**!" Fortunately for me, Pay-dork's "Tormentor" backed down. The problem was solved from that day on, and Pay-dork was extremely grateful.

By this time however, being a little older than when I first experienced the Grandville school system, I was starting to develop an interest in girls, and all of the new faces were a thrill. I made eye contact with one girl my first day at Grandville Junior High, whom (even though I didn't have the nerve to talk to her) seemed to be interested in me as well. Her name was Patricia Kerri Owens, and she was the **prettiest**, most wholesome, healthy, and interesting girl I had **ever seen**, and it felt like I *knew* her from sometime past.

Even though there was always wood to chop, and lots of chores to do, going home to the farm after school was what I waited for. I worked many hours during the summer of 1961 (12 yrs. old), helping neighbors (the Snellers) harvest hay. They were old-timers, who didn't even own a hay-baler, and they harvested their hay loose, with an old style hay-lift, so there was a lot of hot, dusty pitchfork work involved. I received a Hereford beef cow and calf as payment for my summer's work, and since my dad had stopped farming by this time, this was my start into the cattle business. I was allowed to raise cattle and crops on our farm, with the agreement that I keep the freezer full of beef, and I did so from then on. Over and above trapping and raising chickens for eggs, it was my first occupational love, and is still my fondest today.

I have always loved my parents, and all of my family dearly, and I saved the money I made from farming, and gave back to them in ways that I could. Karen and I made it a habit to purchase a gift for each of our parents each year for Christmas, as well as one gift for every other family member, nothing big, but something. This became quite a burden to me, first because I didn't have much money to spend, but **mostly** because I hated to shop, and would put it off until the **last** possible moment. As the stores were closing on

Christmas Eve one year, I realized that I had pushed my procrastination a little past the limit. I had a gift for everyone in our family except my dad, and frantic over not having a gift for him, I buzzed the Puddle Jumper into Grandville. Store after store already had their lights off, and a couple of stores turned them off as I drove up. I pulled into "Prose Five and Dime," which I was delighted to see still had lights on. I pleaded with the clerk at Prose into pulling the key back out of the door, which she had dashed for when she saw me coming, with the promise that I knew exactly what I wanted, and that it would only take me a moment.

Having no idea what to purchase for my dad, and with limited choices at the "Five and Dime," I ran up and down the isles, hoping something would "jump out at me." Nothing did, and with the clerk standing at the door pressuring me, I grabbed a box with the picture of a monkey on it. I remembered that Dad had once been intrigued with the monkey exhibit at the zoo, and let's face it, I was desperate. After I was locked out (in the parking lot), I opened the box to examine my dad's gift, and came to realize that the purchase I had made was a "Barrel-O-Monkeys."

All the way home, I tried to rationalize to myself, how my dad might find some potential value in this gift, never really convincing myself. When Dad opened the gift the following Christmas morning, looking very puzzled, I spent a lot of time trying to explain some caliber of merit to rationalize my purchase. I demonstrated how the small plastic monkeys would all hook together, arm to arm, and form a string. No matter how hard I tried, I wasn't able to get rid of the look of confusion on Dad's face, and before long, rims of laughter erupted from Mother and Karen. The other girls were too young to see the humor, but Mother and Karen were well aware of my "last minute" shopping habits, and soon came to realize what must have happened to me.

One year (in my mid-teens) as an anniversary gift, on August 4 (also my father's birthday), I surprised my parents with a tri-split-rail fence. I purchased the lumber with savings from crop and cattle sales, and put the fence up all the way around the house and garden, with the assistance of my sister Linda, my cousin Bob (Uncle Hank's son), and Doug Ridder (his friend, and neighbor in Grandville), who worked for me on the farm, and along with Linda, were my first Cattle Company employees. Bob and Doug were both around the farm so much of the time (ever since they were very young) that they were really like younger brothers to me. Together, we installed the entire

Bob Schulz as a young boy.

fence (nearly a **quarter-mile** total length) in one weekend, while my parents were out of town celebrating their anniversary, and had it waiting as a surprise for them when they returned home.

9
Sports

The change to the Grandville school system introduced me to many new sports (team and individual) like football, basketball, wrestling, and track. My only previous experience with sports was baseball, at Riverbend. The Riverbend area had a little league baseball team, "The Riverbenders," which became mistakenly titled, the "Riverbend Vegetables," after some kid, at a 4th of July parade in Grandville one year, misread our homemade team T-shirts (with some of the iron-on letters missing). Probably because of all the farmers in the area, the name stuck. This was tough to live down, when we came up against teams with names like the "Wildcats," or the "Rainbow Grillers." What's a *Vegetable* going to do against a "Wildcat," or a "Griller," except get eaten or fried?! Overall though, we were a good team, with a pretty good record. I played shortstop fairly well, and since my dad had ingeniously tied a rope to a ball, with a hole through the center, and had fabricated a mechanical device to spin it in circles, for me to swing at by the hour, I was an excellent batter.

From the time I could first comprehend my father's past, I had the desire to fill his shoes. I loved sports, wanted so much to live up to my dad's reputation (which I had heard about from **many** different people), and I wanted my parents to be proud of me. I also wanted the respect one gets from excelling, so I gave sports 100%, and I remained very active and competitive in sports, as well as other activities (school plays, executive board, varsity club, etc.), throughout my school years. My sports endeavors were not without injury however (knees, ankles, etc.), and at one point I broke my neck in three places, as linebacker on the high school football team.

Mother didn't place much value in sports. She highly respected academics however, so throughout Junior High and High School, I always studied **intently**, and carried a full "college prep" load, with as many extra classes as I could squeeze in. I remained countless nights behind my little pressboard, platform desk, in my tiny 8 ft. by 10 ft. bedroom, in the upstairs corner of our farmhouse, studying Latin, Algebra, History, or other such subjects, until 2 AM. Mother was *demanding,* and difficult to satisfy, however it did motivate me. I always made the "Honor-Roll" (was a four year member of the "GHS Honor Society"), and I clearly recall proudly showing her an **all-A** report card, only to have her point out (with displeasure) that one grade was an A-minus, which I hadn't even noticed.

I love my mother, and I'm sure she wanted the best for me, but I believe that some of her actions came from her desire to have a son whom she could be proud of, and brag about. It was at Mother's hand, with letters of support from organizations like the "Grandville Rotary Club," that I was one of only two boys from Grandville High, who was appointed to, and attended "Boy's State" (with a simulated state government), the summer of my freshman year.

Mother wanted me to attend West Point; she set up a conference, and had me meet with then Senator Gerald R. Ford (later President Ford), *a couple of years* before I graduated from high school, attempting to line up a future appointment for me, which was the only way into West Point. Thank God that never came to pass, because by the time I graduated from high school, the Viet Nam war was really heating up, and a First Lieutenant's set of stripes, which came with graduation from West Point, was a potential "death sentence." First Lieutenants wind up on the front lines in wartime, and "First Lieuy stripes" are frequently the first target enemy snipers will look for, attempting to take away an adversary's leadership.

Dad was a pusher too, in his own way, mostly through setting the bar high, by boasting of his own accomplishments in sports, and expecting the same of his only son. He also made a point of asking the right questions like, "Have you made first string or team captain yet?" I wasn't very large in high school (120 lb. freshman–160 lb. senior), but he was quick to tell me how he hadn't been either. I was often embarrassed about the way he (as a spectator) could be heard above everyone else, at a football game or other sporting event that I was in. My father was "bigger than life" in some ways, and many times I felt that he did things only to draw attention to himself. Nevertheless people accepted him, everyone seemed to love him just the way he was, and hearing him **did** "spur-me-on." My embarrassment was probably just "high school insecurity," and my own self-consciousness.

At one particular time, in the 4th quarter of our varsity "Homecoming" football game, during my sophomore year, Grandville was behind 6-0, against one of our most formidable adversaries, East Grand Rapids. East Grand Rapids was preparing to hike the ball, to attempt a 3rd field goal, on our 20-yard line, with just under a minute left on the clock. Their field goal kicker was deadly accurate, having scored two long field goals already. One more would make the score 9-0, and slim as it was, would leave Grandville with **no chance** of winning its Homecoming game!

I always practiced hard, and played my heart out in our games, with every ounce of strength I could muster. Even after our **most grueling** practices, after everyone else had retired to the locker room, I would run a mile on the dirt track that circled the football field, for extra conditioning. It won me a position playing both ways on the team, as fullback on offense, and right linebacker on defense, got me advanced to varsity already as a sophomore, and earned me enough respect from my teammates to elect me as team co-captain. All of the conditioning and training helped, but nothing inspired me as much as, when "out of the blue," with the clock ticking, I heard my Dad's booming voice, "**BEAR DOWN ON EM SON!**" My dad never gave up, and when I heard him, it did something to me.

I made up my mind, and when the ball was hiked, I went through the East Grand Rapids line like a **freight train**. I was on "**a mission!**" I ran right over their tackle, and kept going. Their field goal kicker kicked the ball into my facemask. I ran right over him, somehow kept my balance, and looking up, saw the spinning ball come down into my arms. I kicked it in gear, and dodging, stiff-arming, and leaping over tacklers, ran it back 80 yards for a touchdown. We made the extra point, and won our Homecoming game against our most bitter rivals, **7-6**! Needless to say, the team carried me off the field, and honored me at the homecoming dance, but **none of it** meant as **much** to me, as the bear hug my dad gave me, in the parking lot after the game.

What I always wanted, **so much**, was for that man to be proud of me, because I loved him so **deeply**! **Everybody** did! He was **so** well liked, and he had no enemies. Dad always told me, "Son, treat others how you want to be treated," and "Life would be better if everyone did that."

I always pushed myself to the limit, often a little *beyond,* in taking my father's advice. I sometimes put myself at risk, in my attempts to earn his respect. In a future football game, which Grandville was losing, faced with an opposing running back who seemed unstoppable, I became very determined. The ball carrier was much larger than myself, but when I finally had a clear shot at him, as my dad had suggested, I hit him head-on (driving my helmet into him), with such force that neither one of us could get up at first. We finally recuperated enough to walk away, but something was wrong, and my right shoulder seemed to hurt.

When our team regained offense, and I received a handoff to carry the ball, as soon as I was hit, I fumbled. I carried the ball in my right hand, and when later questioned by the coach (I rarely fumbled), I admitted to the shoulder pain. Following the game, the team doctor found no sign of "shoulder separation," a common running back injury, and I played two more games, suffering similar pain, and embarrassing fumbles. Finally our coach (Rex Roser) suggested that I might have a neck injury, and ordered x-rays, which revealed a neck dislocation, and three cracked vertebra.

Each time I was hit (with the dislocation, and cracked vertebra), a nerve was pinched, and my right arm would drop (loose function), hence the fumbles. The doctor (specialist) who x-rayed the damage, exclaimed that I came the **closest** that he had ever seen, to becoming paralyzed from the neck down, and yet walked away with no permanent impairment. I sat out the last three games of the season in a neck brace. I was **so** fortunate not to have suffered any paralysis. My neck bothered me somewhat, for quite a few years (still does occasionally), but I have **no** damage that hinders my mobility, and I am very thankful for that.

I also joined the wrestling team, and starved and trained my way down to the 112-pound weight-class my freshman year. Grandpa Schulz passed away that year, and Grandma Schulz moved in with us. Grandma tried so hard to get me to eat more, but I couldn't eat much of **anything**, in order make the 112-pound limit. Grandma would shake her arthritic, bent, twisted little index finger at me, with a plate of food in her other hand, and say, "**Douglas**, you're **skinny**!" I loved my Grandma, and I felt so bad for her, with all the suffering that the rheumatoid arthritis caused her. She would melt wax on the stove, and frequently (with a spatula), I would coat her hands with it, to relieve the pain. Other times I would massage her hands, by the hour, often until she fell asleep.

Grandville High School was fairly large (Class A), with about 300 students in each graduating class, so there was plenty of competition in all sports. In the spring I joined the track team, lettered early, and wore three stripes on my high school sweater. I was fairly popular at Grandville (tied for homecoming king, senior vice president/class executive board member, etc.), I think because I was basically a nice guy. My parents had taught me to treat others respectfully, and equally, and I did.

I didn't fit the "high school mold" too well though, and I didn't like, or fit into "clicks." My childhood pal Dan Tanner came from a large family, where little money or importance was placed on clothes, and because Dan was kind of an unusual guy anyway, he was not easily accepted by the crowd. I put up with flack from some of the "click types" early on, for continuing to hang out with him, a habit that I refused to break, and eventually (once students got to know him) Dan became popular, so then it was "OK," *whatever.* High school kids are insecure, can be so **dramatic**, and everything is **so** important, and such a **big** deal!

Dan and his younger brother Ken were both a little rebellious. On one occasion, as I was seated in a geography classroom, a full minute after the last bell had rung, I and everyone in the room heard someone come running down the hall at full speed (which was clearly against the rules). I looked up, just in time to see Ken Tanner come thundering by, trying to avoid a tardy slip for some class. After he did, our classroom teacher ran out the open door and hollered, **"Halt!"** We all heard the pounding footsteps continue, without even slowing down. Our teacher again shouted out the same command, followed by the words, **"You're breaking the law!"** As Ken rounded a distant corner, still a full speed, we all heard him shout back the reply, **"I'm Billy-The-Kid!"**

The entire classroom broke out in resounding laughter. Our teacher stepped back into the room, and **slammed** his fist down on his desk, after which the only party still chuckling was Dan Tanner. In a very stern, **agitated** tone, the teacher demanded, "What's so **funny**, Mr. **Tanner**?" After continuing to snicker for a few more seconds, Dan responded, in a barely audible, yet clearly **prideful** tone, "That's my brother!" Venting his anger, the teacher ordered Dan, **"To the office,"** where for one reason or another, Dan spent a *lot* of time! As Dan purposely drug his feet out of the classroom, having been repeatedly reprimanded by this teacher (and several other teachers) for "shuffling," his muffled snickering could still clearly be heard, and it became mingled with giggles that his actions drew from the class. The geography teacher commanded, "**Knock it off**, or you'll **all** go to the office! I had to *bite my tongue,* to keep still!

Dan was his own man, and very smart, even though his grades didn't show it. He was wise (especially in the ways of life that matter), and I am certain that he could have done very well academically, had he put forth some effort. He just didn't place much importance on things like grades (or *school*), and he was satisfied as long as he passed. Dan didn't take direction well, **at all** really, and his antics **often** drew laughter.

Early during a tenth grade history class that Dan and I shared, just as the exceedingly boring teacher started into one of his extremely monotonous (and what we could tell was going to be another non-stop) hour long lectures, Dan leaned as far back in his chair as possible, raised his arms to the ceiling, and emitted what had to be some type of a (volume and length) **record breaking** yawn. This naturally prompted some laughter from the class. Midway through Dan's yawn, realizing that Dan had captured the attention of the class, the history teacher stopped in the middle of a sentence, pointed his index finger at Dan, and demanded that he stop, with the word, "**Enough!**"

Dan froze, with his arms still fully extended, looked around the room, and amidst chuckles, with a provocative grin on his face, asked, "Don't **yawn**?" The history teacher commanded, "Not in **my** class you don't! Dan replied, "*OK,*" and then finished his yawn, at only a *moderately* lesser volume, as he lowered his arms. This brought disruptive laughter from the class, and instant **outrage** from the teacher, as he realized that he had been "one-upped." Expressing his wrath, the teacher howled, "**To the office**," as he pointed to the classroom door! Dan got up, and slowly dragged his feet, again *shuffling* (as he had continuously been warned, *by this teacher as well,* **not** to) across the room, and out the door, purposely sporting the same (**slightly intensified**) grin.

Dan was as strong as a **bull**, and actually could have excelled far more than he did in sports as well, had it been important to him. Many times as a teenager, on weekends, I came to pick Dan up in the "Puddle Jumper" for some evening duck hunting. Dan, who was usually out in the Tanner orchards picking apples on fall evenings, would grab two full grates of apples in each hand, and hoist them up, as we hurriedly loaded the apple truck, so we could get in some hunting before dark. Though I tried many times, I could not begin such a feat. I began to coin the phrase, "Dan-Dan, The Strong Man-Man, Two Crates Of Apples In Each Hand." The handle stuck, and eventually, in and out of school, he became know as "Strong-Man-Dan."

Dan lived up to his title many times. One particular time, when both teams got into a full-on brawl, during one of our pre-season football scrimmages with a rival school, I ran over to Dan, whom I noticed still had an opponent in a "bear-hug," a couple of **minutes** after the brawl had been broken up by the coaches. Dan and his (rather large) "captive" were off to the one side of the field, and had gone unnoticed. I hollered, "Dan, let him **go**, he's turnin' **blue**!" When Dan let go, the guy collapsed to the ground. Dan's "bear-hug" was so intense, that the poor guy couldn't even expand his chest, and had passed out from lack of oxygen!

Dan was a powerful football player, and he played offensive tackle on Grandville High's football team. As team co-captain, I often called the plays (sent in from the coach), and many times Dan ran over to me, and asked what he was supposed to do, or whom he was supposed to block, on a play that I had just called. It was each player's responsibility to memorize the plays, and know his own assignment, but I learned that with Dan, that just **wasn't** going to happen, so I memorized his assignments along with mine. Dan could have been a fantastic player, many times he was, but he just couldn't be bothered with small stuff, like memorizing plays. He was so strong that anyone in his path, including **our** linemen, and sometimes **our** ball carrier (including me) was going down, which happened occasionally, when believing that he remembered his assignment, Dan didn't bother to ask me whom he should block.

Dan **was** very dedicated however. At one point, in the middle of the first quarter of a conference game, while I was out on the field, Coach Roser called for a time-out to stop the game. We all came in off the field and gathered around Dan, whom had passed out cold, and had fallen off the end of the bench, where he had been spending time as the result of a missed assignment (from an incorrectly memorized play). When the coach went over to him, Dan was as white as a sheet. Coach Roser yanked off his helmet, and gave Dan some smelling salts, which brought him around. It turned out that a new helmet Dan had been issued was too tight for him, had cut off blood to his brain, and had caused him to lose consciousness. When Coach Roser questioned why he had kept his helmet on, if it was "too tight," Dan replied, "Well Coach, I just wanted to be **ready**, in case you **needed** me!" As he walked away shaking his head, I heard Coach Roser mumble, "I just don't understand that kid at all!"

Dan was also a very good wrestler, and won most of his matches on shear strength. Dan won the conference, and regional titles on the varsity wrestling team, but his lack of speed drove our "hot-headed" Russian wrestling coach, "Zolco" nuts! Time meant nothing to Dan (seemed not to exist)! I never forgot one late afternoon visit to the Tanner farm, which I had made as a young boy, when no-one seemed to know Dan's whereabouts, and I was told that he hadn't even come up for lunch. After searching the premises for some time, I found Dan near the Tanner workshop, sitting in the dirt, with part of an old aluminum shovel in his hands. Next to Dan was a large pile of aluminum flakes (most no larger than the size of coarse ground pepper). When I asked Dan what he was doing, Dan replied, "Oh, I just wanted to see how far I could get with this." Dan was chipping away at the oxidized shovel with his thumbnail; by then, he had three-quarters of the shovel chipped up, and I could tell by his rate of progress, that he most likely had been occupied with his endeavor **all day**!

Dan just would not put anything more into something, than it absolutely required. This included homework and studying, as well as training for a wrestling match, or speed and effort in a match. On one occasion, in a tournament finals match, in the last match of the day, with Grandville's team behind on points, and needing Dan's win to be victorious, Dan was losing. Dan was six points behind his opponent, in the third (final) period of his match, and Zolco was jumping up and down, screaming at Dan to move. Dan would not "**move**" however, until he absolutely **had** to, and he was watching the time clock, saving his strength, and ignoring Zolco.

When the clock had ticked down to the last thirty seconds, and there was no longer a chance of Dan making enough points to win, with Dan on his stomach, and his opponent on top of him, Zolco threw up his hands in frustration, and stomped away from the mat. Dan then did something that neither I, nor anyone else on the team had ever before (or after) witnessed. He reached up slowly, with one of his long gorilla-strength arms, latched onto the back of his opponent's neck, and with his vice-like grip started to pull down. His opponent momentarily resisted, **pointlessly**. There was **no** way **humanly**, of breaking Dan's grip, once he had latched onto your neck, as **I could attest to**, and his opponent had a choice of **giving-in** to the pull, or **losing** his **head**! Still watching the clock as he did so, Dan slowly pulled his opponent head first, up and over his own head, and onto his opponent's back in front of him, where Dan pounced on him, and **pinned** him! The referee slapped the mat, with **two seconds** left on the clock! Dan won the match, Grandville won the tournament, and the team carried Dan into the locker room! Zolco was seemingly happy about the tournament win, but **not** with Dan.

At wrestling practice the following Monday, as punishment, Zolco put Dan and I in a team-trial match against one another, in front of the entire team. This was standard procedure, when a wrestler was challenged for his position on the first string, but made no sense to either of us, or anyone else on the team, because Dan and I were a several weight classes apart, had no intention of challenging one another, and we both already had a position on the first string. Zolco **knew** that we were best friends, and he was **angry** with Dan, and wanted to get between us. When we questioned the point of the contest, Zolco stated, "I just want to see who the better wrestler is." When we protested, he **ordered** us onto the mat, or we both were off the team for **good**.

I was **very** uncomfortable. I didn't want to **win** against my best friend (slim as my chances were), but I didn't want to **lose** to him in front of everyone either! I didn't know **what** to do, but **Dan** did. When the starting buzzer sounded, we shook hands, and crossed over to opposite sides of the mat, as is customary. We grabbed onto the back of each others neck, and began circling one another, looking for an opportunity for a takedown, as is also customary. I was still trying to figure out what to do, when Dan slid under me on his knees, going for a double leg takedown. I recoiled back, by reflex action, and stretched my arms out to hold him off, but he wasn't **there**. Dan had simulated a slip, and was on his back in front of me, rolling from side to side, pretending to have lost his equilibrium, flopping around like a "fish" (which is a term given to the poorest of wrestlers). I played into the sham, and placed one foot on his chest, raising my arms victoriously. The entire team, knowing our relationship, and feeling the intense discomfort in the gym, **roared** in laughter (and relief)!

Zolco was **furious** that Dan had foiled his plan, and sent us both to the locker room. As we walked out of the gym, Dan was sporting his infamous taunting grin, and Zolco shouted out, "Tanner, don't come back to practice for the rest of the week, until you've **made up your mind** whether or not you're going to **listen** to me!" With a monumental grin on his face, Dan responded, "Oh, I've **made** up my mind. I **quit**!" Dan was slow to make decisions in his life, but **solid**. When Dan made up his mind on something that was **it**! He never came back.

I'm sure Zolco regretted his words, which cost him a regional champion wrestler, but it was **too** late. He wouldn't have been able to get Dan back, if he **had** tried. Not long after that, I re-injured a knee, which I had injured in football. The injury required surgery, to remove some torn cartilage, and my wrestling days were over as well.

I think mostly to impress my dad, but also to live up to his reputation, when I turned 16 (the youngest age allowed by the US Amateur Boxing Federation in the 60's) I took up boxing, and I continued all through high school. At my coaxing, my dad took me to a boxing gym (Midtown Athletic Center), which was still being managed by his former amateur boxing trainer Morey Bosman, and Morey taught me the basics of boxing, to the best of his ability. I was not a natural boxer, because fighting is not my basic instinct, and becoming successful took a lot of hard training. My father was of a different era and nature, and I think boxing came innately to him. The fact is I love people, and I had to push myself to hit someone at first, but slowly I learned to. I eventually came to respect the sport (I can **be** competitive, and I am **very** determined), but in reality, had it not been for my father's past, his reputation, and my desire to win his approval, I probably never would have stepped into the ring. Once I did however, I gave it **everything** I had!

I competed in the Michigan Golden Gloves Tournament, the major, and for the most part, the only amateur boxing competition in that time frame. I did **win** a lot of matches, because of my determination, and I was a "crowd pleaser," because of my "no-quit" style. I fought fervently against many superior, and more experienced boxers, long after I probably should have been knocked out, or quit. I sat on my butt on the hard tile locker-room floor of the Civic Auditorium, feeling depressed after a very difficult West Michigan District elimination bout, my first year in the Gloves (my sophomore year of high school). After I had been sitting there for a long while, probably wondering what had happened to me, my father came into the locker-room looking for me. When Dad asked what was taking me so long, seeing my head hanging, with tears running down my cheeks, he asked, "What's the matter son?" I responded, "I just feel so **bad**! I fought as **hard** as I could, and I still lost!"

My dad threw back his head in laughter, and responded, "What are you **talking** about? You **won**! You beat a much more **experienced** boxer, literally **ran** him out of gas, and you had a **standing ovation**! It was the **fight of the night**!" I apparently had fought purely on instinct (had been hit so hard, that my memory wasn't working), because I had

no recall of anything past the first round, including the referee stopping the bout, and raising my hand in **victory**! The following year, I made it all the way to the finals, and lost a very **controversial** decision, for the West Michigan District Golden Gloves welterweight (147 lb.) championship (again after a standing ovation), which was a highly rumored topic at Grandville High, and a real boost to my ego.

10
Dating Begins

I was always a little bashful and nervous, when it came to girls. My older sister Karen pushed me though, taught me to dance, and got me attending Friday night high school dances, already as a freshman. Karen was able to convince me to attend the school dances, by telling me that girls in her class, "**juniors**," thought that I was "cute," and wanted to dance with me. It was fun, and I enjoyed the dances, but boys mature more slowly than girls, and if left up to me, I would rather have been home Friday nights, enjoying all the excitement on the farm.

By late spring term of my sophomore year (at sixteen years of age), I went out on my first date. I still didn't have the nerve to ask a girl out, but Grandville High School had an event each year (as most schools did) known as the "Twerp Dance," held on "Sadie Hawkins Day," to which the girls ask the boys out. I was asked to attend the Twerp Dance by Patricia Owens, the girl whom I had been so attracted to, when our eyes first met a few years earlier, in Grandville Junior High. Pat Owens was **very pretty**, **very popular**, and held in high regard by my male peers, even though she didn't seem to **know** it, or **act** like it, which I found even **more** attractive about her. I was **thrilled** to be going out on a date with **Patricia Owens**, who was to me, and most guys I knew, one of the **prettiest** girls in school!

By this time I owned a vehicle, a blue and white 1957 Ford Fairlane, with a T-Bird engine, which I had purchased from Mr. Zonstra

Karen, Doug, Janice, Patty, and Linda.

for fifty dollars. Patricia Owens and I attended the Twerp dance on a double date, with a couple of classmates (mutual friends). The girls treated us to dinner before we headed off to the dance (as is customary), and when I revved up the engine (producing a series of backfires), my friend "Mac" exclaimed, "**Wow glass-packs!**" I candidly admitted, "No, no mufflers," to which we all abounded in laughter. I didn't have the money for mufflers (rusted out when I bought the car), so I had hack sawed the dual exhaust pipes off, and bent them outside the car frame, just in front of the rear wheels. The motor was tired, burned a lot of oil, and made a lot of smoke, but the T-Bird engine could make the tires squawk, and I was proud of her. **Best** of all, I was driving down the road in my **own** car, on a **real** date, with the girl of my **dreams**! I thought, "If life gets any better than this, I'll **burst**!"

The Twerp dance at Grandville High was held in late May, just before school let out for the summer, and we had a terrific time. We took a drive out to "Tunnel Park" after the dance (a state beach on Lake Michigan), which was a popular gathering spot for high school sweethearts. We took a long romantic walk on the beach, holding hands under the moonlight, and even though I didn't have the nerve to ask if I could kiss her, my heart was melting. A couple of weeks later I asked Patricia out on a second date, for a day of swimming and water skiing with a group of friends at a classmate's cottage, scheduled to take place shortly after the school session ended.

The classmate, whose parents owned a cottage on Kimball Lake, about fifty miles north of Grand Rapids, drew all attending parties a map, and the plan was set. I picked Patricia up in my "57" as arranged, and I had the **time** of my life. It seemed to me that **she** did too, and I was **convinced** by our mutual attraction, that I now had a *girlfriend!* When I returned home to the farm, I affirmed to myself, "Well that's done! I have a girlfriend now, and I don't have to worry about **that** anymore!" Confident of our relationship, I stayed busy on the farm, and never bothered to call her once, the rest of the summer.

When school started again that September, I was **shocked** to hear the news (which some rivals couldn't **wait** to tell me), that Pat Owens had a boyfriend, an **older** boy (*already graduated*), from another school! I was *devastated!* I thought that I had found my **perfect** match, and that this Doug Fenske/Pat Owens relationship was a "**done deal**." I couldn't *believe* that I was going to have to *start over* again, and how **could** I? This was the girl of my **dreams!** Man had I ever **blown** it! My first encounter with the "Ya Snooze, Ya Lose" reality!

I dated a number of girls in my junior and senior year, for rare events like the prom, where everyone brought a date, but nothing seemed to "click," at least for me. A couple of girls in high school were much more interested in me than I was in them, which for me was quite uncomfortable. I was then, and still am a very sensitive individual, and I am cautious not to cause hurt feelings.

One night after football practice in my senior year, I came out to the school parking lot and found two girls (juniors) sitting in the front seat of my car. One of the two (named "Fran"), who was interested in me and had brought a friend, was our varsity football coach's very pretty, and very popular daughter. She let me know that she was interested in me for a boyfriend, and the match was made. We dated exclusively the remainder of my senior year, and for my first year in college, but by mid-year of her freshman year at another college, we broke it off. The relationship just wasn't right for either of us, but we remained good friends.

I had many wonderful times in my high school years, including football games, building floats, parties, dances, school plays, and numerous other events. Somehow, in spite of my somewhat "give it all you have" demeanor (other than the many sports related injuries), I managed to survive relatively "unscathed," and intact. In some ways, it seems as though a person can survive almost anything, if it's not yet their time to go.

One night I was riding as a passenger, with three Riverbend friends, on our way to a high school dance, excited, in a hurry, careless, as sixteen-year-olds often are, when my friend suddenly **slammed** on the brakes, just as we were coming into Grandville. His car slid sideways, with all four tires squealing and smoking, coming to a sudden stop, just inches from a railroad crossing. One of us barely got out the words, "Why did you—?," to which my friend was only able to utter, "I don't kno—," when a very fast moving freight train **thundered** by!

There was no warning, and the traffic signals and stop arms were, for some reason, non-functional. After sitting speechless for a few minutes, covering our ears with our hands, as the deafening train bolted past, there was no question in any of our minds that we all would have **died**, had my friend not instinctively slammed on the brakes the **instant** that he did.

We drove silently the last half mile to the high school gymnasium, and told the dance chaperone, who called in the malfunctioning railroad crossing. I noticed that all four of us were unusually quiet at the dance that evening, and we didn't talk much about the incident ever again. I think we all just wanted to forget that it ever happened. If one believes in guardian angels, we **owe** ours for saving us *that* night!

11

The Cattle Truck

My enthusiasm to make money continued throughout my high school years. I was constantly trying to scheme up new ways to make some money. There wasn't enough profit in raising beef cattle to satisfy me, so I decided to try my hand at trucking, buying, and selling beef cattle as well. There were weekly cattle (livestock) auctions at neighboring towns four nights a week, and I learned the trade through countless hours of observation. When I felt that I was finally ready to risk some cash, I drove my first "home-made" cattle truck to an auction.

Before the cattle truck, my only way of moving cattle on the farm, was on foot or horseback. It sometimes didn't work out too well, especially at weaning time. We always penned the weaned calves at the smaller barn, on a feedlot that the farm-help and I had built across Kenowa, on the old Morry farm, and getting them there was usually very difficult. Calves don't like to be separated from their mothers, and they will do anything they can to prevent that. The horse I rode at the time was a dark quarter horse named "Bigboy," who was good with cattle, and many times he helped me carry in a newborn, which had been abandoned by his mother (usually a confused first-calf heifer). Bigboy was also pretty darned good at cutting cattle. He may not have been "world-class," like the big money winners at the cutting-horse rodeo competition, but he didn't know that. Besides, the calves at the rodeos haven't just been separated from their mothers for the first time, and their determination to out-maneuver a cutting horse, is no-where near the same.

Doug riding "Bigboy" carrying calf.

Once (prior to the cattle truck) out of frustration, after several escapees had made it back to the main herd, for the **third** time, we decided to load the weaned calves into one of the hay wagons, to transport them across the road. The hay wagons had high (eight-foot) sides and backs to catch bales, because I had an automatic bale-thrower on the back of my "New-Holland" hay baler (which could pitch a wagon clear full), and this seemed like a viable option.

After filling up the first load of calves, we tied a farm gate across the front of the wagon to keep them in, and pulled the wagon over to the smaller barn with a tractor. Everything went smoothly, until we were almost there, and I noticed the tires on one side of the wagon start to come off the ground. Too many of the calves had crowded over to one side, and the light framed hay wagon couldn't support their weight. I hollered at Bob and Doug, "**Chase em back!** They're gonna **tip the wagon**!" Misunderstanding me, Bob and Doug jumped onto the high side of the wagon, in a futile effort to try to hold it down, which only chased the remaining calves across to the low side, and **over** she **went**, spilling all the calves!

The force of the tip, which sent the hay wagon right into the road-side ditch, catapulted Bob and Doug (like they had just been launched from a slingshot) twenty feet out into the field, and twisted the wagon tongue like a pretzel! The calves all escaped unharmed and headed **hell-bent** back to their mothers. Needless to say, we were right back to moving calves the old way, with a hay wagon to repair when we finished. I knew that what I needed on the farm was a cattle truck, at least once every year at weaning time. This would also give me a way of transporting finished cattle to the cattle auctions, as well as bringing purchased feeders back to the farm, without the expense of paying someone for trucking. I was convinced that I could also make some money trucking livestock. I didn't have the money to purchase a cattle truck, so I put some energy into alternatives.

My father had allowed the Pepsi-Cola Bottling Company to discard some old out-dated soda trucks (which he thought might be useful for parts) in our farm "bone-yard." With Dad's permission, I was allowed to renovate a '58 Ford soda truck into a cattle truck. It was necessary for me (and my farm help) to remove the sloped truck-bed (badly rusted) steel floor, and replace it with some "used" plywood. We installed used 2-inch by 6-inch boards in the grooves on the sides of the truck box, in which steel roll-up doors had previously tracked, and separated the two by sixes with 2-inch square blocks of wood (to provide ventilation).

We painted the truck black and white, with a small air-spray paint gun. My younger sister Jan hand painted my dba company name ("Doug Fenske Cattle Company") on both cab doors, and on the truck box, and the truck looked petty good. Monday through Thursday, I rarely missed a cattle sale, looking for some trucking work. The sales frequently lasted until 10 PM, and after loading, and delivering cattle, it was often 1AM by the time I arrived home. I was always practicing and competing in some sport (football, wrestling, boxing, or track) after school, but since most auctions didn't start until seven PM, and lasted for several hours, I could still make it to a livestock sale before the sales ended. Because it was rare to find trucking work until the auction sales were nearly over, I had enough time to rush home after sport practice, hurry through my chores, grab some food as I ran out the door, and make the sale. I usually brought homework with me, and worked on it in the auction sale stands, or while delivering cattle (not very safe, but I made it work). I was young, didn't need much sleep, and the inspiration to make money kept me going.

I also watched the paper for weekend farm auctions, in search of additional trucking work, and I usually found some. One very blistery cold Saturday in January, I attended a cattle auction at a farm south of Grand Rapids, near Wayland, MI. I was able to pick up some work, delivering six Holstein dairy cows to an Amish dairy farm (140 miles south), near Shipshewana, Indiana. Even though it was late afternoon by the time the sale ended, and delivery was a long distance, it paid by the mile, so I took the job.

It was extremely cold that Saturday (-10 degrees F), with a harsh wind, that brought the chill index to near 40 degrees below zero. That old Ford cattle truck had an undersized Dagenham diesel engine, which would only push it to 55 mph tops. The heater and defrost didn't work very well (hardly at all), and it was a **long, cold** trip. Fortunately my friend Dan Tanner had accompanied me that Saturday, and having someone to visit with made the trip more bearable. We were only seventeen, and time passes by much more slowly when you're young, especially if you're miserably cold.

We ran out of freeway after we crossed the Indiana state line, and we started down country roads, following the directions the owner of the Holsteins had given us. About ten miles off the freeway, in the middle of nowhere, we came to a stop sign at an intersection. When I pressed down on the brakes to stop, the pedal went right to the floor, and nothing happened. Luckily it was extremely rural, with very little traffic, and no vehicles were crossing, as we sailed through the intersection at a fairly high rate of speed. Frantically pumping the brakes, I down shifted, and finally we coasted to a stop, next to the 10 ft. high windrows of snow, which lined both sides of the road. Dan and I baled out of the truck to find out what was **wrong**!

When we started inspecting under the truck with my flashlight, **to our horror**, we discovered one of the Holstein cows, firmly seated on the rear differential of the cattle truck! The cow was too heavy for the 3/4 inch plywood floor I had installed, and her rear quarters had fallen through the floor. While thrashing around trying to free herself, one of her rear legs had broken a break line, and as I had pressed down on the break peddle (repeatedly) trying to stop, all of our break fluid sprayed out on the road. It was actually a good thing the Holstein had broken the break line, or we probably would not have discovered the problem until we arrived. However, we were now burdened with coming up with a solution. There were no farm lights, or even vehicle headlights in any direction, so we knew that it was up to us to get ourselves out of this dilemma. We didn't have enough money between us anyway, to pay someone to fix our problem, even if we could have found help.

Pacing back and forth, I began to fret about our situation, but Dan always had a way of calming my nerves. Just as he had throughout my life, each time I would start to get all worked up about something or someone, Dan latched onto the back of my neck (with one of his gorilla-grips), and while firmly squeezing and rocking my head from side to side, uttered the words, "Oh Ouser, don't go getting all bent 'outta' shape now!" This usually was enough to prompt a chuckle, bring me back to reality, and cause me to realize the insignificance of my current trauma. This time however, I was **exceedingly** worried.

We knew the first order of business was to get the 1200-pound Holstein cow back into the truck. The end of her tail (the very tip) had been severed, after becoming entangled in the universal joint of the drive shaft, there was blood everywhere, and the situation appeared desperate. The Holstein dairy cow was worth nearly 1000 dollars, and I carried only the bare minimum vehicle insurance on my cattle truck, which covered nothing on its contents. It's a good thing that neither Dan nor I are very reactionary individuals, because the unfavorable conditions in which we found ourselves required **100 per cent** of our wits.

Dan and I are both farm boys, with an instinctual ability to manifest solutions, when none seem probable, and we both have strong backs. Knowing that our legs had the strongest muscles on our bodies, we crawled under the cow, with our backs flat on the ice covered country road. With both legs, we each pushed up on the cow with all our strength, and amazingly, with the cow's cooperation, we were able to get her back up into the truck. Incredibly, the cow had no broken bones, and other than a slightly shorter tail, and splattered blood, she was fine. We then crowded all the cattle to the front of the truck, covered the hole with the cattle-loading ramp, and tied it in place.

We turned the truck around, and cautiously (with no brakes) headed back toward the freeway, where we had seen a service station, which fortunately (after 11PM, when we arrived) was still open. The service station had no mechanic on duty, and was not large enough to get the cattle truck inside, but they did carry break-line repair tubing, and break fluid. Dan and I were **bone** cold, with numb fingers and hands, but after we warmed ourselves a little on a space heater in the service station, we were able to make the necessary repairs (in the service station parking lot). It took forever to bleed the air out of the break-lines manually, taking turns, with one of us lying on our back on the ice covered parking lot, opening and closing the air bleed valve with an end-wrench, while the other one pumped the break pedal in the cab. Eventually we developed some pedal, the brakes became functional, and we were back on the road.

We finally arrived at the delivery farm, around one AM, and woke up the farm owner, by knocking loudly on the front door. I was concerned that he would be very upset, and may have even called the authorities on us; however he wasn't at all angry. I had discovered at other times that the Amish are normally very warm and forgiving. The farmer and his wife were very understanding and hospitable, and stated that they figured we must have had some trouble, but that they had remained confident, "We would be along, in due time."

Dan and I had cleaned up the blood on the cow, with a bucket of warm water at the service station, and my fears over the farmer's potential anger, regarding his cow's injured tail, were immediately dispelled by his statement, "Oh, with a shorter tail, she won't swat me in the face when I'm milking her." The Amish do not use electricity, tractors, or any other types of mechanization, and chores like milking cows are all done by hand. Dan and I had both had our fair share of milking cows by hand, had felt the sting of a swat in the face by a cow's tail, and we knew what he was talking about, as we nervously chuckled. Mostly, we appreciated his understanding, and compassion.

After we unloaded the cows, the farmer insisted that we come into the house, warm ourselves, and fill our bellies, before starting the long cold trip home. His wife had warmed up some delicious roast beef, potatoes, and gravy leftovers for us, which Dan and I ravenously devoured. We were paid in cash, given warm hugs goodbye, and finally headed for home around 2AM. Dan and I made it home nearly frozen around 5AM (the temperature dropped to -15 degrees F. that night), split the cash, and were **very glad** to have warm covers to crawl into.

I made money hauling cattle with that old Pepsi-Cola cattle truck throughout my teen years, nothing big, but enough to have some cash to invest. I started buying a few feeder cattle here and there (at live-stock auctions), using the knowledge I had gained to make what I felt were good purchases. Sometimes it would be a feeder bull that hadn't been castrated, or a steer or heifer that hadn't been dehorned, or a feeder that was a little too thin, had a little mange, or a cough, and needed a little TLC. I knew how to doctor them up (with antibiotics, etc.), dehorn, delouse, de-worm, castrate, whatever it took to make them healthier, put on some weight, and look and do a lot better. Most of the time, I could bring them back to an auction in 6-8 weeks, and resell them as a feeder, for a few cents more per pound, plus make some money on the pounds gained.

Once in a while I'd find a good weight gainer, and I'd "finish the feeder out" (as cattlemen say) to 1000–1200 pounds, on my own feedlot. I maintained two feedlots on my parent's farm, on which I finished out feeders (sorted by size) from my own cow-calf herd, and I turned loose any "keepers," into the appropriate lot. There were very few nights that I didn't find one or two good buys at a cattle auction, and I'd load up my purchases with others that I was paid to truck that night. I had a separation gate in the cattle pen on the truck, and I usually locked my purchased feeders up in the front of the truck, to avoid having to re-sort them. I would sometimes haul finished beef cattle off my own feedlots with me to the cattle auctions, although as time went by, I sold more and more beef by the side.

By word-of-mouth, I developed a reputation for high quality beef, at a fair price. I was able to cut out the middle-men (wholesalers, supermarkets, etc.), and Doug Fenske Cattle Company almost always had a waiting list of orders for sides-of-beef. It was a good business, and I did all right for a teenager. I may not have made it into the cattle business, had it not been for my parent's farm, but I worked fervently, put in long hours, kept our family supplied with beef as I had agreed, and I was proud of the business I had built.

There were few times that I got "stung" on purchases, but once I took a bad "hit" (along with many mid-west farmers). One night I ran into what I felt was a very good buy. Some Black Angus heifers came through the Wayland Livestock auction ring one Tuesday evening, and were sold all together. I was shocked at how low the bids were, probably because the heifers appeared to be bred, and most all bidders were either buying feeder cattle, or finished "butcher beef" cattle. Since I owned a brood cowherd that I could commingle these bred heifers in with, and eventually make some money on the calves on my own feedlots, I bought all thirty head, at a cost of around $10,000 (nearly everything I had in savings).

All of the cattle seemed fine at first, but after a couple of weeks they started to lose weight, and began dying. The heifers kept going down hill no matter what I did, or what I fed them. None of my usual antibiotics were effective, my veterinarian had no clue what was wrong, and as they started to calve, they all needed help with delivery. Every calf was stillborn, and eventually I lost every last heifer. I took some of the carcasses into my vet to determine the cause of death, with no conclusive results. I was **baffled**. The news soon started to be filled, with stories of farmers all through Michigan, and several surrounding states, experiencing the same thing. Stories surfaced of huge dairy farmers losing their entire herds, with some farmers even driven to suicide. Eventually it turned out to be the "PBB Incident."

A company called "Michigan Farm Bureau Services" had inadvertently mixed vast amounts of fire-retardant chemicals into cattle (hogs, and other farm animal) supplements. The fire-retardant PBB (Poly-Bromated Bi-phenols), which was mistaken or mislabeled, caused hundreds of millions of dollars in damages, including birth defects and stillbirths in animals, and health problems in humans (as the dairy and beef products were consumed). The loses drove many farmers into bankruptcy, and cost MI Farm Bureau Services millions of dollars. Retesting on a couple of very week, but still live heifers detected PBB as the cause of death in the cattle I had purchased, and I tried to collect some damage restitution, but since I had not personally fed the supplements to my purchased cattle, I was not able to collect anything.

As I was burying the last couple of head on our farm, my dad stated, "Remember son, a fool and his money are soon parted." I never understood why Dad said that to me. Thinking back years later, he may have felt a little threatened by my youthful success. His remark hurt **worse** than the $10,000 loss, because I always cared so much what he thought of me. I didn't stop buying cattle to make a profit, but I did become much more cautious from then on.

12

Linda the Cowgirl

My youngest sister "Linda" was the most "Tom-boy-ish" of all my sisters, or so she became. Actually as a little girl, Linda was always the most demure, and "feminine" of my sisters. Mother would dress them all up in their bonnets, and Easter Sunday dresses, and Linda seemed the most content of them all in that attire. Sometimes I have had concern that Linda changed (was actually accused of causing changes in Linda), as a result of the rigorous demands of working for Doug Fenske Cattle Company, or because she thought that was what I expected or admired. I guess I shouldn't flatter myself so much, but I loved Linda dearly (still do), became closest to her, and always felt that she strongly loved me too.

Linda helped me tremendously on the farm, eventually as Doug Fenske Cattle Company (DFCC) "Foreman," but she was really a partner, and a **good** friend. I love all of my sisters, but Linda and I became very close, working shoulder to shoulder for many years, and putting our heads together to solve "many-a-problem." If we weren't hooking a cable-winch to an oak tree, to pull out a buried tractor in a downpour, on a spring day, when every last tractor we owned was stuck, we were laboring side-by-side, trying to pull out a breach-birth calf in the middle of the night. At the end of a long week, we would drink a few beers with the cattle company employees, and laugh at our struggles and ourselves.

Linda, Patty, and Janice—"The Three Little Pigs."

Linda driving the tractor.

Linda riding her horse, "Cone," with farm dog "Bear."

On one occasion Linda was trying to make it back to the main farm, late in the day, late in the year, with a full wagonload of round bales of hay. The homemade bale wagon she was pulling was way over legal width and length, was over the limit on weight, as well as height; it was nearly dark, and the wagon had no **brakes**, let alone tail or break lights! Linda got caught in heavy traffic on a freeway overpass, which was under construction, and the bale-wagon would not fit between rows of concrete abutments. It was impossible to back up the swivel-tongue wagon she was towing, even if she could have seen around the fourteen-foot wide stack of bales on the wagon, or didn't have 50 impatient vehicles behind her, with horns blasting.

With no other option, Linda began to inch forward, and attempted to squeeze between the yellow blinking lights mounted on top of the abutments. As she did so, the first two blinking lights snapped from the steel brackets fastening them to the concrete abutments, and shattered as they fell defunct to the concrete road. With the tempo of the shrieking horns escalating, Linda crept forward, only to witness the next two lights suffer the same fate. A traffic director, manning a radio, helping to control the two-way traffic over the single lane open on the overpass, hollered out to Linda, "Take 'er on thru Honey, yer gonna break 'em all!" Two young construction workers ran ahead of Linda, attempting **fruitlessly** to unfasten and save the remaining lights. Because of the time involved in disconnecting the lights, and the ardent fever of the crowd, the workers threw up their hands in anguish, and watched as Linda destroyed every last one of the yellow blinking lights. Later that evening, the entire cattle company crew and I all roared in laughter, as Linda shared her story.

There were times that Linda and I took shifts relieving one other, as we worked throughout the night, planting corn 24 hours a day. With Michigan's short growing season, a corn crop could be a total loss, if it didn't have the few months necessary to mature before the first fall frost hit, sometimes as early as September. We became fair size corn growers as time went by, planting several hundred acres per year, continually leasing additional acreage. We also grew wheat, oats, and many acres of hay, mostly alfalfa, timothy, and brome grass, usually some combination. Our hay eventually was harvested mostly all in round bales, easier for feeding to the brood-cow herd (initially wintered out in wooded lots).

Linda and I saw eye to eye on most issues, but we differed on one in particular. Linda always said to me, "Doug, I'm only a *cow*girl," but at one point in time, fairly early on in the cattle business (when my younger sisters were still quite young), I decided to try my hand at raising pigs. I had heard that feeder pigs, penned in with cattle on feedlots, did well. Pigs will root through cattle manure, eating any silage spilled by cattle, and also eating any undigested corn cornels. The presence of a few pigs can have a calming effect on feedlot cattle, and they often do better with pigs mixed in with them.

As a teenager, I purchased my first batch of 25 feeder pigs, at a Monday night livestock auction in Ravenna (a burg about 40 miles NW of the farm). My transportation that night was the old family Chrysler station wagon, handed down to me by my parents, to transport my sisters and I to and from school. I hadn't really planned to buy any feeder pigs that particular night, only to observe prices, so I had left the cattle truck home. However, prices were much better that night than what I had been seeing, I couldn't resist throwing in a bid, and sure enough it stuck.

Feeder pigs are auctioned right out of the back of trucks, and the feeder pig seller looked very surprised, when I backed my station wagon up to his truck, in which to load the 25, 40-pound feeder pigs. When I pulled out of the sale yard, the hood of the car was aimed at the stars (with 1000 pounds of pigs on board), and the windows quickly steamed up. At a stoplight on the way home, in the small town of Coopersville, a police cruiser happened to pull up along side of me. My rear springs were bottomed out, and the restless pigs were rocking the car from side to side. I could see the officer straining to see through the fogged windows on my station wagon, trying to figure out what it was I had on board. I had the driver's door window open, so I could see the outside rearview mirror, and of course **breathe**! Just as the light turned green, a feeder pig stuck his head over the front seat, right next to mine. I quickly gave the pig an elbow, and drove off, with a friendly wave and smile to the officer, who (I was relieved to see) sat motionless, with his jaw dropped open, and a bewildered expression!

After finally arriving home, and unloading my new purchase, I was burdened with the task of hosing and scrubbing out the back of the station wagon, which was never to be the same. The next morning, with windows wide open, the wails of complaint from my younger sisters could be heard throughout the neighborhood, as we headed up Kenowa on our way to school. Despite routine scrubbings with soap and bleach, and many pine-scent air fresheners, I never completely got rid of the pig stench, and the scene replayed itself many times. The best I could do was to attempt to disguise the odor. If we had a passenger, there was always the question, "What is that smell?" If I was alone the response was, "What smell, I don't know," but if any of the "Three Little Pigs" were along, it was, "Yeah, doesn't that **stink**?! **Ask Doug**!"

I continued to raise feeder pigs on the farm for years, purchasing them at 20–40 pounds each, and finishing them out to sell, at 200–220 pounds, never venturing into sows and litters. We eventually fattened as many as 200 pigs at a time (far more than the cattle feedlots could support), and we used a number of different products for feed. Being close to town, we had access to quite a few food-scrap products, including carrots, celery, and dairy products, from food processing companies, which were anxious to unload scrap waste, free of charge. There was a huge potato processing plant, located only a mile and a half

from the farm, which generated many tons per day, of potato processing scrap. In the process of making french-fries, potato chips, powered potatoes, and several other types of potato products, tons of
potato slurry waste (potato peels, and pieces) are generated.

We experimented with the potato slurry, in attempts to find the best
way to handle and feed the product. The hogs did best with it dumped
out in the open, in the dirt. Linda and I, along with Bob and Doug
constructed a hog fence. To save money, we used scrap wood pallets,
placed side by side, partially buried in a trench, which we furrowed
with a one-bottom plow. We fenced in about seven acres with pallets,
and the pigs ran freely. The truckloads of potato slurry were dumped
in the open, or over the fence, throughout the hog pasture. The pigs
would wallow in belly-deep, and gobble potatoes at will. They got
really messy, and at times, only the whites of their eyes remained mud
free. In the heat of the summer, the potatoes would rot, which caused
the pigs to smell plenty foul, but they fattened up rapidly on the
potato waste.

We had many wild hog-roundups on livestock sale nights, with
some of the landfill employees (described ahead) helping us after
work. I have laughable memories of an occasional member of the
"hog roundup crew" losing his footing, knee-deep in the potato slurry,
while trying to cut off the escape route of some pigs. It was all in
good fun, and though not nearly as humorous to the rotten-potato-
slurry enameled victim, as to his co-"hog-roundup crew" members, it
worked out fine. Once the roundup was complete, the victim was
hosed off along with the hogs that had been sorted for sale, and he
would enjoy a beer and laughs along with the rest of us.

Beer Drinkin' Buddies

Actually on one occasion, we discovered that **pigs** like beer too. I
got wind of a truckload of beer that was on a semi-trailer, which had
caught fire, and needed to be discarded. Insurance had paid the dis-
tributor, the beer was in cans and bottles, most of the cases weren't
even singed, and having sampled the beer myself, I could attest that it
was fine. I thought the beer would probably help fatten up the pigs,
and it was free, so I took it. The pig feed-troughs were steel half barrels, split lengthwise, and connected end to end, located in the open
main barn. After penning up all the pigs, Linda, Bob, and Doug
endured an afternoon of snapping pop tabs, and un-capping bottles,
tediously filling the barrels. When I looked in on them about quitting
time, the feed troughs were nearly full.

We pulled the barn doors closed, and turned the pigs loose. The pigs ran up to the barrels, and at first just looked, and sniffed at the beer. Just as I thought Linda, Bob, and Doug may have wasted an afternoon, one of the pigs took a sip, and word spread **instantly**! Within seconds the pigs were squealing, and fighting to get their noses into the barrels, so much so, that they were crawling on each other's backs! There were jam-packed rows of pigs on either side of the barrels, and a row of pigs in the middle standing **straight up and down**, with their noses in the center of the barrels! Who **knew**! They **loved** beer! All four of us roared in laughter at their antics, and we were amazed at how quickly they emptied the barrels!

Once the barrels were empty (which only took minutes), it became **deftly quiet** in the barn…for about a minute or so, with all of the pigs just looking around in pure silence, seeming rather confused. Then one of them let out a **loud** snort, and all at once, they **all** took off running, and grunting, and squealing, in different directions, all **over** the barn. They were **drunk**! At first we laughed, as pigs ran nose to nose into each other, and others ran head-long into steel support pipes, oak support posts, or the closed heavy wood doors at the end of the large barn.

When they kept it up however, I became **alarmed**! I shouted at Linda, Bob, and Doug, "Come-on, we've got to **stop** them!" I was concerned they would hurt themselves, or at the very least, run all the fat off themselves!" We ran in amongst them, trying to calm them down, corral them, or stop them somehow, but it was **hopeless**! We weren't able to slow them down one iota, and we were run into, knocked off our feet, and even had pigs run right over us from time to time. Finally we just gave it up, and let them run themselves sober. The pigs undoubtedly ran off more weight than they put on from the beer, and I learned the hard lesson, that pigs and alcohol **don't mix**!

We had plenty of hog roundups of escaped hogs as well. Linda used to say that (unlike cattle) hogs, "Had their head built on the wrong end of them." Pigs always wanted to go the opposite way that you wanted them to go, and they always wanted to be, and frequently were, where you didn't want them to be, which was the main reason Linda despised raising hogs. Pigs have a snout that is built to root, and we couldn't bury the pallets on the hog fence-line deep enough to keep the pigs from excavating an escape route. We tried adding an electric fence, which worked fairly well, until the electric wire shorted out, which happened constantly. It was necessary to keep the hotwire close to the ground, to keep the pigs from mining an exit under the wire. However when soil rooted up near the fence-line came in contact with the hotwire, the wire shorted out, and it never took the pigs long to discover the fence was shorted out. As soon as the first pig escaped, and sent out a freedom snort, all the rest were soon to follow.

One Sunday, on our return from church, when the family station wagon rounded the corner into the farmhouse driveway, **all seven members** of the Fenske family **gasped**! Our farm lawn, consisting of a huge front yard, nearly the size of a football field (bordered by a long gravel driveway), wrapping around the farmhouse, breezeway and garage, connecting to the side yard, running laterally forty yards to the bunk house, circling to the back yard, extending 100 yards straight back to the barn, was no longer a sea of green. The pigs had escaped while we were in church, and had tilled the entire lawn with their snouts. Our fearless watchdog "Hercules," whom had accidentally been locked in the garage when we left for church, was unable to intervene. Apparently one of the pigs discovered a grub, or something delectable, that he had rooted up in the soft early spring sod, and the word spread. Needless to say, I and my "Cattle Company" employees would spend numerous hours in the days ahead, turning over clumps of sod, rolling out bumps, and righting the pigs wrong.

The Mighty "Hercules"

"Hercules" was a black-lab-mix dog that my father brought home once, given to him by a business which was unable use him as a night watch dog (for which he had been purchased), because he was **too fierce** (none of the employees could handle him)! Actually Herc just had some issues, and a **bad temper**! On one occasion, we had to replace a cast (several times) that the vet had placed on Herc's badly broken front foot, because he kept **attacking** his **own foot**, as a result of the shooting pain he felt whenever he put weight on it!

Herc is the only dog I have ever seen, or heard of, that would attack an electric fence. Most dogs will yelp and run if they touch an electric fence, but if Herc's tail touched an electric fence, Herc would turn on the fence, and start ferociously barking at it, running up and down the fence line, snapping at it. One day after a heavy rain, my father heard some loud hissing noises, and upon walking out the farm shop door, found Hercules sitting in a mud puddle, with his jaw locked on an electric fence he had bitten. Because he was sitting in the puddle, and so well grounded, the electricity caused Herc's jaw muscles to lock down, and he could not let go.

My father stomped the wire to the ground, shorting out the current, and Herc was finally able to open his jaw and release the wire. It probably saved his life, but the incident resulted in a trip to the veterinarian, when for several following days, Herc would not eat. The vet discovered that Herc's only problem was constipation. He was so sore in his rectal area, from the electric current shorting out on the water he was sitting in, that he would not let his bowls move. After a few days on an enema, and with the application of some salve, Herc was back to normal, and right back to occasionally attacking electric fences.

Herc loved to ride around in the cab of the pickup truck with me, but he liked to hang his head out the window, and he didn't like sharing his seat. Once when I picked up Doug Ridder, by then tagged "Easy Ridder" (after Peter Fonda in the '69 movie "Easy Rider"), from a fence-line he had been working on near the western end of the farm, Easy Ridder jumped into the cab of the truck, and pushed Herc (who uncooperatively resisted) over to the center of the seat. As we began to travel down the two-track back toward the farmyard (at the end of a long hard day), I heard a growling sound, and I looked over to see Herc's nose, right in Easy Ridder's face, **clearly** letting him know of his displeasure with the seating arrangement.

Even though pound-for-pound, not much larger than Herc at the time, Doug (a young teen) was not someone to be bullied around however, and before I could intervene, Easy Ridder grabbed Herc right by the throat, as you would grab someone by the shirt collar. He held a fist right in Herc's face, and commanded, "**Shut-up** Herc, or I'll **bust** you **right** in the mouth! Easy Ridder apparently was convincing enough, because that put an end to the issue, and to any future disputes between them regarding seating.

Arnold the Pig

At one point in time I owned a pig, which would not stay fenced, and as a result, eventually became a member of our family. I had purchased a truckload of thirty feeder pigs at a livestock auction, and turned them loose in the barn for the night. The following morning at breakfast, one of the feeder pigs had escaped, and was at our back door, "chirping" for attention, or a handout. Amazingly, this was the only pig that had escaped, and I never could discover how, or where. That same feeder pig repeated the stunt continually (daily), over the next week, no matter what means of keeping him penned up I employed. I **swear**, this pig could **untie** knots, **flip** gate latches, and **push** thumb buttons on barn doors!

While he was out, he never did any damage; he just seemed to want to be with people. Over time we named him "Arnold," after a pig on a popular sixty's TV show called "Green Acres," let him run free, and had loads of fun with him, for years. Arnold would follow us everywhere we went (even on long hikes), just like Hercules, and the other farm dogs. The dogs weren't crazy about Arnold at first, but as time went along, the dogs (even Hercules) accepted Arnold, and they would be seen napping side by side with him in the back yard. Before long, Arnold even took up residence in one of the dog-coops, and he was always the first to greet any visitors who stopped by.

Arnold grew to be much larger than the dogs, and eventually reached about 400 pounds. We didn't find out until years later, after Arnold had met his "Waterloo," what a "wanderer" he really had become. On one of his daily expeditions, Arnold was hit by, and totaled out a 1969 Camero, on Wilson Ave, a half mile east of the farmhouse. Arnold loved being scratched behind the ears, and I think he got lonely for human attention, when all the Fenske kids went to school. He also loved "handouts," and after he was killed, neighbors as far as two miles away asked, "Where's Arnold? We haven't seen him at our back door begging for a treat, in a long time!"

Other than Arnold, Linda far preferred cattle to hogs, and I must admit so did I. To me, cattle just plain smell better, sound better, and as well, are much easier to keep fenced in. Also cattle are far less difficult to round up, if they do get out.

Over time we also found cattle to be very fond of scrap products, like carrots, celery, and even melons. Naturally, most food scrap products are very seasonal, but we did learn how to preserve potatoes, which cattle are also very fond of. Linda and I and the farm employees constructed four large bunk silos (40 ft. by 100ft. by 12 ft.), made of walmanized (wood-preservative treated) tongue and groove two by six boards, with railroad tie supports, and asphalt floors. As we harvested corn each fall for silage, we dumped truckloads of the scrap potato pieces onto the concrete aprons in front of the bunk silos, and mixed, and packed the potato waste in with the corn silage, as we filled the bunk silos. We fed the corn/potato silage to the feedlot cattle with an old Lorain front-end loader, into fence-line feed troughs, which we had constructed on the edge of the feedlots. The cattle loved it, did very well on it, and the potatoes (along with other vegetables) became a stable food-source in the feedlot cattle diet.

Cattle also have an inherent wisdom, as I learned from time to time. I always wintered the first-calf heifers separate from the main brood cowherd, so that when it got near calving time, we could keep a better eye on them. Usually once a cow has birthed a calf, it will deliver a newborn each year on it's own, with no problem, but they sometimes need a little help with the first one. As I drove past the first-calf heifers one early spring evening, I noticed a heifer bellowing, and prancing up and down a creek bank, which ran through the old "Morry" barnyard, and provided fresh water for the cattle. It was still March, and a few weeks before I expected any calves, but the heifer was so persistent, that I stopped my truck to see what was up. When I got to the creek bank, which dropped down about six feet at a forty-five degree angle, to a shallow one-foot deep by three-foot wide creek, I saw the problem.

There laying flat on its side in the frigid water, with thin ice on the edges (it was 25 degrees Fahrenheit that evening), was a newborn calf, struggling to hold its nose up for air. Born just above the creek, the calf had slipped down the bank, before it had even learned to walk. I dragged the calf out, and up the bank, and tried to dry it off with some burlap sacks, but the first-calf heifer (the calf's mother) kept pushing me away. It was very unusual for any of the cattle to get close enough to touch a person, let alone push them, so I was a little surprised. I swatted at her at first, but she was so tenacious in her desire to get me away, that I gave-in, to see what she wanted.

To my amazement, the heifer pressed her snout into her newborn's side, over and over, and blew her warm breath all up and down the calf's body. She kept it up for twenty minutes while I watched, and she continued when I left. I figured the calf had a slim chance of not catching pneumonia and surviving, but the heifer must have kept it up long enough, because when I checked later, the mother had nursed the calf, led it inside, and was snuggled up with her calf, in a warm straw covered corner of the barn. The calf lived, and did just fine. In fact, the calf was a female, and she eventually became one of my best brood cows.

It wasn't that the cattle business didn't encounter problems; just like pigs, it had plenty. As the herd grew, we didn't have enough storage space for the entire brood cowherd to get in, out of the harsh winter weather, so Linda and I, and the "Cattle Company" crew improvised. We built a windbreak on one westerly corner of a fairly thick, approximately five-acre woodlot, on the southwest side of the farm. We scattered a two-foot thick layer of sawdust and straw down for bedding, and fed the brood cows baled hay in a feed bunk we built behind the windbreak. The brood cows were well protected from the severe Michigan winter winds, and the windbreak worked out well.

Prior to having a round baler, we carried baled hay back to the brood cows in a pickup truck, but one-year, an early snowmelt and huge flood of the Grand River cut off our route. The brood cows were stranded on an 8–10 acre island, with 5–6 foot deep water all around. Night after night, Linda and I stacked as many bales of hay as possible (3–4 bales high to save trips), into a little 10-foot rowboat, and paddled (precariously) the 100 yards, through the ice-cold, swift water, out to the island. After several weeks, the water finally receded enough for us to carry the hay back to the cattle in the bucket of the Lorain loader, which had large tires, and could tread through much deeper water than a pickup truck.

Although we tried not to get attached to any of the cattle, like we had to "Arnold," it sometimes happened, and they sometimes became attached to one another. At one point in time I purchased a black baldy (Hereford/Black-Angus cross) bull for breeding, and from day one, the bull teamed up with, and hung out with a Hereford steer, calved from our own cow-herd. The steer and the bull battled each other constantly, head-to-head, but were always together. Though the bull performed well, with a nearly perfect breeding record, after almost a year of continual fighting, I decided that I better sell the steer to avoid future interference. Once I did, I learned a hard lesson.

My breeding bull didn't eat much for weeks after I sold the steer, was continually bellowing for his missing companion, and his breeding suffered. By trying to improve the situation (fix what didn't need fixing), I had harmed things. The bull eventually calmed down, but he was never quite the same, never looked as healthy, and never performed as well. He just seemed sad. I could see it in his gate. I think I learned something valuable, not to judge one's relationship with another. No matter how it may appear from the outside, we **all** need a friend, even a **bull**!

During my teen years, I made a good friend myself, named Gus Bulma, who remained my constant companion throughout my twenties and thirty's. Gus and his brother owned an excavating company, Bulma Excavation, which they passed on to Gus' sons, about the time Gus and I became acquainted. I soon became close friends with Gus' wife Jo, and their sons, Ray and Ron, who did a significant amount of contract excavation work for Fenske Enterprises (to be described), Doug Fenske Cattle Company, and another private company of mine

(CRRI, *to be described*), over the coming years. I also became good friends with Gus' grandsons (two of whom, Ron Jr., and Craig, worked for me, *Craig for a number of years*), who like their fathers, Grandfather, and Great Uncle, were dedicated, hard-working individuals.

About the time Gus retired, he and his brother purchased a piece of farmland. Neither one of them had much experience with farming or cattle, so I helped where I could. My friendship with Gus grew strong, and as the years went by, we were seldom seen apart. Gus had a similar habit, that I had developed as a boy, of showing affection for another, by lightly touching foreheads, which we did frequently, and I miss that. Gus continually helped me in my business (daily for years), and he played on the Doug Fenske Cattle Company softball team, golf team, and bowling team. He and Jo attended all Fenske Enterprises, and Cattle Company events, dinners, and parties, and it was rare that Gus and I weren't seated side-by-side, at most any event.

I had a lot of good friends; however, even though Gus was my father's age (actually a few years older than my father), our relationship was **special**. We were very close friends, **bonded**. Linda got along well with Gus also, and she remarked about how connected Gus and I had become over-time, with statements like, "Neither one of us could function without our 'shadow' (the other one)." I spent endless (non-work) hours with Gus and his beautiful wife Jo, and we often vacationed together, sometimes driving as far as Florida together. We enjoyed countless weekends together at a retirement cottage Gus and Jo built, sixty miles North of Grand Rapids. Whenever I had a problem, I would discuss it with Gus, to come up with a solution. When Gus passed on, I felt the pain my bull must have felt, at the loss of his companion.

13

First Taste of the West

There were times when the cattle truck was useful for something more than just a work truck to haul livestock. I had made trips to the state of Wyoming, a couple of times in my mid-teens, with a friend and his father, hunting mule deer and antelope, and I thoroughly enjoyed it. One particular fall, a group of five of us decided to make the hunting trip. The group included me, my friends Dan Tanner, Easy Ridder, Don Cass and another Fenske employee. We sent in early for permits, which (since we were out-of-state applicants) was done by draw. We were successful in the draw, and set about trying to make plans of how to afford the trip.

One of us came up with the suggestion of converting the cattle truck into a "motor-home" temporarily, for the hunting trip. We scavenged up some used plywood and pressboard, fastened it to the inside of the slat-board sides, covered the plank floor with old carpet, and brought in some old bunk beds from the bunkhouse (fka the "play-house"). After wiring interior lights and stereo speakers, powered by a portable generator, mounted in an outside compartment, it didn't look too bad. We loaded a couple of Honda mini-bikes up the cattle ramp, for ground transportation, loaded up all our guns, sleeping bags, and coolers full of food and beer, and that October we set out for Medicine Bow (100 mi. NW of Cheyenne).

With two of us up in the cab (driving), rotating with the three in the back, who were usually playing cards, and drinking beer (when they should be sleeping), we made the 1300 mile trip, with no mishaps, other than a starter that went out, about halfway to Wyoming. Unfortunately a new starter for the old '58 Daganham diesel engine would have to come from Germany, and would take a week at best. The engine started fairly easily though, and with a little slope, and the four larger of us pushing (with "Easy Ridder" behind the wheel), she would fire up within a couple of turnovers, so we pressed on.

We had a fantastic time, a successful hunt, and my love for the West grew even deeper than it had on my two previous trips. The smell of the sage, and sounds of coyotes at night, felt **so** familiar to me. Maybe it was from childhood memories of our trip to California, or from some past life, I don't know, but I felt strongly that the West was where I **belonged**! I would daydream (have visions) about owning and living on a ranch out West, and meeting a beautiful blond on a California beach, who would become my wife. Maybe these were the dreams of many young men my age, but they felt and were **so real** to me.

One night we drank a little too much beer, and celebrated a bit too fervently at a tavern in Laramie, from which we were abruptly escorted out (thanks to "Easy Ridder," whose demeanor frequently became combative, in direct proportion to alcohol consumed). This particular night, Easy Ridder decided that it would be entertaining to knock ten-gallon hats off cowboys, which he proceeded to do (unwise in a **cowboy** bar). Within a few minutes of Easy Ridder's amusement choice, after being systematically hurled out the front door, all of us found ourselves with fat lips, lying on our backs in the parking lot, in the *rain!* All in all however, our trip to Wyoming created magnificent memories, which I will forever cherish.

On our last night before heading home however, we found ourselves in a crisis situation. About three AM we were startled awake by a pounding on the cattle truck door. It was some neighboring hunters, also "out-of-staters," who had been parked in our same canyon above us, warning us, that it had started to rain, and since we were parked in a steep canyon, which would soon turn into a river, created by runoff from the mountains above us, we better pack it out **fast**, as they already had!

We thanked them, and began picking up camp, which took us about 45 minutes, working as fast as we could. We were getting very concerned by the time we were ready to leave, because by then, the rain was coming down in torrents, and the canyon bottom in which we were parked, was already becoming a stream. Water lines higher than the truck, on the canyon sidewalls, clearly depicted what we could expect!

We were parked on a gentile slope, as we normally always did, ever since the cattle truck starter went out. However this time, to our **horror**, when we popped the clutch to start the engine, the rear wheels of the cattle truck only slid, in the rain soaked clay soil of the canyon bottom, and the engine never even turned over. We came to rest on a flat spot at the slope bottom, where water had already accumulated several inches. We were thirty miles from the nearest town or phone, and cell-phones were at least a decade away. All three of my employees asked me "now what?" I looked at Dan, who only shrugged his shoulders, shook his head, and let his chin come to rest in his palm, as he had a habit of doing, whenever he needed an answer requiring contemplation.

Fortunately, either I had found myself in enough seemingly impossible situations in the past, already in my young life, or I had been blessed with enough "Yankee Ingenuity" to come up with solutions when I had to. I quickly came up with the idea of jacking one rear tire up off the ground, and attempting to start the diesel engine, by spinning the tire, and popping the clutch. After several failed attempts, and realizing that we were not going to be able to spin the tire fast enough by hand, I was back to brainstorming. I had an **idea**, and we placed "Easy Ridder" in the driver's seat with the ignition on, in fourth gear, ready to pop the clutch. The other four of us fired up one of the mini-bikes, and balancing it on it's side, running full throttle in fourth gear, held as much pressure as we could, with the rear mini-bike drive wheel, against the bottom of the jacked up rear truck tire. After several sputters of smoke, on our first attempt, the old Daganham fired up!

We were cold, wet, and exhausted, but we all had the energy to cheer in celebration for a few seconds, before we went back to work. Time was limited, because the water level was close to a foot deep already, and the downpour continued. We jacked the truck down, reloaded the mini-bike, threw everything inside, and took off. The cattle truck had pretty good drive tires, and under the clay mud layer, the canyon bottom was gravel and stones, so we were able to move fairly well, even in the foot deep water. We were so exuberant when we reached the county road (1/4 mile away) that we all cried out in relief.

The county roads were clay, with almost no gravel; they were constructed with an extreme crown for drainage, and were very slippery.

The only way to travel the county roads in wet weather (which locals knew enough not to try at all) was to travel very slowly, and cautiously, right in the center of the road. We had one more mishap, when a front wheel slid off a saturated clay covered bridge (in a bend in the road), which I traveled over too fast, in an attempt to maintain enough speed to be able to climb an approaching slick clay hill, directly on the far side of the bridge. I got my "innovative engineer's" hat back out again. We removed the front tire, placed a section of steel pipe (which we found near one end of the bridge) under the front axle, and used a chain-binder and chain, to winch the truck back onto the bridge, then jacked the truck up, and slapped the tire back on. A four wheel drive pickup truck, which came along and had to wait to cross the bridge we had blocked, chain-towed us over the next rise, and finally we made it back to pavement, and headed for home!

"Cattle Truck" on bridge in Wyoming. Dan Tanner, foreground, Doug, on truck.

14

Injury Changes My Life

By 1961, my parents had stopped farming completely, became involved in a small amount of land development in the Riverbend area, and were successfully selling sand, gravel, topsoil, and clay (mined on the farm), which was when I had first started into the cattle business. Whenever I wasn't farming, I worked for my parents in their business, throughout my teen years, summers, nights, weekends (whenever I could), operating equipment, shoveling, mixing cement for building cinder block manholes, whatever was needed. However, we had a horrific fire on the farm during the winter of my senior year in high school, which destroyed most of my parent's uninsured excavating equipment, and trucks. Since the fire occurred on the very night that I was boxing in the Golden Gloves West Michigan District finals, my mother (who was **very opposed** to my boxing) blamed me for the fire. Mother claimed that my father had been so "worked up" (distracted) over my boxing, that he had neglected to turn off a space heater in our farm shop, which (during a wind storm that night) had caused the fire.

That business was our family's only income, and with myself and three younger sisters still at home, and one older sister being supported in college, I felt the burden of responsibility for the devastation this tragedy caused our family. Countless silent tears rolled down my cheeks, as I labored endless hours in the weeks following the fire, shoveling and sifting through tons of ashes, in a futile attempt to find

Farm shop destroyed by fire.

anything of value that had survived. Although I found many wrenches and metal tools, the intense heat of the fire had removed their "temper," and rendered them useless. I hand painted a sign, "Firewood For Sale," and spent the rest of the winter cutting, splitting, and stacking dead wood on the farm, trying to come up with some form of income for our family, and trying to right the wrong that I felt (and had been told) I was responsible for.

During the summer of the year I graduated from high school (1967), a few months after the fire, my parents started into the solid waste landfill business. Open dumps were being closed, and there was a need. Permitting was handled at the time by the Michigan Department of Public Health (soon switched to a newly formed MDNR, *Michigan Department of Natural Resources*). Since our farm and property were located on the outskirts of Grand Rapids, and had an abundance of impervious clay, not long after we applied, we were issued a permit, and it was an income solution.

My father and I were the only two "employees" initially. We didn't have a backhoe, so we used dynamite to excavate the first keyways, through the overburden soils, and into the underlying clay layer. The keyways sealed the clay dykes we constructed around the perimeter of each landfill cell, to the impervious base clay layer, to prevent any potential contamination of groundwater, or of the adjacent Grand River. As Dad and I worked the first day with dynamite, the dynamite exhaust smoke hung in the humid still air, under the dense canopy of the surrounding trees. As the afternoon wore on, my head began to **pound**, and I experienced the most **horrific headache** of my entire life. A friend of my father's who stopped by, explained that the dynamite smoke was the cause, and that the only sure cure, was for me to eat a pinch of the saltpeter, out of a stick of dynamite. When I looked at my father for an opinion, he shrugged his shoulders, with his hands palms-up. Since he had been out from under the canopy, bulldozing clay down to me as I blasted open new sections, my father was unaffected.

My head hurt **so** badly that I was ready to try anything, so I broke open a stick of dynamite, and in spite the horrendous taste, I ingested a sizable pinch of the saltpeter. Within a few minutes I was vomiting profusely, to bellows of laughter from my audience. My father's friend exclaimed that his remedy **was** effective, which it **was**, but **only** because I was then so **nauseous**, that I didn't even **notice** my headache! I never again tried, or advised that remedy, I just made certain to always steer clear of dynamite smoke.

Our only landfill equipment was a single old worn-out TD14 International bulldozer, which had survived the fire, because it was not valuable enough to park inside the farm shop. The old dozer had badly worn steel tracks, which came off the dozer continually (an ordeal to put back on), and had no cab or roof, so when it rained or snowed, we got wet and cold. We made our first (three-sided) landfill building, to keep rain and snow off the dozer at night, out of large (3ft. × 4ft. × 6ft.) stacked bales of scrap fabric (which came into the landfill as waste).

My father and I cut and trimmed the branches off some large diameter, tall trees, to stretch across the bales as timbers, for a roof. As my father was lifting one of the last timbers into place, with a very old Case farm tractor, which had a loader bucket, I stood on top of the bales, poised to remove the chain, once the timber was in place. This timber was larger, longer, and heavier than the others we had been placing all afternoon, and since the farm tractor barely had the power and reach to handle many of the previous timbers, I was a little concerned. Just as my father was ready to lower the nearly vertical timber into place, to my horror I noticed that the timber had past center, and was starting back toward the **tractor**! I ran for the timber,

Building made of bales.

desperately hoping to somehow be able to stop it, screaming "**Dad— Dad look out!**"

That old Case had a high back, "U-shaped" seat, and large heavy fenders, which sandwiched the operator in, making a fast exit very difficult. To my relief, my father dove free, in the last split microsecond, as the timber crashed into the tractor, totally flattening the seat, the steering wheel, and part of the hood.

As he had on previous occasions, my father made it very clear to me, that this incident was to remain between us, and that my mother was **not** to be informed! We found a used seat and steering wheel, off a scrap tractor in the bone-yard, and other than a flattened hood, dented fuel tank, and widened rear fenders, although it didn't much resemble a tractor any longer, the old Case was operable. Once it was repaired, we used it to hoist up rolls of PVC plastic, which we rolled out over the timbers, and cross support branches. We then held down the PVC with dozens of scrap tires. The building was crude, and cold, with a frozen dirt floor, and a roof that leaked in many places, but it was a far cry better than no shelter at all.

Winters are bitter cold in Michigan, with howling winds, and just having a place to park the dozer out of the elements for repairs and oil changes, was such a relief. It was necessary to wear many layers of clothes, and really bundle up to stay warm. I wore "long-johns," a wool shirt and pants, down coats, covered by insulated "Car-Heart" coveralls, a scarf and wool stocking hats under my hood, with Korean ("Mickey-Mouse") boots on my feet. When I went into Grandville for a beer after work one winter Friday evening, I ran into my high-school friend Tom Vandermullen, who laughingly remarked to me, "Wow, look at **you**! Where you been? Out huntin' **buffalo**?"

Eventually we needed some help. An employee (Phil Armsted), who had worked for my dad off and on for years, even helped him milk cows before I was old enough, came to work for us. My dad initially acquired a small shed (discarded in the landfill), which we mounted on an old equipment trailer, and moved around the landfill site with us as a ticket office. Later we were given an outdated used car-lot, eight foot by ten foot wooden building, which we located on the entrance road, and used as our ticket office. Phil, even though he had been seriously wounded in World War II, could work unbelievably hard (bussed firewood at the rate of five men), was a great employee, and a friend. Phil manned both ticket offices for us for years, as well as helped operate, and maintain equipment.

Landfill fees were fifteen cents per cubic yard, work was difficult, days long, and money scarce. We were lucky to gross $100.00 per day, before any expenses, such as fuel and parts, in those early days. We made a go of it though, and the following fall, I came home from college (Michigan State University, in East Lansing) every weekend to help. I chose Civil Engineering as my major, believing that it would be the most beneficial to the business, which we named "Fenske Sanitary Landfill," later (at my request) "Fenske Enterprises."

With hard earned money, which I saved from cattle sales and Fenske Enterprises wages, I paid $3000 cash, for a nearly new (demo) 1968 ('Corvette-bronze,' T-top) Chevy Corvette, my second year in college, and appeared to have become, as a buddy put it, "Joe College." I dated a few different girls in college, and I had one relationship for a couple of years (with a wonderful young woman named Pam), but nothing that I thought of as permanent. Maybe it seemed like I was just too picky, but I knew what I was looking for. I did go out on dates occasionally, with a girl whom I knew wasn't "the one," just to have a date, and to get my Mother (who was always pushing me to get into a relationship) or my buddies off my back, but the **truth** is, I always preferred to be *alone,* as opposed to with someone I wasn't *drawn* to. I wound up the only single at a lot of couples events, but I still had fun.

It used to upset my buddies, when we would be out as singles for an evening, attending a huge college dance, or in a bar full of people, in East Lansing or Grand Rapids (sometimes with several hundred people present), that after fifteen minutes of looking through the crowd, convinced that the "one I was looking for" wasn't there, I wanted to leave. I was never insistent about it, and I liked to have fun like anyone, but I wanted a relationship, and I always thought that maybe that "special someone" was right around the corner at our next stop.

I continued to box in college, and I picked up the name "Sundance," to some extent because of my dance-like, "Ali-style" footwork. Just as I did most everything I tackled in life, I gave boxing everything I had, and I got into the best physical condition I possibly could. Boxing had been an intercollegiate sport, but was banned as a result of a couple of deaths, prior to the start of my college career. MSU had been the start for some world famous boxers like "Chuck Davies," who later turned pro and made history, with his "still talked-about" world championship battle against "Kid Galahad." MSU had beautiful, "mothballed" boxing facilities, rings, and equipment, which they allowed a few friends and I (who formed the "MSU Boxing Club," *fall 1967*) to use, once we signed liability wavers.

I was able to train and work on my conditioning on campus, but none of my teammates had any boxing experience, so I needed to look elsewhere for any challenging sparring competition. I found a gym in Lansing (MI Capitol), and many nights I ran the five miles from my room in East Lansing, to the gym downtown Lansing, trained for a couple of hours, and ran the five miles back to my room. The roadwork and training got me in superb condition, and the manager of the gym in Lansing (Al Vanet), often made the statement, "Just as sure as you can count on the **sun** to come up tomorrow, you can count on Fenske to be **dancin'** every round!" The tag stuck, and I used the Dane part of my last name, boxing with the ring name "*Sundance Dane*" (embroidered on my boxing robe). Interestingly, a couple years later (1969) the movie "Butch Cassidy & The Sundance Kid" came out, and my tag "Sundance" gained a new popularity. Even though I trained in Lansing, I still competed in the Golden Gloves in Grand Rapids (training weekends at Midtown), my freshman year in college. Al Vanet wasn't too happy about it, but he allowed me to train at his gym (the "Capitol Caravan Club") that first year, provided I agreed to fight in Lansing, under him in subsequent years.

That year, Morey Bosman had moved the Midtown Athletic Center to a new location on Madison Avenue, one of the roughest areas (with the highest crime rate) in Grand Rapids. The first night I walked into the gym, I felt uneasy, kind of nervous. There was a lot of racial tension (in the sixties), especially in this section of Grand Rapids, and other than Morey, I was the only Caucasian in the gym. Everyone stopped working out, and it became dead silent as the door closed behind me. Morey wouldn't let me spar with anyone for a couple of weeks, and he warned me to go straight to my vehicle, lock the doors, and leave immediately after each workout. It wasn't long before I found out why.

After my third night of working out at Midtown (my second weekend), there were half a dozen black guys waiting for me in the parking lot as I was leaving, blocking the path to my truck. I could see a couple of them had a short length of chain in hand, others had a club, and I heard the words, "Think yer pretty tough, do ya' 'Honkey'?" Bracing for the worst, with clenched fists, just as I thought I was in for the fight of my life, I heard the words behind me, "Hey man, leave **him alone**!" James Washington, an Open Division welterweight had just walked out of the gym.

James was one of the best, most experienced boxers at Midtown, and his words carried a lot of weight. James went on to state, "He ain't hurtin' **nobody**, and he's **my** friend!" That's all it took for me to be accepted. James and I became sparing partners, and good friends, and I learned a lot from James Washington, who was one of the fastest boxers I had ever encountered, as well as one of the nicest guys. James went on to win the state championship that year, and I was looking forward to a lasting friendship, and celebrating his championship title with him. However, just a week after the tournament ended, before we ever got the chance, our plan was disrupted.

I came home from MSU, to an article in the *Grand Rapids Press*, about a young black man mistakenly shot by two Grand Rapids policemen, who were responding to a burglary on South Division, at a drugstore not far from James' home. It turned out that James had walked into the drugstore to make a purchase, shortly after the burglary had been called in. When James stepped out of the store, he was shot and killed. The officers claimed they had believed him to be armed, and that he had ignored their orders to freeze, and drop the weapon in his hand, which turned out to be a tube of toothpaste. I was very sad to read that it was James, who had been pointlessly killed, and I was angered over the actions of the trigger-happy officers, who had shot and killed a wonderful human being, and one of the most **unlikely** people to **ever** be involved in an armed robbery. James had been decorated, and survived the jungles of Viet Nam, only to come back and be shot dead, two blocks from his own home.

A trainer at the Capitol Caravan Club (Eddie Doran), an ex-pro heavyweight who lived in Lansing, really took an interest in me, and tried to convince me to quit college and turn professional. Eddie gave me a rub-down every night after training, with his own concoction of "Witch Hazel," "Amigo Oil," and a few other ingredients (Eddie said were "classified"), and he stated many times, "Sundance, give up this college **crap**, and we'll **go** places, and make some **big** money!" I really wanted my Civil Engineering degree though, and I was able to hold Eddie at bay, by explaining that by quitting college, I would lose my 2S student draft deferment, and I would wind up in Viet Nam in a heartbeat.

Eddie worked hard with me throughout my years at MSU, I believe banking on me getting sick of college and being broke, or the war coming to an end. I liked Eddie, and always gave him and boxing my very best. I won the Lansing District Golden Gloves Championship a couple of times, and runner-up in state, but the award that meant the **most** to me, credited me personally for more than my boxing skills. That first year in college (competing in the 156 pound division), I won the **very coveted** West Michigan "Golden Glove Award," only awarded to **one** boxer per year, out of **all** contenders, in **all** weight classes. The trophy is inscribed with the words "TO THE BOXER WHO MOST EXEMPLIFIES THE SPIRIT AND DESIRE OF A GOLDEN GLOVER," and in West Michigan, is described (captioned) as amateur boxing's "Heisman Trophy."

I believe that I won the Golden Glove Award, more as a result of my determination and "never-quit" style, than skill. I know in my heart, that I won a lot of fights against far more skilled opponents, because I kept going (no matter what), even after I had been hit with much of what my opponent threw at me, and we both were "out-of-gas." I continued to box all through college, and for several years after, winning numerous awards, but **this** award meant more to me than all the others combined! I played a little football at MSU, joined the wrestling team, ran a bit of track, even did some fencing for a while (mostly to satisfy my mother), who was constantly trying to get me interested in something else (anything other than boxing), but I always continued to box.

I suffered many injuries from boxing over the years, numerous times broken nose, broken knuckles, broken ribs, and several broken eardrums, which reminded me of the first one I had suffered as a boy.

Prior to a headgear being required in amateur boxing, trainers would use "Vaseline Petroleum Jelly" on boxer's ears, in an effort to cause punches to slide off, and help prevent "cauliflower ears." However when a left hook is landed squarely, the air trapped in the ear canal, sealed by the Vaseline and the force of the punch, can cause the eardrum to burst. An eardrum usually will heal, if kept uninfected, but each time some additional scar tissue, which forms, can further impede ones hearing. Once I finally realized the cause of the injuries, I refused further use of Vaseline on my ears. I didn't like the injuries caused by boxing, but still something always drew me back.

Mother desperately attempted to convince me not to go the Grand Rapids Civic Auditorium, on the very night I won the "Golden Glove" award. With tears in my eyes, I stated, "Mother, I **have** to fight! I'm in the **finals**! They're **counting** on me!" As she sat beside me on the edge of my bed, after she had found me in my bedroom gathering my boxing gear, and preparing to leave, Mother told me a story. "I don't understand men, and their desire to fight. I tried so **hard** to get your father to stop, and he did, just before we were married, but did he? One evening, about six years after we were married and living on the farm, when you and Karen were babies, your father was late for supper. I left you and Karen in your highchairs, and walked out to the barn to see what was keeping your father.

The cattle were still all stalled up, but I could see that he was done milking. I walked into the granary, where I heard some noise coming from above. When I climbed the stairs, I found your father with his boxing gloves on, punching a gunny-sack full of grain, which he had hanging from the rafters! He had been practicing there continually, ever since we were married, planning on staging a **comeback**! I made him cut it down that **instant**, and told him that if I ever found him practicing boxing again, I and the kids were **leaving**!" I'm not sure why Mother told me that story, but I never forgot it. She did agree to relent for that night, but she firmly stated, "This is **it**! After tonight you are **done** boxing!" I wasn't.

My sophomore year in college, I rented a room on the third (top) floor of a fraternity. The fraternity (Tau Delta Phi) had purchased an old apartment building, and converted it into a fraternity house. All of the rooms were accessible from inside the building, and were fully equipped apartments, with a stove, refrigerator, washer, drier, etc. The fraternity, having more beds than members, ran an add for a spare bedroom in one apartment, and when I found out how reasonable the rent was compared to a dorm room, I grabbed it. I was doing my utmost to pay my own way through college, and even though my parents helped me, I did all I could to save enough money from cattle sale profits, and from wages at Fenske Enterprises (earned on weekends and summer breaks), to pay for books, tuition, and living expenses at college.

When I moved into the fraternity, I shared my apartment and split living expenses with Steve Newmer, who haled from Chicago, and who was actually a fraternity member. Steve, who was nicknamed, and called "Rou" by all the other fraternity members, and I became good friends. Rou was short for "Roundo," which bespoke Steve's physical stature, and since we split the grocery tab each week, I discovered that he came by his physique honestly. Steve was the only guy I had ever met, who could reach in the frig, grab a full two-quart container of milk, tip it up and guzzle the entire jug, without even coming up for air! He would then let out a belch, and a fart, grab a drumstick, and ask, "What's for dinner?" Steve was a big guy, and everything he did was "big." When he got up in the morning, he always headed straight for the toilet, and cut loose a stream that sounded like a racehorse (probably from drinking a full two-quart container of milk, as if it was a **juice-glass.**)

Each semester fraternities take on new members, to fill openings left by graduating members. Sometime before I knew him, Steve earned his abbreviated nickname, during "Pledge Hell-Week," which was when new fraternity "Pledges" were put through any kind of miserable hell the existing fraternity members could dream up, to "see if the pledges were hardy prospects." As the story goes, Steve was once positioned on a toilet, supposedly wiping himself with his right hand, as new fraternity pledges were being shown around the fraternity house. Then as the bathroom door was opened to display the bathroom to each new prospective pledge, the tour guide would exclaim, "Oh excuse us! This is fraternity member Roundo." Steve would then pull out his hand, shake off some slightly wet sticking toilet paper, and extend his hand in greeting. Most all pledges caught on quickly, and stepped away chuckling, but apparently one "gung-ho" new pledge was caught off guard, shook Steve's hand, and uttered the words, "glad to meet you Rou..." At that point, the pledge realized it was a setup and stopped. Everyone who witnessed the event burst into laughter, as did all who heard the story repeated for months to follow. The name "Rou" stuck, and became Steve's new handle from that day forward.

I got along great, with all the guys at the fraternity, and even though I couldn't afford to join, they treated me just like a member, inviting me to all of the fraternity functions, parties, etc. A lot of fraternity guys are "jocks" (athletic type guys), and I fit that mold. I tried to be a triple sport guy in college, just like I had been in high school, but in college the seasons intersect. The football coach didn't like the wrestling coach, neither of them liked the track coach, and when I started showing up for practices with black eyes, none of them liked boxing. Once I joined the Rodeo Club, I think they just figured I was nuts, and they all gave up on trying to control me.

Most all of the fraternity members loved very physical sports, in my case boxing, as well as Rodeo. When I joined the MSU Rodeo Club (as a founding member), my sophomore year in college, I learned to ride bulls and bareback horses, and I coined the phrase, "I'm a Lover, a Fighter, and a Wild Bull Rider," which I used all the time (still do at times). Our MSU Rodeo Club was permitted to use the MSU Livestock Stadium, with an indoor arena and bleachers, and we sponsored two rodeos per year, to "sold-out" crowds, earning us traveling money to attend other college rodeos. I had a lot of frater-

Doug riding bareback horse in rodeo.

nity fans cheering me on at MSU Rodeos, and at the Lansing "Civic
Center," when I won the "Lansing District Golden Gloves (165
pound) Championship" that year. My fraternity buddies carried me
over their heads, into a surprise victory party back at the frat house,
complete with a huge monogrammed trophy cake, and a couple of
sororities in attendance, with one bikini clad sorority member who
came **out of the cake**!

The Civil Engineering curriculum at MSU was really set up as a
five-year course of study. Even though I was concerned about having
to face the draft and Viet Nam once I graduated, constantly hoping
that the war would end, for reasons of expense, and to obtain my
degree as soon as possible and help my parents with the business, I
was determined to make it through in four years. This ambition however, required a heavy credit load, with many twenty plus credit terms
(the college average was fifteen), and many late nights studying. The
guys at the fraternity knew that I didn't have much money to spare,
and they just looked the other way when my stomach sometimes
prompted me to raid the basement frig. On one given occasion however, as I was running back up the stairs from one of my midnight
"study-break frig-raids," I got caught.

As I thundered up the second flight of stairs, a room-door burst
open, and out jumped "Big Bad John," the Fraternity's duly elected
"Sergeant-At-Arms," blocking my path. "What's that you got in your
hands?" he inquired. "Nothing" I responded, as I held my fists behind
my back, with an egg in each hand. "**Come-on**, let's see it," he
demanded. Big John wasn't a tough guy at all, and I didn't really
believe I was in any trouble, so I showed him. "Aw you've **had** it,"
said Big John, "I'm turnin' you in, unless you **eat** both of those eggs,
right here, **right** now!" I wasn't really worried about getting turned
in, and I responded "**Raw**?" I'm not eatin' these eggs **raw**!"

Big John had been in a poker game in his room, and was slightly
inebriated, but sober enough to realize that his idle threat wasn't
going to provide him with any entertainment, so he came up with a
second plan. Big John proposed to give me all the change in his pants
pocket, which was bulging from his poker winnings, if I ate the raw
eggs. I was really broke, and didn't even have fifteen cents for a
McDonald's burger (the price at that time), which was still open at the
end of our street, so I went for it! I speculated that he had five to ten
dollars in his pocket, and one at a time, I popped both eggs in my
mouth, and chewed them up (shell and all) and swallowed them, on
the spot! The last laugh was on me though, because Big John had

been in a "pennies only" poker game, and my winnings only amounted to **$1.83**.

All through college, I devoted most weekends to traveling home to the farm. I needed the wages to pay for college, my parents needed my help in the business, and I always had farm work waiting for me. One of my cattle company employees fed the cattle for me during the week, but there was always manure to clean up, corn to grind, fence repairs, and endless other chores to catch up on. Also, my father came up with a mechanical idea, and he and I started developing an attachment to a piece of heavy equipment known as an "earthmover" or "scraper," which would assist in loading clay, to be moved to the landfill. The heavy blue clay on our farm was so dense, that loading it without a dozer pushing behind the earthmover was next to impossible, and that created additional expense. Since the blue clay also had fairly large rocks (boulders) embedded throughout it (as did parts of the sand hill), self-loading with a conventional elevator-scraper wasn't practical either, because the rocks would constantly become jammed in the elevator.

My father's mechanical prowess came into focus again, the device we developed worked very well, and my parents patented the invention under the name, the "Fenske Load Booster." Somehow the *Grand Rapids Press* got wind of the patent, and ran a story about it. Since we devised the attachment on a Terex (formerly Euclid) earthmover, my parents began patent sales negotiations with General Motors (Terex parent company). Once GM's attorneys became involved however, things got ugly. My parents wound up spending a year in court, and thousands of dollars in legal fees (which they really didn't have to spare), trying to keep GM from "jumping" our patent. After meeting with my parents, GM had filed for their own patent on the device, trying to get around having to pay my parents anything.

When GM finally lost the case in court, with no chance of appeal, GM officials came back to my parents, and attempted to reopen negotiations. However by this time, neither my parents nor I wanted to have anything to do with GM. My parents eventually obtained a world patent as well, and wound up selling the patent rights to Caterpillar Corporation, which is now building and selling earthmovers, with the "Fenske Load-Booster" attachment, all over the world. Caterpillar attorneys were also very shrewd however, and as a result of a contract glitch, my parents unfortunately received a pittance of what they should have. We all **did** learn some valuable lessons about attorneys, contracts, and **patent laws**.

Tragedy Strikes

While we were in the developmental stages of the device, during spring break of my sophomore year in college, an accident occurred which changed my life. One April morning, on my first day home from college, my father asked me to watch as he demonstrated the effectiveness of some recent changes he had made to the "Fenske Load-Booster" (which consists of a hydraulically operated auger, mounted in the bowl of an earthmover). I explained to Dad that I didn't have time, because my high school buddy Fred was due within the hour, and I was busy packing for a trip to Daytona Beach, Florida (a hip "college spring-break" town).

Dad convinced me to take one quick trip up to the sand-hill on the farm, and as I watched him excavate the first load, the auger suddenly stopped. I ran and leaped onto the side of the moving earthmover, to see if a rock had become wedged under the auger. My father saw me jump onto the side of the earthmover, but didn't think anything of it, because I had done the same thing many times previously. This time however, I landed on such a precarious location, that my right foot became trapped between the equipment frame, and the hydraulically lowering earthmover bowl. Thankfully, when I jumped on, my left foot landed slightly farther back on the frame than my right foot, and wasn't enmeshed. There was only about a half-inch clearance between the scissors action parts of the earthmover, where my foot was snared, and as my father lowered the cutting edge to load soil, I internally heard and felt the crushing and tearing of my bones and flesh. I screamed at the top of my lungs for my father to stop, but he could not hear me above the roar of the dual engines, and my foot was slowly severed from the ball forward (note: we later discovered the auger had stopped due to a faulty electrical switch).

When my father did finally look back, and notice me frantically waving my arms, and motioning for him to raise the earthmover bowl, he stopped, and pulled on the hydraulic lever, which raises the bowl. I fell to the ground. We could not see the extent of my injury, because the high top rubber work boot I was wearing had only stretched, as the end of my foot was literally torn off. I knew that it was very bad, because my boot quickly filled to overflowing with blood. Even though I was only twenty years old, I had sense enough to immediately remove my belt, and make a tourniquet around my leg (which probably saved my life). In spite of my father's insistence, I refused to remove my boot, pleading with him to take me to the hospital. I believe because he did not want to face the severity of what had happened (regardless of my appeals), my father drove me to our family doctor's office in Grandville.

When we arrived, I refused to leave the truck, **demanding** that he take me to the hospital. My father brought the local doctor out to the truck, and the doctor stated after one quick look, through a section of the rubber boot he cut away, that we needed to go to the hospital. The doctor exclaimed, "I can see **bones** and **tendons** and **everything**! There's **nothing** I can do here. Get down to the hospital emergency! I'll call and tell them you're on the way!"

After a **long painful** wait, for several hours in the hospital emergency (with no pharmaceuticals), I was finally taken to a room. There had been two hand injuries that afternoon, and even though one came in after me, the emergency room attendants explained that a hand takes precedence over a foot. Doctors (specialists) at the hospital reattached everything to the best of their ability, and (in spite of pain medication) I suffered **immensely** through the next **agonizingly painful, sleepless** ten days in the hospital.

One evening, at the end of her shift, a day nurse (about my age), whom I would have been attracted to had I not been in so much misery, came into my room in her street clothes. When she asked me why I couldn't sleep, I told her that a guy across the hall was keeping me awake with his constant moaning. The nurse explained to me that the moaning was coming from **me**, and that I was keeping the **entire floor** awake! After looking both ways down the hall, she reached into the pocket of her fringed, tan, suede-leather jacket, pulled out a blue and yellow capsule, and said, "Here take this." I was in so much agony, that I didn't even ask what it was. I didn't care. Forty-eight hours later, as I peered up at the blurred images of two doctors leaning over my bed, I heard the words, "He's coming around!" I never saw the nurse again, and I'm afraid that she may have been reprimanded, but I am grateful to her for the only uninterrupted sleep and escape from the pain, that I had experienced in over a week. I have no idea what she gave me (LSD was popular at he time), but I have memories of freely floating up in the clouds.

I stayed home on the farm, for the following several weeks, trying to cope with the pain, and hoping against hope, that somehow there was life inside my reattached toes, which had turned coal black, and were as hard as rock. I was still a young man with dreams, and I didn't want to go through life without my toes. I had heard and read of instances, in which reattached fingers and toes eventually shed a black lifeless layer of skin, and were fine underneath. However, because of the crushing, tearing nature of the accident, and the severity of my injury, gangrene set in, and amputation was necessary. When I pleaded with my doctor (on the Saturday that I was told), to delay the amputation of my toes, in the hope of a miracle, my doctor told me, "If I wait until Monday, I will have to take your **foot** above the **ankle**!" I lost my big toe to the ball of my foot, as well as most of two others, and a fourth no longer bends (only my "pinky" toe remained unscathed). Following surgery, my doctor emphatically stated that I still would be able to walk (with a limp), but I would no longer be able to **run**, and my **boxing** days were over.

Four days after the amputation surgery, during a visit to my hospital room, my doctor informed me that I could remove the bandages (when I felt ready), and view the appearance of my foot. Shortly after he left, I told my father, who was at the hospital visiting me at the time, that I wanted to look at my foot. Dad helped me remove the bandages, and after staring at my foot for a few minutes (in shock) I started, very quietly, to sob. All of us "Fenske kids" had been taught by both of our parents to "be tough," and not to cry at **any** type of pain, emotional or physical. Only once, had I ever seen my mother shed a tear. That was at her father, Grandpa Schulz's funeral. On a few rare occasions, I had seen my father cry. He was a little softer, and more emotional than Mother; he was just good at hiding it.

Even though my toes had turned black, before this they were still **there**, and I was **stunned** at the freakish appearance of my foot. Memories returned to me, of thoughts I had entertained, and statements that I had made to myself, several years earlier as a young teen, "I wish I didn't **have** these crooked toes!" I shuddered at the **horror**, that I may have **created** this! That was not what I had **meant**! I hadn't wanted to **lose** my toes! I would rather have **crooked** toes, than **no** toes! I quickly changed my thoughts, and **blessed** all my remaining toes. I wanted so badly to be "normal," and my voice cracked as I wiped the tears from my eyes, and uttered the words, "So this is how it's going to look?" My father commanded, "Oh **cut** it out!" Embarrassed, I dried my eyes, and stated, "Oh, don't mind me; it's just the pain medication; they've got me all doped up." As I said so, my father left the room, and I figured that he was disgusted with my childish reaction. Not until several years later, in an emotional discussion with my mother, did I find out that Dad had left my hospital room, because he could no longer hold back **his** tears, which streamed from his eyes as he passed her, seated on a chair in the hospital hall.

15

Injury Repercussions/Making Things Work

I missed that spring term at MSU, and as a result, I lost my student deferment. It was 1969, and the Viet Nam war was in full swing. Males were deferred from the draft with a 2S (student deferment), as long as they went directly from high school to college, and maintained a full-load curriculum. However, it did not take long for the Draft Board to find out if one missed a term. I wasn't even out of the *hospital* yet (following the amputation), when my draft notice arrived. The notice required me to report for a draft induction physical examination the following Saturday (a few days away) in Detroit. My mother, to no avail, attempted to convince the Draft Board that I would not be able to attend the scheduled physical exam. A couple of weeks later, a second notice arrived, with a warning that a warrant for my arrest would be issued, if I failed to report. On the required date, I rode the scheduled bus to Detroit (with 60 other "draftees"), crutches in hand. My foot was **excruciatingly** painful whenever I did not keep it elevated, and I had been warned by my doctor that it was **essential** for me to keep my foot raised above my heart, twenty-four hours per day, to avoid potentially lethal blood clots, which could kill me if they broke loose and traveled to my heart or brain. I kept my foot propped up on the bus seat in front of me on the long ride to Detroit, but I was in **unbearable** misery, when standing with my crutches, for the many long hours throughout the ordeal. In spite of numerous agonizing explanations of why my (*by now blood soaked*) foot was heavily bandaged, the Draft Board "physical examiners" refused to remove the bandages from my foot and look at my injury. Even though I had a letter from my doctor explaining the extent of my injury, I received a 1-A (first draft-able) classification. In 1969, if you had a **pulse**, you were **draft-able**!

After having stood in line for many painful hours to challenge my classification (fruitlessly), I missed my bus ride back to Grand Rapids. My wallet had been stolen from the "flea-bag" motel room, which the Draft Board had provided for us to spend the previous night in, so with no money or ID, I hitchhiked the 150 miles home, on crutches, in the rain. When I was finally dropped off near downtown Grand Rapids around 10 PM, I proceeded to hitchhike the last eight miles to our farm. I was in **extreme** pain by this time, it was cold, the rain was coming down increasingly harder, and no one would pick me up for the first mile or so. Finally a car pulled over, and when I saw that it was a squad car, I was relieved, believing that I would receive a ride all the way home. When the officer ordered me into his vehicle, and asked for my ID, I explained why I was on crutches, what I had just experienced, how my wallet had been stolen, and that I did not have any ID, or even a dime to call for a ride.

I explained that I had knocked on the door of several homes, but was unable to convince anyone to allow me to use their phone, probably as a result of the blood soaked bandages on my foot, and my saturated and homeless appearance. When the officer handed me a ticket for hitchhiking, expressed that he had been a marine, and referred to me as a "**draft dodger**," who probably had "shot-gunned his **own foot** to avoid Viet Nam," then ordered me out of his vehicle, I had **reached my limit**! As I crawled from his squad car, I firmly declared, "It's officers like you that give cops the name **Pig's**!" I **tore** the ticket in half, threw it down, and hobbled away on my crutches. The officer jumped from his vehicle, drew his weapon, and ordered me to **halt**, stating that he was placing me under **arrest**! I turned and faced him, with a crutch pointing at his gun responding, "If you're going to **use** that thing, then you better **do it**, because **without it**, you are **not** going to get me **back** into that car!" I had **had** it! I spun around on my crutches, and continued my journey home.

I was a little nervous with a gun pointed at me, but I could not imagine how the officer would explain, that he had shot someone **in the back** for hitchhiking, **on crutches**, in the rain! The officer responded, with a somewhat nervous, shaky voice, "Well you better be in to pay for this tomorrow, or there will be **warrant** issued for your **arrest**!" I stuck my thumb out again, as soon as he left, and I received a ride the rest of the way home, shortly thereafter. My mother took care of the ticket, somehow (over the phone) the next day.

I spent (most of) the rest of that spring and summer home on the farm, reading in a hammock, with my foot elevated above my heart as advised, to avoid blood clots. I was young however, and at times restless. All my younger sisters were in school, and Karen was attending college, so whenever mother was away, after groceries etc., I would grab my crutches and go hunting for morel mushrooms, which came out about this time each spring, and I was very fond of. The problem was that mushrooms grew in places where the soil was soggy, and would not support my crutches very well. More than once I had to explain a mud-covered butt, which was the only way for me to maneuver through some of the best mushroom prone areas.

I anxiously awaited the sound of racing motorcycles each afternoon, which signaled the return of Andy and Rich Zoonstra, from their assembly line jobs at GM in Grand Rapids. That spring they had purchased a pair of matching new 350 Honda road bikes, and every afternoon there was a test to see whose bike was the fastest, for the last mile down Kenowa. Their first stop was always my hammock, and before long, regardless of Mother's protests, we devised a way to keep my foot elevated (with a homemade prop), so that I could enjoy a motorcycle ride as a passenger. Promising to travel very slowly, we inched our way out the drive each day, only to crank the throttles wide open as soon as we were out of sight, which I'm sure was quite audibly apparent.

One particular afternoon that spring, as we raced down one of the dirt farm roads, Andy was in the lead, going a little faster than Rich could with me on the back. As we rounded the top of a blind knob, with a sharp left turn at the bottom, we heard skidding tires and gravel. Rich and I had time to break, and to witness Andy's motorcycle skid to a stop in waste deep water. Andy was thrown off his bike, and he sailed through the water for about forty yards on his back, with an image resembling a torpedo, as the water streamed over his bubble face shield.

The Grand River had flooded overnight, with a late spring second flood as it sometimes did, and what had been a farm road, was now covered with four feet of water. When Andy finally came to a stop, he stood up in his leather jacket, chest deep, with murky river water gurgling out from under his facemask. Rich, who had brought our bike to a stop at the waters edge, waited momentarily for things to settle, then proclaimed "Andy, you **stupid shit!**" He then turned his bike around, and we rode off. I felt a little bad leaving Andy behind, but it was just Rich's way, and other than a wet one-quarter mile push of his motorcycle back to their farmhouse, it was clear that Andy was fine. We did enjoy many laughs however, in the years that followed (to Andy's dismay), retelling the story.

Andy, who was only a year older than myself (and closest to my age), and I became pretty good buddies over the years. There were times that I awoke Andy, by tossing pebbles at his upstairs bedroom window at five AM, to leave for a canoe trip, after we had closed the bars together the night before. Andy wasn't crazy about getting up early in the morning, but he loved to have fun, and was always glad he did. Andy, who was small (skinny) when the Zoonstras first moved to Riverbend, grew up to be a much larger guy than his older brother Rich. By this time in our lives he was already six-two, 220 pounds, with a set of shoulders, and a natural physique that resembled Charles Atlas (although Andy had never lifted a weight in his life). Even though "Big Andy" (his "Handle") was not really much of a fighter, "more a lover," as he always put it, his shear size helped me out of more than one jam.

On July fourth that year, as Andy and I were enjoying the afternoon strolling the streets of the tourist town of Saugatuck (on the shore of Lake Michigan), forty miles south of Grand Haven, we came upon a number of "awesome" Harley choppers. I crawled onto the seat of one of them, to see how it felt. As I was bouncing up and down, playing with the throttle, imagining that I was "Rollin' Down The Highway," two of the most gruesome looking characters I had ever seen walked up to me. One of them, with a half-bottle of whiskey in his hand said, "Hey **man**, what are you doing on **my** bike? You're a **dead** man!"

Saugatuck is very popular, and it draws people from all across the nation, especially on holiday weekends. As I was fumbling for words to explain myself, I noticed the lettering on the back of their dirty sleeveless denim jackets read, "Hell's Angles—LA Sector!" The Hells Angles had a pretty bad reputation in 1969, and just as I figured I had met my undoing, Andy, who had been wandering around through the rest of the bikes, walked up. As he kicked the front tire of the chopper I was sitting on, Andy stated, "What's up guys? Nice **bikes**! My friend and I **like** um!" As he stuck out his dinner plate sized hand to shake theirs, Andy stated, "We don't have a **problem** here do we?" The guys were obviously very intimidated by Andy's size, and simply stated, "No man, no problem. Glad you like um." In a street fight, **size** means everything! I grabbed my cane, and the two of us were on our way, without any further ado.

The fact is, Andy didn't have any fighting experience, and in a boxing match between us, I would have undoubtedly come out the winner, provided I was skillful enough not to get hit with one of his cannon ball sized fists. The previous fall, after Andy and I had been cruising the downtown Grand Rapids circuit one night, trying to meet some girls to invite to a party (at Andy's cousin's house), I found that out.

There was always a continual stream of teens and young adults in cars, which ran in a loop from the Pearl Street Big Boy restaurant parking lot (near downtown), to a city parking lot a couple of miles away. The cavalcade circled through downtown Grand Rapids every weekend evening, providing numerous opportunities to meet the opposite sex, whenever the various stoplights on the route stopped the procession. We were following a car with four girls in it, whom we had met on the circuit, and whom had agreed to follow us to the party, after they dropped off one of the girls (with a curfew), who had to be home.

Just as we arrived at the home of the passenger they were dropping off, a car screeched in front of my corvette at a forty-five degree angle, blocking our path. Four guys jumped out, and two of them ran to either side of our car. As I asked, "What do you guys think you're **do...**," one of them reached through my open window, and slapped me in the face. As I asked, "Hey, what the Hell...," I got a second slap, as did Andy. One of them was probably an estranged boyfriend or something; it was obvious they had been drinking, and they had undoubtedly been following us from downtown.

Andy and I took one last look at each other, and in resolve, in unison, burst open our doors. Adrenaline enabled me to ignore my foot pain, and with my boxing experience, it didn't take too long before I had both of the guys on my side, on the ground with bloody noses. It's not that I was some rough, tough, macho fighter, and I wasn't even a very big guy (I hadn't finished growing yet), it's just that most guys don't know much about boxing, and a little ring experience is a real advantage. As soon as I was confident that my two opponents were incapacitated, I ran over to "Big Andy's" side of the car, and to my

shock, found Andy on the ground, close to unconscious, with one of our opponents **kicking** him in the **face**!

I like to box, and I'm pretty good at it, but I'm not a violent guy. To me boxing is a sport. I have always been able to control my temper (which is imperative in boxing), and I have always said, "In the best knock-down drag-out battles of my career in the ring, I have been able to throw my arms around my opponent after the fight, because I don't hate the guy; I **admire** him! I know what it takes to get into the condition necessary to be able to do that!" This confrontation was not a boxing match however; this was a **war**!

This was one of the first and only street fights I had ever been in. Young guys just challenge each other a lot. I think it's a male hormone thing. The human species isn't really much different than any other species in this way, but I never saw any sense in it. I would always do everything in my power verbally to walk away from a fight, even one that I *knew* I could easily win, because it seemed so foolish to me, however I was not one to be pushed into a corner, and when I saw my friend injured I went ballistic.

As I ran toward the guy kicking Andy, the other adversary on Andy's side of the car, who was standing along side watching, with a brick in his hand (which he had probably hit Andy with), stuck out his foot to trip me. I noticed it in time however, and dropped him with a left hook. Fortunately, none of our opponents had much boxing prowess, my opponent didn't even throw up an arm to block the punch, and when I hit him, with the full force of my body weight as I was running forward, he went down like a bucket of mud! I tackled the guy kicking Andy, landing on his chest, where I punched him a few times, then with a raised fist, warned him that he better stop fighting, or I would punch him again. The guy stopped struggling, and said, "You know, you really aren't a bad guy!"

Just as my opponent finished his statement, someone grabbed my raised right arm. Thinking that it was one of the other three who had regained their feet, I spun around with my left fist, to the face of a cop, with a night-stick in his other hand, who said, "Go on, and I'll break this right over your head!" Somebody in the neighborhood, must have called the police, who probably had a cruiser in close proximity, based on how quickly they had arrived. I helped Andy (who was still out of it) to his feet, and the cops, who ordered us all to stand next to our vehicles, seemed a little surprised that the four guys with bloody noses, were all on the same side. They let Andy and I leave, and retained the other four for questioning, but I'm sure they also let them go shortly. This was the sixties, fists were most often the only weapon used, and it was highly unlikely one would get arrested for fighting. Times were different, life was simpler, there was a lot less stress in the world in general, and in a lot of ways it was a better time.

I don't know what happened to the girls, who probably had split when the fight broke out, and needless to say, we never made the party. Andy had a fat lip for a few days, and one of his two front teeth had been knocked loose. His tooth finally tightened up again after a few weeks, but apparently the nerves to the tooth had been broken, and over time his tooth turned a dull shade of gray. I feel bad about what happened to Andy, but I'm glad that I saw him and intervened when I did, or he might have had some off his teeth knocked clear out!

Gradually I healed to the point, where I could put more weight on my foot, and walk without a cane. My friends (Dan, Fred, Jim, and Dave) and I were inseparable in those days, and we were together most every weekend (Andy Zoonstra frequently joined us). Fred, who's nickname was Derf (Fred spelled backwards), had a new Ford Torino, always drove, and usually brought Jim and Dave (all three from Grandville) with him, when he came to Riverbend, to pick up Dan and I. Dan Tanner and I had graduated with, and become close to all of them in high school. Since I lived at the dead-end of Kenowa, I was usually the last stop.

One Saturday night my friends came to pick me up for a night on the town, just as the Fenske family was finishing my father's "flap-jack" (pancake) dinner, which was a ritual every Saturday night. Late, as I often was, I rushed upstairs to clean up, and my father invited my friends to sit down at the table and enjoy some pancakes, which they did.

Dad always prepared far more batter than he needed, and not want-ing to waste any, he kept filling their plates with pancakes. When I came down the stairs, I saw all of my friends in the living room, with the exception of Dave. We found him still at the kitchen table, with a stomach bloated, as though he had swallowed a watermelon **whole**! We watched him finish the last bite on his plate, only to see my father slap another stack in front of him, with the firm command, "**Eat** um!" Dave had been overfilled for some time, and was imploring, "No more Mr. Fenske, *please*," but he was intimidated by my father, who was having a blast using up his batter (I think he had even made more, while Dave was occupied). We got Dave out of there, and had a good laugh about it, but we had to take him home, because he was "too stuffed" to do the town with us *that* Saturday night.

I had quite a hitch in my stride that first year following my injury, but I still made it out to the beach often that summer. Grand Haven, or Holland State Park were fun places to be, and were great places to meet girls. We would often try to interest some girls into joining us for a party, coco-cola, hotdogs, (even a little beer) on the Fenske 7, if my parents weren't around. At my pleading, my dad moved the boat to the Saugatuck Harbor, for my buddies and I to stay on that Labor Day weekend. We docked right behind the Coral Gables Bar, and had a fantastic time. We even had a band playing on the front deck (some guys who came to town for a "Battle of the Bands" competition at Coral Gables). We had more people dancing on the docks, than there were inside the bar! A couple of years previous, the drinking age had been lowered from 21 to 18, amid citizen protests that being drafted, and sent to Viet Nam at 18, should entitle one to be old enough to drink. The drinking age was changed back to 21, several years after it had been lowered (just two weeks before my twenty-first birthday). We weren't big drinkers, but we liked to have fun, and like many young people, we sometimes took dangerous risks.

We often rode our motorcycles to the beach, no shirt, shoes, or helmet, which even though risky, was legal in those days. I rode a Honda 350 Scrambler, which I had purchased used, but in fairly good condition. As we raced our motorcycles the entire thirty miles back home, single file, in the twilight one evening (on two-lane M-45), something happened that I will always shudder to recall. I was topped-out at about 85 mph, second in line behind Andy Zoonztra, with the rest of our pack behind me. I noticed a car (which obviously didn't see us) pull out in front of Andy, from the right side of the road, intending to make a left hand turn, to travel in the opposite direction that we were traveling. Too late, the driver saw us and stopped, **directly in the middle** of our lane. There was not time enough to break before hitting the car, so Andy swerved to the left oncoming lane, narrowly missing the front of the stopped car, and just barely making it back into our lane, before the approaching traffic arrived, with horns blaring! With no other choice, I swerved to the right road shoulder, fishtailing **at 85 mph** in the loose gravel. To my **alarm**, immediately in front of me was a diamond shaped metal road sign, supported on each side by steel legs. I had **no chance** of stopping, and with a deep ditch to the right, **no chance** of missing the sign! Somehow my fishtailing left me straight up, just as I reached the sign, and I instinctively tucked in my elbows, and ducked my head. **Miraculously**, I made it through without a **scratch**, and I was able to slowly come to a stop.

The other riders behind me had time to come to a stop, and Andy circled back to see if I was okay. The car just sped away, without a word. When I stopped shaking, we took my motorcycle back to the sign, to see how I had managed to get under it. When we sized up the situation, I had only **1/2 inch** of clearance on either side of the rubber handgrips on my handlebars and only about an **inch** of clearance above, with my head tucked in the lowest position **possible**! If either of my handlebars had caught one of the angle-iron legs, the sign would likely have bent forward, and with the force of momentum, at my rate of speed, could have sliced me in half like a tomato! If I had **even** been wearing a **helmet**, I wouldn't have had the clearance to make in under that sign! I guess it just wasn't my time to go! Anyway, I spent the rest of the trip home, **again thanking** my guardian angels!

Following my injury, I was always embarrassed by the appearance of my foot, so whenever we went to the beach, I wore my shoes, even when we walked in the sand. Invariably this would evoke questions from strangers as to why I was wearing shoes, so I learned to carry my shoes, and step quickly whenever we were walking, keeping my right foot buried in the sand when we were standing. That way I had my shoes handy, in case we strolled across some pavement, or concrete. On one occasion, while walking on the shoulder of the road, single file past a long line of cars waiting to get into Holland State Beach, I noticed a lot of strange stares. We usually parked a mile or so back up the road and walked in, rather than wait in line with our bikes or our vehicle, for several hours (which it sometimes took) to get into the Park. My foot started to throb, after the first quarter mile of hiking, and I was walking with a pretty heavy limp. I was leading the pack, and unaware of all the stares we were getting, until I observed some of the onlookers **pointing** at us, and **laughing**. When I turned around to see if the other guys had noticed, I discovered my friends marching like a row of penguins behind me, all limping in perfect unison with me. When I saw what they were up to, I understood the gawks and giggles from the crowd. Embarrassed, I uttered, "**Real funny** guys!"

Most of us are very insecure at twenty, and things bother us that we would hardly notice later in life. I **was** humiliated momentarily, but I knew my friends meant no harm by their prank, and I did see the humor in their stunt. On some level, I knew that my friends were more accepting of my injury than I was myself. We had a good hoot about it, and my friends retold the tale on numerous future occasions, fantasizing about what thoughts some of the puzzled onlookers might have had like, "Maybe those guys were all in the same platoon in Viet Nam, and had the same foot injured by the same landmine!"

The beachside community of Muskegon was a place we rarely visited, except once each summer, when we attended the annual motorcycle hill-climbs. This event is the "National Finals," and is **huge**, drawing thousands of contestants and spectators, from all across the nation. We rode our motorcycles that year, with a cooler full of beer (strapped on the back), so that we would have a chance at getting a close enough parking place, that I could make the hike in without too much discomfort. It seemed so ironic (and unfair) to me, that the pain from my foot injury was intense enough to keep me from attending a concert we had heard about, and that I **passionately** wanted to attend (named "Woodstock"), to be held later that summer in August, but yet my injury was not "serious enough" to keep me out of Viet Nam!

We got there early, were able to park fairly close, and we found a decent spot to sit, right near the base of the hill. We knew a guy who supposedly had qualified to be in the climb, although I had my doubts, because our "friend," who we really only knew from some parties we had attended together, didn't seem the type. He seemed kind of "sissy" and frail to me, like one of those people who would never have dirt under his fingernails! The hill climber, whose name was "Bill Laury," was actually the boyfriend of a waitress, at one of the pubs we frequented. The waitress, whom I was somewhat attracted to (and whom I could always tell was attracted to me), had invited us to attend the previous parties, at which we had met her boyfriend, and she also had asked us to be sure to attend this event.

The bikes that make the finals are super modified, with enhanced engines, most mounted at a forty-five degree angle in the bike frame, so that they stay closer to level when climbing. We had a great time all day, and saw some good climbs, with plenty of radical crashes. The hill was very long, and steep, with numerous constructed ditches, and hurdles, and well over half the bikes didn't even make it to the top. We never saw our acquaintance "Bill," and I figured he hadn't even shown up, until late in the afternoon, when I heard his name announced as the last climb of the day. We started to cheer, but quickly stopped, when we saw him roll his bike into the "starting pit." His bike, in contrast with all the other "chopped up" radical looking bikes we had been watching all afternoon, (although very "modified" looking) was painted a shiny, spotless florescent green. He wore a spotless matching florescent green leather **jacket**, **pants**, **helmet**, **gloves**, and even **boots**, unlike the soiled, worn blue-jean, leather, and bandanna-clad contestants we had been watching all day. Nobody seemed to know this guy. Nobody cheered, and I heard a lot of comments like, "What the **hell** is **that**," coming from different places in the crowd.

"Bill," who had a prissy, feminine style walk, took longer than **any** other contestant had taken all day! He even had **assistants** (a couple of guys with shovels, and a **broom**) to prepare the pit area, before he would even start his bike. He wasn't the "type" to **personally** handle a broom or shovel. By the time he finally quit pointing to more spots for his assistants to smooth out, I was embarrassed that I had even acknowledged I knew him. By this time of day, many people were drunk and impatient, almost **everybody** in the crowd was booing, and some were already leaving. After the longest delay between climbs that we had experienced throughout the entire contest, he finally fired up his bike. I saw a few heads take notice when we first heard his engine throttle up, because it sounded pretty **powerful**, and a little **different** than anything else we had heard all day.

Before we, or anyone else even had a chance to comment, the start man dropped the flag, and Bill was off. I, all of my friends, and the entire crowd sat in awe, as Bill went straight up that mountain, **gaining speed** the entire way! He barely **touched** the tops of the moguls, and threw a dirt rooster-tail **twenty-five feet** behind him, the **complete** distance to the top! When Bill crested the top, and broke the finish light (rooster-tail intact), he was at such a speed, that he had **no** chance of stopping his bike before the immediate backdrop, that the announcer had previously described, and he just pushed himself away from his bike. All that I and the entire crowd saw, was Bill and his bike separate, and then drop out of view in the sunset, as we heard the crash of his $100,000 florescent green bike, named "The Mountain Slayer!" The entire crowd came to their feet in applause, and soon after, the announcer broadcast a time that shaved *10 seconds*, off the best time we had heard **all day**! All of my friends and I quickly got **real** busy, telling everyone we talked to, that we were **buddies** of "Mountain Slayer Bill!"

I reported to MSU that next fall, even though I had lost my 2S student deferment, and one could not reacquire a 2S, once it was lost. I **wanted** my Civil Engineering degree, and I felt that I might just as well stay in college, and earn as many credits as possible before my inevitable induction into the army, and have less to obtain when I returned home. Several acquaintances, and a high school classmate, had already been shipped home from Viet Nam in pine boxes, and a couple of others were missing, but I had **every intention** of coming home **alive**!

Shortly after MSU started that September, the United States came out with the draft lottery. All 365 days of the year were drawn randomly out of a tumbler (pre-computer), and those with a 1A classification were drafted in the order that their birth date was selected. My birth date (Dec. 16) was drawn out #187, and that first year, Uncle Sam called for the first **184** numbers! I missed being drafted (inducted) by **three** numbers! The following year December 16 was drawn #226, and the first **220** numbers were called (drafted)! I graduated from MSU with a Civil Engineering degree in 1971, and missed again by a handful of numbers. I had a good draw again in 1972, and in 1973 the Viet Nam war ended (*at least US involvement*), and so did the draft. I guess I wasn't supposed to go. Anyway, I was lucky.

My friend Dan Tanner attended Grand Rapids Junior College after high school, and as always, studied just enough to keep his 2S student deferment alive. Dan didn't have much use for education in general, and he was in college purely as a means of avoiding the draft. When the United States came out with the draft lottery, Dan dropped out of college immediately. I tried to talk him into changing his mind, but Dan said, "No, don't worry about it. I'll get lucky on the lottery!" As it turned out, Dan's birth-date (Dec. 30) was drawn out **number 2**! Needless to say, Dan was destined to ship out on the first boat to Viet Nam. Fortunately however, Dan quickly signed up for the Paratroopers, he was assigned to Germany, and avoided Viet Nam entirely.

The fall of 1969 (the first fall after my foot injury), I hiked over to Jenison Field House (on the MSU campus) every night, and ran on the dirt track. The pain in my foot was **agonizing**, and at times I would fall on my face, with dirt sticking to the tracks of tears, from the pain, and **sorrow** over what I had experienced, but when it eased, I would get back up, and pound out another mile. I was **determined** not to let this injury cripple me, and I was "Holding On" to my desire to be normal, and to my *dream* of being a famous boxer. Because I am right handed, I box with my left (lead) foot in front of me and flat, and my right foot back, and up on my toes (which were no longer there). To compensate, I took my boxing shoes to an old shoemaker in Lansing, who fashioned a piece of spring steel into the sole of my right shoe, to support my foot.

I continued boxing, and running all through college, and for several years after, until age twenty-six, which was mandatory retirement from amateur boxing in the nineteen seventies. I didn't want to retire from the ring at such a young age, but I didn't want to turn pro either, I guess because I did not want to make a livelihood out of boxing. Boxing was my sport, my recreation, and I didn't want to turn it into my job.

Four or five years after my surgery (at his request), when I paid a visit to the surgeon who had worked on my foot, the doctor was amazed that I had no limp, and at the lack of scar tissue, and the pliability of my foot, stating that I was "**very lucky**!" Actually I knew that it wasn't luck at all, but it was the blood, sweat, and tears that I had shed in Jenison Field House, pounding out endless miles around the track, and down the road, along with all my hard work in the ring, that had gotten me to where I was.

It wasn't until years later, when the true story movie came out about a football player named "Rocky Blier" (portrayed by Robert Urich), who played fullback for Notre Dame (only a few years before I played football for Michigan State), then later for the Pittsburgh Steelers, and helped them win the Super Bowl four times, that I realized I had injured the same foot, the same year that Rocky Blier had injured his (and also his leg), on shrapnel in Viet Nam. Although I haven't accomplished anything like Rocky Blier, we both made a comeback, and I hope to meet him someday.

I really never even thought much about my right foot being any different than any other boxer's right foot. Sure it hurt quite a bit at times, but not bad enough to cause me to want to quit. My belief in myself, and my dream, were strong enough to get me through the pain, and keep me going, and they **still are**. I have always believed that any pain or handicap has only as much power and control over us as we give it, and one of my favorite quotes is, "Whatever doesn't kill us, only makes us stronger."

16

Building a Life after College

Doug graduating from MSU, December 1971.

I proudly graduated from MSU, with a BS in Civil Engineering in 1971. After I graduated, I continued to help build the family business (Fenske Enterprises), and for the first summer I lived with a good friend, Dave Welsh (a fellow Civil Engineer) from Detroit, who moved back to the farm with me. We did a survey of the Grand River that summer (required by the MDNR, to determine the flow rate), which was a bit treacherous (with one of us in a row boat), but it saved my parents a lot of money, and allowed us to obtain an expansion permit. Dave fit in well, and became another family member, joining us at all family functions. The two of us moved into the bunkhouse, and converted it into a total "seventies" bachelor pad, with a US flag on the wall, and plenty of "pin-ups." I know my "little brothers," my cousin Bob Schulz and Easy Ridder, learned how to drink a few too many beers, and learned some other things (they probably weren't quite old enough for) by hanging around that bunk house, but we created some great memories.

Over time, my friend Dave formed a relationship with a neighborhood girl (a former Riverbend, and Grandville High classmate), whom he eventually married. I went back to MSU that fall, making up a few credits I still needed for my BS degree, and taking some graduate courses, toward a masters (MS) degree. I decided not to continue pursuing a Masters Degree after that fall term, and I moved back to Grand Rapids, putting my energy into our business. I took up residence with a couple of buddies at a bachelor pad (and later with a girlfriend) in Grand Rapids, until my late twenties.

I enjoyed being single, and five years flew by. However by age twenty-eight, Grand Rapids, MI being steeped in tradition and religious values, with family at the center, I started receiving a lot of pressure from my mother (and others), to get married and raise a family. Mother often stated, "You're the **only** boy! **Who's** going to carry on the family name?!" When I replied, but "Mother, I haven't met the **right** girl," Mother responded, "Oh, don't be so **fussy**! What about that girl you're dating now? You've been dating her **long enough**! **She'll** be fine!"

Schulz/Fenske families with Dave Welsh.

Doug (left) on Bigboy, and Dave Welsh (right) on Bronk.

Somehow I **knew** better. I did want **eventually** to be married and raise a family, and I **had** searched for years to find a compatible mate, with no success. Throughout my twenties (**incessantly**), I experienced a **strong** feeling, a "**voice-thought**" inside my head, which said, "You've already **met** whom you're **supposed** to be with!" The "voice-thought" didn't make sense though, because for a very long time I had harbored dreams (and **visions**), of meeting a blond woman, who was beautiful, and who lived on a beach in California, and I had only visited California once, as a very young boy. The "voice-thought," "**feeling**," was so **strong** however, that I looked up a number of girls whom I had dated in high school, and in college. I traveled to several places in Michigan, and to South Bend, Indiana, Champagne, Illinois, and Toledo, Ohio. I located some of the girls I had dated, and several were still single, and interested, but it's easy to romanticize a relationship, once you're no longer in it. Each time I would reacquaint myself with an old girlfriend, memories would return of what wasn't right, and why the relationship had failed.

Finally, reluctantly, I ignored the "voice-thought, feeling," wrote it off as just a dream, and asked the girl I was dating, named Ruth Ann, to marry me. I had been dating her for several years, although turbulently (we argued, and broke up frequently). **Mostly**, I felt a sense of responsibility. I didn't want to let my mother down, and also, Ruth Ann's older brother Dick (whom I held in high regard), and whom on various occasions had bluntly pressured me to marry his sister, had recently been diagnosed with terminal leukemia, and I wanted **him** to **know** before he died, that we were going to be married. Unfortunately, on the weekend I proposed, Dick slipped into a coma. He never knew of our upcoming wedding, and he died within a few months. Dick was forty-two years old.

We were married in the spring of 1977, for a rocky ten years. My good friend Dan Tanner was my "best man," and several other neighborhood friends stood up for me. My company sponsored a men's "DFCC" softball team, golf team, and a men and women's bowling team (on which we both participated). We were friends with the members of the teams, which were comprised mostly of guys I grew up with, and their girlfriends and wives.

They were good athletes, as well as good friends. They included guys like ballplayers/bowlers/golfers, Doug Ridder, Dirk Drevis, Jim and Chet Casper, Doug Fenske Cattle Company, and Fenske Enterprises Maintenance Manager Bob Mench, our excellent infielders, first baseman Huey Meinmen, second basemen Jerry Degard, and our top pitcher/first-baseman, Ed Hasbreck, and of course Dan Tanner, who played catcher, and outfield (as well as golfed and bowled), and who's powerful long arms allowed him to throw to home plate (sometimes over the backstop) from the farthest corners of the field. Ed Hasbreck ("Auto Ed") was in the automobile sales business (Jerry Degard eventually became a partner), and Ed (a confirmed bachelor) threw many terrific (frequently wild) parties at his place, with all the trimmings (often a full turkey meal), which parties I will never forget (*nor I am sure* will some of his **neighbors**)!

My good friend Gus Bulma played on the teams, and stood up for me in my wedding, as did Glenn Cass (as mentioned one of my father's first employees). Glenn was a close friend of mine, who played softball with us, and bowled with us, in spite of a serious injury (compound fracture of his leg) he had suffered years earlier in a vehicle accident. Glenn and I both had an interest in agriculture, and often helped one another. Glen's brother Mel (a team member), was a good athlete and friend, and did the same. All of Glenn's sons (and one daughter), and Mel's son, were DFCC and Fenske Enterprises employees at one time or another, as well as team members. We often golfed with our neighborhood friends, partied with them on a regular basis, and even vacationed with some of them.

One of the events, which became a yearly outing with a number of our neighborhood friends (including ball team members) as couples, was a weekend canoe trip each year, down a northern Michigan river. We scheduled the event in July or August of each year, and we all headed up together, packing sleeping bags, tents, and lots of beer. It was always a wild weekend, with most of us consuming a little too much alcohol. None of us were expert canoeists, and we actually expired nearly as much time in the water, as in the rented canoes.

Dan Tanner could always be relied upon to create some type of humorous situation. One year, as Dan was canoeing with his girlfriend Char (who later became his wife), Dan and Char's canoe hit a partially submerged log sideways, at a fairly fast moving section of the Pere Marquette River, and immediately flipped, spilling Dan, Char, and all of their contents. They both went under, with the exception of one of Dan's hands, clutching a full can of beer. Dan surfaced fairly quickly, and he began dog paddling around in circles with his other hand, watching for Char to surface, grabbing a couple quick sips of his beer as he did so. We were close enough behind him to see what was happening, but not close enough to assist.

After a few seconds had passed, and Char hadn't yet surfaced, I hollered, "**Dan**, you better go down **after** her!" Dan just continued to paddle around for a few more seconds, muttering a nickname he had given her ("Jive Mama?"), a couple times, as if there was any possibility that someone submerged could hear him. Finally Char popped up, spitting water, and **hopping mad**! Char spewed, "The current had me **pinned** under a **log**, and you didn't even **come** down **after me**!" Dan just replied, "Oh Jive Mama, just relax. I'd have been comin' down after ya, if ya hadn't come up pretty soon! I had **just** opened a **full** beer, and I didn't have any place to set it down!"

Our marriage produced one child, a boy named Brandon, born in 1981 (who was six when we divorced). I was ecstatic to become a father, and I was in the room when he was born. Brandon came out calm, and was so perfect and silent when I first stared into his sweet little face, that I was spellbound. However one look at me, and he let us all know that he had a set of lungs! My heart melted at first sight, and I loved that little boy with every fiber of my Being (as I do today).

Brandon as a baby.

When Brandon was still a baby, he would spend entire afternoons in the cab of a farm tractor with me, totally content, with only occasional stops for food or a diaper change. We were continuously together in his pre-school years, and Brandon instigated some good changes in me. Once, while strapped in his car seat in my pickup, right after I had shot at a starling, which was feeding on corn in one of the farm corncribs, Brandon pleaded in a tearful tone, "Daddy, don't shoot the Birdie!" I tried to make excuses but caught myself, realizing that I was trying to **explain** my behavior to a child barely out of **diapers**, who really understood more about life (on this issue) than I did. There were other ways that I could protect my corn, if it became too big of a problem, which it wasn't. I never forgot that incident, and I slowly started looking at life differently. It wasn't long after that day that I no longer shot at birds "stealing corn," and within a few years, I gave up all hunting.

Brandon spent many entire weekends with me alone, when his mother would travel up to Rockford, to visit with her friend Raquel. We fished endless hours together in a little ten foot dingy before Brandon could even bait a hook, but he loved it, and so did I. Raquel was single, and she and Ruth Ann loved to go out and party. I knew they were going to singles bars, which I accepted because Raquel was single. The irony however, was that I was the one continually accused of going out to singles bars, which was untrue, and in fact Ruth Ann was very threatened by me going *anywhere* with my friends *at all.* **She** eventually had an affair with a good friend of mine, whom she was always attracted to, and flirtatious with. I became aware of the affair, but never confronted either one of them about it. I think that we will only let ourselves believe the things in life that we are ready to deal with. Something inside me died however, the night I found out. In a way, once I learned of the affair it released me, because somewhere in my deepest heart, I knew that this was not the right person for me, and I believe that if Ruth Ann was honest with herself, she knew it too.

We had good times of course, but no matter how we tried, the relationship just wasn't right. I had ambitions, and dreams, and I was constantly developing something new. Ruth Ann was continually opposed to my efforts with another business that I had started before we were a couple (CRRI, described ahead), as well as to my expansion plans for Fenske Enterprises. She was also resistant to many of my personal goals, such as a barn I took down and moved to our home property.

I had always admired this particular barn in the many years I had passed by it. It was a Quonset style (hip-roof) barn, similar to the barn I had grown up with on my parent's farm, just not quite as large. It was forty feet wide by eighty feet long, of all-wood construction, and was located on Ivanrest Avenue, in Grandville, about five miles from where I lived. The owner started to subdivide the farm on which the barn was located, and one day driving past the farm, I drove in and talked to the developer, who had entered into a partnership with the farm owner. It was a Wednesday afternoon, and when I asked the developer what they were going to do with the barn, he told me, "Monday morning, it's coming down. We have a street going right through the middle of where it sets, and eight AM Monday, a bulldozer is pushing into a pile of rubble, to be loaded into trucks, and delivered to your landfill!" I said, "Oh no! I love that barn! Let me take it down, and save it!" Believing I wouldn't, he stated, "Go ahead, but you better move fast, because in five days we're putting a street right through there!" I jumped into my truck, and headed straight over to "Gelock Heavy Movers," and lined up a crane, with truck and operator, to meet me at the barn at 6 AM the following morning.

I knew that the barn was too large to move in one piece, but I didn't have time to dismantle it, so I decided to cut it into large sections, to be reassembled once it was delivered to my property. Unfortunately, it was extremely windy the following morning, with wind gusts reaching forty miles per hour, but I knew we had no choice, or I could lose the barn to demolition. I decided to quarter the barn, and I directed a couple of DFCC employees with ladders and chainsaws, to the midline we had chalked on either side of the barn, to cut the barn in half.

Since it was too windy to ask anyone else to climb up to the roof peek to split the barn lengthwise, I did so myself. It was a little tricky with the strong wind gusts, and a few times I had to quickly hit the chainsaw kill-switch, drop the saw (tethered to me with a rope), and grab onto either side of the roof peek with all fours. I slowly made my way along, with one foot on either side of the barn peek for stability, and cut the barn in half, right down the center. Employees simultaneously dismantled all of the wood stalls and pens inside the barn, and removed them. After my workers completed the crosscut, and I completed the peak-cut, we were ready. I then knocked two holes in the roof of each quarter section, and we chained a heavy beam inside, against the roof timbers, to enable us to pick up 1/4 of the barn at a time.

As the crane put cable-tension on the first quarter-section, we all worked around the edges with crow-bars, checking for any missed anchor bolts, and helping to break the barn free from the concrete slab it was setting on, which was quite difficult, since the barn had been constructed seventy years prior. Finally, as darkness neared, it broke free, and the crane began to swing away the massive forty by forty foot square (arched) section of timber, which from the underside, resembled a giant section of rib-cage, from some pre-historic dinosaur. We all cheered, as the crane operator slowly circled his swing toward the flatbed trailer that I had parked on site for moving the barn sections. All seemed to be going very smoothly, however, as the operator circled his swing, one of the strongest (and longest) wind gusts of the day, grabbed onto of the enormous barn section. When the wind got under the roof, I immediately knew we were in trouble, but there was **nothing** I could do!

The wind continued to howl at an unforgiving rate, and escalated, until the cable was strung out nearly parallel to the ground! I was standing right next to the crane operator, to whom I had been offering advice. At the start of the day, the crane operator had admitted to me that he had never before been involved in such a project as this, but he had seemed comforted by *my* confidence level. As the incessant gust of wing seemingly, **endlessly** continued, I observed the far side crane-stabilizing jacks pull up off the ground, a **clear foot** or more! I looked up at the crane operator, to see if **he** had noticed, but his eyes, which looked like saucers, were fixed on the colossal sail on the end of his cable, and his knuckles turned white on the crane control levers. I noticed a string of cars starting to line up out on Ivanrest Avenue to witness the event, and with one hand pulling down on either side of my hat, backing away, and poised to run out of the way if the crane went over, I uttered the words to myself, "Oh **Fenske**, you did it **this time**!"

After what felt like an eternity, the mighty wind gust let up, the barn quarter section swung back to perpendicular, and the crane stabilizers settled back to the ground. The crane operator quickly let the barn section settle to the ground, jumped out of the crane, and walked straight over to me, as fast as he could. He stated, "You probably don't remember me, and I wasn't going to say anything, but now, what the **hell**! I fought you once in the "Golden Gloves," about eight years ago, and you knocked me **out**!" After standing speechless for a few moments gathering my thoughts, I replied, "Oh **no**! I hope you haven't picked today to get **even**!" We shook hands, enjoyed a good laugh, and were both obviously relieved to be through the ordeal we had just experienced. We called it quits for the day, and my employees and I cabled the other barn sections together, to help them make it through the rest of the windstorm that night.

The following day the winds died down, and moving the next three sections was much smoother going. We loaded all four sections on the trailer, on top of each other, with support blocking between the sections. The third day we loaded all the loose lumber from the barn interior into roll-off containers, cleaned the site, and moved the trailer (out of the construction zone) to the edge of the property, where I had to leave it, until I obtained moving permits. In three days we had the barn down, loaded, and moved, and the site ready for road excavation, which started on schedule the following Monday morning.

The permits to move the barn (two because we had to cross the county line) took forever, because the barn sections were way over width, and actually would take up most of the road. Winter set in, and heavy snow fell before I got the moving permits. Finally, on a mild

February day, we moved the sections to my home site, where they sat, snow covered, until the following spring. Many times over, I heard rumors of statements that neighbors, and passers-by had made, "That barn will never stand again!" By mid-May however, I hired a building erector company (owned by a friend) to assist me in reconstructing the barn. My friend Denny is a "master" at his profession, and it went back together marvelously well. I poured a concrete floor, built beautiful oak stalls inside, stained it dark brown to match the house, and it turned out magnificent. More than once, when complete, observers remarked how it reminded them of a "Kentucky Blue Grass Country" barn.

Gus Bulma's son Ron was raising registered paint quarter horses at the time, he needed a place to board them, and before very long, the barn had tenants. I was **so** proud of that barn! I paved the driveway right up to the entrance of the barn, strung electric to it, and built a tack room inside. On many weekend nights, while Ruth Ann was away, and Brandon and I were home alone, rather than sit in the house and watch television, we would go out to the barn. Brandon and I danced and sang, as we played together for entire evenings in the barn, building forts in the hayloft, wrestling, and telling stories. It reminded me of my own childhood, and the endless hours of entertainment the Tanner boys and I had enjoyed in our barns.

In the following few years, I began to understand what had drawn me to that barn, and the significance of having moved the barn became crystal clear to me. That barn became a temple to me, in the loneliness I felt in my marriage, as I sobbed many hours alone up in the loft. Something was terribly wrong, and I didn't know what to do to correct it. It was another three years before I did finally leave, but our relationship continued to disintegrate throughout that time. My dreams and plans would constantly aggravate Ruth Ann. She just didn't want any more, and would often say to me, "What's the **matter** with you! Just **stop**! We've got **enough**!" Our differences caused a lot of arguments, which we explained away to Brandon's objections as "discussions." No matter how hard we tried to hide it, our disagreements would sometimes surface. It used to break my heart when Brandon was just a toddler, who could barely speak, and he would grab each of our pant legs with a chubby little hand and state, "You guys don't always **discust**!"

Concern for his well-being, as well as his mother and I, helped me to eventually leave, and file for divorce. Actually I never missed the relationship once I left, and I felt a freedom and lightness I had almost forgotten, but I painfully missed being with my son each night. The relationship was hard on Brandon, Ruth Ann, and I, and I believed that we **all** deserved something better. It was nobody's fault. Ruth Ann and I just weren't right for each other, and wanted different things. I was never going to be the nine-to-five husband she wanted, and she was never going to be the "go-for-it-all risk-taker" I wanted. For Brandon's sake, I did my utmost to, and told his mother that I wanted to remain friends when we divorced. To my sadness, it did not happen that way, primarily because Ruth Ann opposed the divorce, became angry, bitter, impossible to communicate with, and extremely difficult to deal with, especially with issues such as "shared custody."

17

Building the Business

For many years, Fenske Enterprises cooperatively shared the entrance to the business with Rieth-Riley Inc., an asphalt paving company, which leased five acres from my parents for an asphalt plant. The owners of Rieth-Riley had approached my parents in the late-fifties, wanting to purchase some acreage. When my parents refused to sell (at my mother's fortunate resistance), Rieth-Riley signed a long-term lease. Fairly soon after Rieth-Riley had moved on site, my Uncle Hank went to work for them, and eventually he became plant operator. One afternoon (early 70's), I was on the phone in the Fenske Enterprises office, when I heard a huge explosion. I ran to the window and saw flames coming from the Rieth-Riley plant. I dropped the phone and took off running.

Several men had gathered around a person on the ground by the time I got there, and I could hear sirens from an ambulance and fire trucks in Grandville, already on their way. It was my Uncle Hank, who had been blown off a platform (close to thirty feet high), near the top of the plant, by a gas explosion, which happened while he was making some repairs. Although in severe pain, he was conscious when they loaded him into the ambulance, and I insisted on riding with him. As I had been instructed (to keep him conscious), I kept him talking all the way to the hospital. I loved my Uncle Hank dearly (as I do today), and having always thought of him as my older brother, I accepted that he at times didn't seem to have much use for me.

Uncle Hank has probably always thought of me as a "pain-in-the-ass" kid brother (although I know he loves me). I'm sure he though of me as a "ratchet-mouth-pain" on this trip, and I learned some new four letter words, but I kept him talking. Unbelievably, other than a badly shattered heel (on the foot he landed on), Uncle Hank was fine, and through hard work, and many painful miles of hiking (after months on crutches), other than a slight limp (through his incredible determination), he completely recovered, and remains in good health today.

Fenske Enterprises continued to grow and prosper throughout the years. The volume of waste we received continually increased, and I was constantly amazed and appalled at what a "throw-away" civilization we are in the United States. Michigan has four distinct separate seasons, and at the change of seasons, we would frequently see brand-new, perfectly good items come into the landfill (such as $100/each, fishing rods and reels, camping items, etc.), which had not sold, and were discarded by large volume retailers, to clear shelf space for items (such as snow skis and ice skates), which were in demand in the upcoming season.

Occasionally we received perfectly good items, which were discarded for other reasons. One Monday morning, we received several truckloads of perfect, new, $1.25/each, "name brand" golf balls, packed in gunnysacks, 750 balls per sack. Inspectors were present to insure that the golf balls, which had been (as explained to us) inadvertently manufactured under an "expired" India rubber contract, were properly disposed of. The loads of golf balls continued to come in all week (in excess of 1,000,000 balls total), and the inspectors became bored and left after the first couple of days.

Needless to say, none of us golfers needed to buy golf balls for quite some time. In fact we discovered new uses for golf balls, such as target practice. At times after work, we shot the golf balls up over the landfill with a slingshot, and found that if they were hit squarely with shotgun birdshot, they would burst into a spray of rubber fragments, which would float down to the landfill surface, resembling fireworks. This provided myself and other employees with hours of entertainment, as well as improved our marksmanship significantly.

I ate, slept, and lived the Fenske Enterprises business, focusing on recycling. With very little money to purchase new materials on the farm, like my parents, I had learned to recycle, and I knew there had to be a better way to handle waste, than burying it in a landfill. At one point in time, while auguring a corner fence posthole on a finished section of the landfill, the augur extracted a section of newspaper, with a date over fifteen years old! I became aware that we were simply "entombing" discarded materials in our landfills all over the world, and creating potential "time-bombs," with a continual threat of contamination for future generations to deal with.

In time, the Fenske Enterprises recycling business grew to such size, that we owned over forty semi trailers to collect cardboard, newspaper, plastic, and other materials for recycling, from all over the state, as well roll-off containers all over Kent and Ottawa counties. We collected recyclables from as far as Traverse City in northwestern Michigan (150 miles NW of Grand Rapids), to Ypsilanti in southeast-

Grand Rapids Press, May 7, 1984—Fenske Enterprises recycling advertisement.

ern Michigan (200 miles SE of Grand Rapids). We also received source-separated recyclables (materials separated at the source of generation), which we purchased, and commingled recyclables (separated in our Paper Plant), delivered to us by our own trucks, and by approximately forty private (and two public) waste hauling companies, as well as numerous companies (and individuals), that hauled their own scrap materials.

After processing (sorting, grinding, crushing, shredding, baling, etc.), we sold and delivered recyclables to recycling mills (paper mills, steel foundries, glass factories, plastic forge plants), all over Michigan, Ohio, and Indiana. Fenske Enterprises soon became the largest solid waste recycling business in West Michigan, and won numerous recycling and environmental awards, in which I took a lot of personal pride. The awards included the "MI Industrial Recycler of The Year" award, presented to me individually (on behalf of Fenske Enterprises) by the active Governor of Michigan, as well as the "Environmental Leadership" award, granted to Fenske Enterprises by the "West Michigan Environmental Action Council." WMEAC was the *most powerful* and effective environmental action council in Michigan, with a dynamic Executive Director (Ken Sikkema), who later became a Michigan Senator (and nearly Governor of Michigan). WMEAC worked vigorously to improve environmental standards in the state, and at my insistence, Fenske Enterprises joined their membership in the early seventies.

By the early to mid-seventies, Fenske Enterprises had grown to the point, where we needed some management assistance. We hired a Paper Plant manager, who did not work out because of some dishonest activity. We discovered (after he had been working at Fenske Enterprises for a couple of years) that he had started brokering and selling recycled paper on the side, and delivering it to recycling mills in Fenske Enterprises trucks, with the cash going directly into his own personal account. I could not take on any more responsibilities, and my father (in his mid-fifties) wasn't willing to. My sister Karen, and brother-in-law Dick, both schoolteachers, had expressed that Dick was sick of teaching, and would like to give it a try. I convinced my parents that we should give Dick a chance as Paper Plant manager, and for a number of years Dick (Kamisch) managed the Paper Plant superbly. Dick had grown up in a city (near Detroit), was not very hands-on, and he had a lot to learn. Karen and Dick met at Western Michigan University, and married shortly after graduating (at twenty-

10F—   Advertising Supplement To The Grand Rapids Press, Monday, May 7, 1984

Fenske Picks Up State Recycling Award

The founder of Fenske Enterprises learned that the old adage "waste not, want not" made good sense long before recycling became a widespread public concern.

Howard Fenske's desire to salvage reusable materials tossed into his landfill resulted in one of the state's largest and most highly regarded recycling operations. He is committed to the recyling cause.

"We're running out of space for landfills and we're using up our resources and wasting them," said Fenske.

His operation reclaims plastics, paper, wood, metals, and glass to sell it for reuse rather than burying it in the landfill.

Fenske's recycling efforts earned him a statewide award presented by Gov. James Blanchard on May 2. Blanchard presented the award on behalf of the Michigan Recycling Coalition, which named Fenske the state's Industrial Recycler of the Year.

This is no mean feat for the family-owned operation at 2537 Wilson Ave. SW, in Walker, pointed out daughter Karen Fenske. Karen, her mother Leona, brother Doug and his wife, Ruth Ann, take an active role in the business.

"We beat beat out some big companies for the award," Karen said.

Fenske is in the process of con-structing a large new building, 200-by-300 feet, and new equipment to process reclaimed materials. The new facilities will allow Fenske to save even more materials.

He currently reclaims abut 50 percent of the so called "garbage" dumped at the landfill.

"We hope to reduce the material being buried in the landfill by at least 50 percent by the ened of the year through recycling alone," he said.

Fenske is proud to receive the honor from the coalition and Blanchard, but his pride does not eclipse his environmental concern.

"It makes me snd that there is nobody doing more then we are," he said.

His concern about waste and his ingenuity in making use of society's discards accounts for his business success.

Fenske launched his operation as a 193-acre farm in 1946, then expanded it to 300 acres. A portion is still used for agriculture; his son has a 100-head herd of cattle.

Fenske branched out from a dairy-cattle farm to selling sand and topsoil. When the need for a landfill surfaced in the area, his land was a likely spot because of a high amount of clay. Clay inhibits liquid run-off from polluting ground water and other water supplies.

Howard and Leona Fenske have built a recycling operation that urged Gov. James Blancha name Howard "Michigan's Industrial Recycler of the Year."

As the garbage came in to the landfill, he was disturbed by the amount of useful material also dumped out.

"It just bothered me there was so much good stuff coming in here," he explained.

So in 1968 and 1969 he began to reclaim or recyle metals and then

other materials for sale, the first business around here to do so. Since then he has consistantly tried to reduce the amount of material going into the landfill.

With the expanded recycling facilities and an eye to the future, Fenske hopes to keep the need for landfills at a minimum. He plans to

install a mass-burn incinera convert the nonreclaimable rial for energy.

"It's the only way to go," h "We hope as time goes on able to burn anything we do for electricity and steam fo But that's a few years dov road."

Parents, *GR Press* article "MI Industrial Recycler of the Year" Award.

one years of age). About eight years earlier, when Mother broke the news to me that they were to be married (in 1968), I had responded, "It's **my** fault"! I stated, "I haven't been paying enough **attention** to her lately," after which Mother burst into tears of laughter. Karen and I were quite close at that time in our lives, but I had started my first year at MSU, and I had not been communicating with Karen as much as I had previously. I thought that her young marriage was a bad thing, which would break our family apart. Mother assured me that it would be fine, and that we weren't **losing** Karen.

Dick is a great person, and turned out to be a fast learner, which was a good thing, because he had some hard lessons ahead of him. At one point early on in their relationship, when Dick was visiting at the farm for a weekend, **I learned** a tough lesson, about how little Dick knew of farm life. I had a couple of full size horses at the time, and while Dick and I were taking a horseback ride one afternoon, we noticed that about twenty head of beef cattle had managed to push the barn door open a few feet, and were grazing in a nearby alfalfa field. I asked Dick to help me round them up, which he did very well, however once we had them headed back in the direction of the barn, Dick began to yell loudly, and spur his horse on. I had taught Dick a little about horses, but nothing yet about cattle, and before he heard my warnings, Dick had the herd of cattle stampeding toward the barn. Needless to say, the cattle took the partially opened barn door in with them.

Karen and Doug, late teens/early twenties.

As I was shaking my head, noticing my father coming out the back door of the farmhouse (**shaking** his), and heading our way, all Dick could say was "**Wow**!" When Dad got out to the barn, and had a look at the damage, with his arms folded at his chest, he declared, "**Well**, as long as you boys had a **good time**! That's the **main** thing!" Without saying another word, he spun around on his heels, and stomped off. Dick and I passed all of our time the rest of that weekend honing our carpentry skills, again rebuilding the same barn doors that Sugarbabe had destroyed, six or seven years prior.

Dick was a hard worker, and willing to try most anything. One summer, when we had a drought, I was in quite a bind for hay. My Uncle Ken had a field of Sudan grass growing on his farm, which he said I could harvest if I wanted it. The Sudan grass was near the banks of the Grand River, growing in a field with a high water table, and was thick, in-spite of the drought. It was so thick, with such a slippery texture in-fact, that it would not bale. It kept plugging up the hay baler every few feet, so I came up with the idea of using our paper baler.

When the oil boom had hit Michigan in the early-fifties, my parents had drilled and struck oil on a half-dozen oil wells (only one unsuccessful try on our farm). None were big-producers (average 1–2 barrels/day), except for one, which was a "gusher" at first. I was a young boy (preschooler), waiting in the car with my mother and my sister Karen (the "Three Little Pigs" weren't born yet), while my father walked over to check on the drilling rig, the evening the "gusher" hit oil. I clearly remember crying (believing he was in big trouble), when my father came back to the car covered in oil, with streams of oil dripping from his raised arms, and tears of joy streaming down his cheeks.

That well pumped *100 barrels/day* at first, and even though oil was not worth anywhere near what it is today, a dollar was worth more then, and it made my parents a lot of money for a number of years, before it slowed down like the other wells. My parents maintained and pumped the wells for many years (about 30), before they eventually sold them all.

Because my parents had been in the oil well business, we had a lot of used steel pipe stacked up on the farm. The farm help and I built a large buck rake out of used steel oil well pipe, mounted it on a bucket-loader farm tractor, and used the farm tractor to push the Sudan grass into truckload size piles all over the field. Working after hours each night when the paper baler was free, we hauled the Sudan grass back to the Paper Plant, with Fenske Enterprises roll-off trucks and containers, where Dick (equipped with a dust mask) baled the grass into 2000 lb. bales. Linda loaded the roll-off containers with an International skid-loader, and always had a full container waiting, each time that I or another driver came back to the hayfield with an empty container. The paper baler packed the bales so tightly, that the excessively dry grass, which I had worried was **too** dry, even **fermented** a little (like silage), and the cattle **loved** it, and did very well on it. This was pre-large square hay-baler days, and I'm sure it was not cost-effective, but hay was extremely scarce that year, and it got us through.

The Paper Plant was a Quonset style building, which my parents had built as warehouse rental space in the mid-1950s. My father built it with his own employees, and I remember all of the Fenskes (although Linda wasn't born yet, and Janice and Patty were too young to help much), sitting around the farmhouse kitchen table, night after night, placing black rubber washers on bolts, which were used to hold the metal ribs of that building together. The company that had been leasing the building had gone out of business, and the building was vacant, so when we decided to get into the paper recycling business (in the early 1970's), it was the logical place to start. My parents purchased a Harrison baler and conveyors, and we eventually expanded into the recycling of plastic, metal and other materials in that building as well, however its name always remained the "Paper Plant."

The winter of the first year that Dick started at Fenske Enterprises was extremely cold, with an excessive amount of snow. The Paper Plant was not heated, and as a result of a rust preventive fiber paint that a traveling salesman had talked my father into, which we had applied (two coats to the entire building) the preceding summer, too much of the snow stuck. About mid-winter, the building **caved in** from the excessive snow-weight. What a **mess**!

We had contracts with some large volume waste paper generators, many tons of paper were delivered to us daily, and paper quickly started piling up outside the building! Dick and I and my dad put our heads together. We used front-end loaders, and boom cranes to raise the roof, by lifting cables, which we strung through torched-holes burned in the steel roof, and wrapped around and clamped to barn beams inside the building. We supported the roof with stacks of paper bales, once we got it lifted, and even though it didn't look too appealing, we were able to get functional within a couple of days.

It took a week or so, to catch up on baling all of the accumulated loose paper (which was minimal, compared to what we faced in the near future). After a couple of years, on a limited budget, we completely revamped the building. My father eventually located a number of used steel trusses, and over time the Paper Plant was enlarged, and completely rebuilt, to a more functional flat-roof style building. We constructed it with two high bays for off-loading tall forty yard roll-offs, which rise to over twenty feet when dumping, and the building worked out excellently.

There were plenty of other challenges in the recycling business as well. One challenge, as in any business, was hiring good employees. Several of the employees we had started out with at the Paper Plant were brought in by Dick's predecessor (the former Paper Plant manager), and came with him from his previous position at PCA (Packaging Corporation of America). One employee (with plenty of problems) whom I will never forget was "**Von Jon Shamole**," as he always introduced himself, which translated as "One John Shammel.

John Shammel was a German immigrant (spoke very broken English), and had actually been a Nazi pilot in World War II. Although I never accepted his short temper, I felt empathy for John Shammel, and what he must have endured in his prior life experience.

Both of John's hands had very short fingernails. Reportedly, at some point during his tenure as a Nazi pilot, John had received what was termed a "Nazi Manicure," undoubtedly for refusing to follow some orders he had received, a habit (we came to discover) he never quite conquered. The Nazi manicure was an extremely cruel and painful custom the Nazi regime habitually practiced, when a soldier disobeyed orders. The Nazi tradition consisted of immobilizing a victim, then clipping off the ends of all his fingers, about **midway through fingernail** of each hand, probably with some type of heavy-duty bolt cutter. With all of the nerves in the end of each finger, I can't even imagine the pain John must have endured (probably for months), until his fingers healed.

In addition to a hardheaded attitude, and a refusal to follow orders, John Shammel had a **very** quick temper. On one occasion (after being alerted of a disturbance), I ran from the office into the Paper Plant, to find that "Von Jon Shamole" (while operating a small International Front-End Loader) had chased my cousin Bob up the conveyor leading into the paper baler. Bob (who worked for Fenske Enterprises part-time while attending Grand Rapids Junior College) was operating the paper baler, and John Shammel had refused to listen to Bob's instructions on how to feed paper onto the conveyor. Apparently, when Bob came down from the baler operations station to explain what John was doing incorrectly, John Shammel lost his temper, and went after Bob with the loader, shouting, "**You not tell me vot to do! I am an enganeer! I bale you up!**" John Shammel had a habit of telling others that he was educated as an engineer, knew more than they did (on whatever subject), and was not going to take instruction from them. There were plenty of occasions when he (as well as other employees, over the years) should have been fired, but my parents never fired anyone!

The paper market (which was our largest volume recyclable material) fluctuates seasonally, and this was often another challenge. Sometimes the market will drop right off, for a short time. At one point, a year or two after we reconstructed the paper plant, the paper market dropped **dead**, and stayed there for many months! With the large contracts we had to pick up paper from around the state, the paper **kept** coming in, and we couldn't sell **any**! Mills just would not buy recycled paper, for **any** price! We had no **choice**, but to keep trucking paper in, and baling it! It wasn't long before every square foot of unused space under roof was used up, so we started stacking baled paper outside. Over a period of months, acres of flat ground around the Paper Plant were covered with baled paper, stacked four bales high, packed tightly together, and covered with black PVC, held down with tires. At one point the *Grand Rapids Press* ran a front-page picture of the stacked bales, with a headline story, titled "Fenske's Folly." We weathered the storm however, and in time the paper market finally came back around. We wound up selling every last bale of stored paper, a lot of it for **premium** prices!

Dick was a friend, as well as my brother-in-law. At one point in time, he asked me to help him take down, and move a forty-foot by sixty-foot hay barn to his farm, and reconstruct it there, which I did. He played on the "Doug Fenske Cattle Company" softball team, and partied with us. Dick was a good athlete; in fact he had been on the Western Michigan University track team, when he and several team-mates broke the world record, in the "Shuttle Hurdle Relay." Dick's legs were **so** developed, and strong however, that I believe they were the cause of a serious injury that Dick suffered playing softball with us. Dick was **very** fast, and during one of his numerous attempts to stretch a double into a triple, which his speed allowed him to accomplish frequently, he pulled up short, midway between second and third base. Dick had snapped his Achilles tendon, clear in two, a couple of inches above his heel. It was a very serious injury, however after a painful operation and a number of months on crutches, he fortunately recuperated fully, and eventually was able to play ball again.

18

Personal Endeavors/DFCC

It bothered me that my parents never offered me a partnership in Fenske Enterprises. My parents are fairly conservative, and in spite of long hours (sixty-plus hour weeks), my salary was pretty modest. My parents were not demanding of my time; they just relied on me to get things done, keep the business permitted, and everything rolling smoothly, which I did. I wanted more out of life though, so by my mid-twenties, I started putting some of my energy in other directions. I developed, owned, and operated a land application business (incorporating land applicable liquid waste into agricultural ground), which I operated as part of my beef cattle/agribusiness (DFCC, Doug Fenske Cattle Company, *by this time a MI corporation*). I also developed (along with a partner, whom I later bought out), owned and operated a 415-acre "Hazardous Waste TSD (Treatment, Storage, Disposal) Landfill" business at another site (CRRI, *Cascade Resource Recovery, Inc.*), prevailing through fourteen lawsuits (two of which went to the Supreme Court). During the permitting process of CRRI, I personally inspired two new state laws, which I helped write (described ahead), and which (amended versions of) are the current existing solid waste, and hazardous waste management laws in Michigan today.

DFCC

I continued to lease more ground, and grow more crops each year, eventually tilling/cropping/pasturing close to 1000 acres. I increased my cattle numbers, continually selling finished beef to individuals (cutting out the middle-men), over time selling the majority of finished beef in this manner (by-the-side). Linda and I and the farm employees built the four large bunk silos (described earlier) for storing corn silage, for feed to finish out cattle, on the two separate feedlots on the farm. Each fall we harvested silage corn, and shelled corn into roll-off trucks, driven through the cornfields alongside the chopper or combine. We dumped the roll-off containers of chopped corn onto the concrete aprons on the front of each bunk silo, and then tightly packed it into the bunk silos with an all-wheel-drive log skidder, mixing in scrap potatoes, and varying amounts of other types of processed vegetable scraps. The cattle seemed to love the silage mixture, and finished out (fattened up) excellently on it.

The land application business was a very profitable business of surface application, and injection of different types of land applicable liquid wastes, which municipalities and businesses paid DFCC to dispose of by the gallon. The waste material helped me and other farmers, by adding humus to the soil, as well as by cutting fertilizer costs (costing DFCC about $30–40,000/year, by the late seventies). The land application business was permitted, regulated, and closely monitored by the Water Resources Division of the Michigan Department of Natural Resources (MDNR), a different division of the same state regulatory agency that regulated landfills. Our customers (some of whom I became aware of through managing the landfill), were companies which generated a lot of organic by-products, such as tanneries, vegetable/fruit processors, wastewater treatment plants, and even acetylene production plants (gas used with cutting torches). A by-product of acetylene production is liquid lime, which is useful for raising the pH of acidic soils, greatly enhancing crop production.

I was young, had little investment capital, and I started into the business very slowly. I was interested in saving money on fertilizer, as well as making money on disposal. I borrowed a small Case bulldozer from my parents, and initially Linda and I spent many long hours, often in the dark, on short, bitter cold winter days, spreading Waste Water Treatment Plant (WWTP) filter cake on rented agricultural ground.

One initial WWTP customer (the City of Wyoming) eventually went to liquid sludge disposal. I had nowhere near enough money to purchase the equipment necessary to accomplish liquid disposal, but I was very interested. Not realizing how creative thoughts are, I followed tanker truck loads of liquid sludge from the Wyoming WWTP many times, and tried to learn the trade, **visualizing** doing so myself. A few months later, the liquid waste hauler, who had been awarded a hauling / disposal contract with this particular WWTP, drove into Fenske Enterprises one morning, and approached me for disposal options. I made an offer, and we cut a partnership deal.

I purchased all of his land application equipment, two large farm tractors (a four-wheel drive John Deere, and a two-wheel drive Allis Chalmers), along with two ("home-made") vacuum tanks, all paid for over time (since I had little cash). Before long, with money earned, I also purchased a new four-wheel drive 4890 (300 hp) Case tractor (the largest Case on the market at the time), and two new calumet vacuum tanks, equipped with injectors. We (DFCC) took care of all of the permitting, and land application. The hauler delivered the liquid sludge (8–10% solids) from the WWTP to permitted locations (I was responsible for permitting), with several semi-trucks towing tank trailers.

Transfer Tanks

The liquid hauler (Tony Rosebud), whom I bought out within a year or so, had his-own welding shop. Tony was an excellent equipment fabricator, and with his skill and my inherited ingenuity, we developed ways of cutting costs, to give us a competitive edge over other bidders (WWTP's generally award contracts on a bid basis). One of the things we did was to construct two 30,000-gallon transfer-tank trailers. I purchased the massive ten foot diameter/forty-five foot long steel tanks new, from a tank manufacturing company in Detroit, and with help from Tony, and excellent (DFCC/Fenske Enterprises) welders/fabricators Bob Mench and Huey Meinmen, mounted them on steel frames, and installed hydraulic cylinders, which raised the tanks on heavy-duty truck axles (on the rear of each tank), for transportation. We equipped the tanks with a fifth-wheel hitch on the front for towing, and mounted a fifth-wheel dolly on a single truck-axle trailer, to support the weight of the massive tanks when they were towed from one location to another.

Before we constructed the transfer tanks, we had discharged the liquid sludge into small constructed ponds at each farm location (as Tony had been doing when I started into the business), and then vacuum loaded the liquid sludge out of the ponds, into the vacuum tanks (towed by the farm tractors) for land application. The MDNR had approved of this practice temporarily, but it was messy, unsightly, and required continual new holding pond construction, each time we switched to a different location.

On my very first day in the business, Tony was standing with me, next to a vacuum tank I was loading from a pond, when I pulled a valve lever to dislodge a clog, at the wrong time. Just as I was pulling the lever, I heard Tony (who was much more experienced with vacuum loading than I) start to warn, "No, **don't op—**," as a fast moving stream of sludge shot out of the coupling I had loosened, and implanted a foot wide black streak on Tony, from head to toe. The sludge blasted off Tony's hat, covered his face, and some even went into his mouth (which was open, issuing me the warning). When I realized that my actions had created a leak, I closed the coupling as quickly as I could. Since I was standing out of "the-line-of-fire," not a drop landed on me, and I had no idea what had happened. Embarrassed, I started to state, "Boy, I didn't know -," as I turned and saw Tony's blackened condition. Tony was spitting sludge, and broadcasting various profanities, as he stripped off his sludge covered jacket and threw it down. Even though I didn't know Tony very well yet, his appearance was so **hilarious**, that I could not **contain** myself from bursting into laughter. Fortunately he forgave me, and over time, we became very good friends.

The permitted land application rate, which varied with soil type, was generally in the 20–30,000 gallons per acre range. Because the WWTP averaged 125–150,000 gal/day, depending on farm size, and permitted acres, we were required to move every two to three weeks. We moved the transfer tanks (empty) with the 4890 Case tractor, and kept them at two different locations. Since precipitation happens in Michigan twelve months a year, I attempted to keep one transfer tank at a sandy location, saved for wet days, when heavier soils were very difficult (often impossible) to traverse. The WWTP had very little storage capacity, and by contract we had to move sludge under all conditions, rain, snow, sleet, whatever.

The advantage of the transfer tanks, which were equipped with high volume transfer pumps, is that a 9000-gallon tanker truck could be off loaded in a matter of minutes. The semi could then get back on the road to collect another tank load, as opposed to remaining parked at a farm for 45–60 minutes, while being nurse-unloaded by the 3200-gallon land application vehicles. This meant that we could get the same volume of sludge moved per day with three semi-tanker trucks, and three land application vehicles, for which our competitors needed at least six trucks, and six land application vehicles. There was nothing like the transfer tanks on the market, they worked excellently, and I was very proud of our invention. We painted the transfer tanks with silver and white DFCC company-colors, and labeled them with large black letters, which read "Harvest Booster," in an attempt to deflect protests, of which there were always plenty.

I sat on the "hot seat" at various "Town Hall" meetings, which were frequently called to answer concerns, whenever I applied for permits in a new township. Usually however, if we promised to deliver "free" organics to the loudest protestors, whom were almost always owners of farms, neighboring the farms on which we had requested "land application permits," protests were quelled, and permits were granted. I never charged farmers a fee for the organics applied to their fields, in exchange for the damage of compaction and wheel ruts, sometimes caused by the heavy trucks delivering the materials, and the land application vehicles applying it, and the trade-off worked out well.

We worked exceedingly hard, long hours, under extreme conditions. On a specific winter night that I will never forget, with high winds, and a 40-degree below zero Fahrenheit chill-index, Linda (who was DFCC foreman, over more than a half-dozen men) and I worked in the field most of the night, unloading a transfer tank. It took us a very long time, because it was **so cold** that the diesel fuel in the farm tractors would gel (solidify/freeze), even though we had fuel-line antifreeze in the tanks (apparently just not enough)! All that we could do when the tractors would stall out, was empty the gelled fuel from the fuel filter canisters, refill them with fresh fuel, bleed the lines, and work to get the tractors restarted, which could be difficult under the best of conditions. This all had to be done numerous times, in the pitch dark, usually in howling wind in the center of the farm field. Our fingers and hands were numb, and along with our ears and parts of our cheeks, suffered frostbite. It was an extremely long, **painful** night, but we had no choice except to keep going, or the 30,000-gallon transfer tank would have been a solid block of ice by morning, and Linda as always, was a "die-hard trooper" throughout the ordeal.

The AG-FIL

A second successful attempt at achieving a competitive edge was a self-constructed land application vehicle, which I named the "AG-FIL." We had started land surface applying, and land injecting liquid waste materials with the Calumet vacuum tanks (following the home-made tanks I had purchased from Tony), which are designed for handling liquid manure from cattle, hogs, chickens, and other farm animals, much lighter per gallon than most of the material we were handling. The liquid lime, tanning wastes, and wastewater sludge that we trucked and injected, contained a high percentage of sand and other solids, which raised the liquid weight significantly above that of livestock manure. As a result of the excessive weight, we often blew out tires, had wheel bearings fail frequently, and occasionally had a wheel break completely off a tank.

We also worked the tanks ten hours per day, six days per week (way beyond farm-use design), so we were down for repairs continually, and I knew that we needed something more durable. We pulled the Calumet vacuum tanks with the farm tractors; they had a valve that could be switched from vacuum to pressure (for injection), and they worked well under good weather and field conditions. However, good weather and field conditions in Michigan are the exception, and since it was necessary for us under contract to land apply under all weather conditions, we were often stuck in the mud, which was another reason for constructing the AG-FIL.

The AG-FIL name came from the vehicle components. It had an *A*llison transmission, and a *G* MC diesel engine. It was built by *Fen*ske, with an *I*nternational semi-truck cab, and it had a *L*orain undercarriage. I started with a Lorain all wheel drive construction crane, which I purchased from the Wellet's scrap yard (Wellet Truck Parts, Inc.). The crane, which was late model, had actually been nearly new when the swing lock accidentally let loose, as the crane was being transported on a lowboy trailer. When the truck towing the lowboy trailer had traveled under a freeway over-pass, the crane boom swung sideways, and hit the concrete bridge pillars, damaging the extendable boom beyond repair. Since it could no longer be used as a crane, I was able to purchase the Lorain at a premium discount price.

I removed the crane and scraped it out. The mobile crane had been a rear engine, which did not work for me, because I needed to mount a tank on the rear. To compensate, we flipped the axles completely over (left to right), so that the machine would travel in the opposite direction (with the ring gear in each differential on the opposite side), and we reversed the location of the drain plugs and vents on each differential. Next, we mounted an International semi-truck tilt cab (also purchased from Wellet Truck Parts) over the engine. We then mounted a 3200 gallon vacuum tank, and land injection rippers (from a subsoil tiller) on the rear. I equipped the AG-FIL with monstrous 66 inch high, by 48-inch wide tires, which gave great flotation, and even though when loaded, the AG-FIL topped out at 25 tons, it could work under almost any field conditions. Observers often commented, "It could keep going on rough water!"

Even though there were just starting to be some similar types of equipment on the market at the time, with names like AG-GATOR, the price tags were enormous, and nothing available had the power, flotation, or size of the AG-FIL. With the assistance of my skillful fabricators, once complete and painted, it looked very impressive, and it had a total cost of approximately $100,000, as compared to the $250,000 price tags of comparable equipment on the market. I ran the DFCC land application business for quite a few years (10–12), and the AG-FIL and transfer tanks paid for themselves, many times over. Eventually, I purchased several end-dump trailers, for hauling different types of soil with semi-trucks, and DFCC also went into the aggregate trucking business.

There were many memorable (some terrifying) experiences in the DFCC farming, cattle, and land application business. The time I moved the AG-FIL on black ice was one of them. On a severely cold January day, late in the afternoon, I drove the AG-FIL as we moved to a new land application site. I was traveling south on Division Avenue, near the small town of Wayland. I was in a hurry, because it was near dark, and I had hoped to have some daylight left, to get the new site set up. As I came over a steep grade and started down, I immediately noticed a small truck halfway up the hill, with two men standing

AG-FIL next to rear of portable Transfer Tank.

beside it holding shovels. Simultaneously, the AG-FIL began to slide sideways, as to my **horror**, I realized that I had hit **black ice**, which is the term for a sheet of ice that has formed on bare (black) pavement. Black ice is not visible (it looks like wet pavement), comes from freezing rain, and you usually do not know you are on it, until you begin to slide.

The brakes did nothing to slow me, and as I sashayed from one side of the snow-bank lined road to the other, closing in on the small truck, which had been unable to climb the hill from the opposite direction, the eyes of the two men widened like **saucers**! I frantically pumped the brakes, and cranked the steering wheel from side to side, in a hopeless attempt to control the AG-FIL. The last vision I have of the men, was the two of them diving headfirst over the snow-bank, as the massive AG-FIL slid straight at their little truck. I fully expected to flatten their tiny truck like a pancake, and braced myself for the impact; however at the last second, the AG-FIL miraculously sashayed the other way, and somehow made it around the little truck without touching it. I made it to the bottom of the hill, was able to straighten out, and I cautiously continued on down the road, slowly catching my breath. I never did find out who the two men were, but I had fun retelling the story for years, as I'm sure they did (only a slightly more panicked, less humorous version).

On another occasion, late in the year (January 31 to be exact), my friend Huey (Hugh Meinmen) stopped by the Fenske Enterprises office, late in the afternoon. I stated "Huey, just the man I'm looking for!" Huey (nicknamed "Baby Huey," *being the youngest in his family*) immediately became leery, since I had a habit of soliciting help from people who stopped by, Huey in particular, and Huey had found himself in numerous precarious situations, on past occasions. I grabbed Huey's arm as he headed back out the office door saying, "I just **remembered** something I have to do!" I talked Huey into helping (as I usually did), stating, "There's a **snow storm** on the way, **winter's setting in**, and I still have some **farm equipment** I need to get home. With both of our trucks, it'll only take a **minute**." Reluctantly, Huey followed me out the front gate, to a farm field seventeen miles away. I expected that it wouldn't take **too** long, if everything went **perfectly**, however it started to snow as soon as we headed out, and traffic was always a problem that time of day. In addition, Huey's little Chevy truck was **excessively** small for the implements we were going to be towing, and just as Huey had feared, he had let himself be roped into another preposterous situation.

When we got to the field, Huey stated, "You expect me to pull **that**," as I motioned for him to back up to a large wing-drag (which probably outweighed his little Chevy S-10 truck). I stated, "Yeah, no problem. This drag is on wheels. I've pulled this thing with little more than a **go-cart** (which I hadn't)." I actually was a little curious, as to whether or not Huey's truck could even get out of the field with the drag attached, but I figured I could come back later, on another trip with my 3/4-ton truck, if he couldn't move it. We hooked my truck up to a large wing-disc, and I headed for the road. I had no problem pulling out of the field with my four-wheel drive, and I watched in my rearview mirror, through the ever-increasing snowfall, in amazement, as Huey made it to the road, in a cloud of smoke, with his engine roaring full boar, and tires screaming. Even though it usually took a little persuasion to obtain his assistance, one thing about Huey was, once he committed, he would give it everything he had.

The first mile or two back toward the farm was gravel, and before we even made it to a paved road, the storm really hit. The heavy snowfall turned into a full-on blizzard. The further we went, the roads became nearly impassable, and we witnessed many abandoned cars, as we traveled along at a glacial rate. After a couple hours, at a stop sign about half way back, Huey hollered, "Can't we just leave these things, and come back tomorrow?" I stated, "No, the snow plows will hit them in the middle of the night, we've **got** to keep going now!" We had to travel very slowly because of the road conditions and visibility, but also because the drag that Huey was pulling was so heavy, that it was like the tail wagging the dog! The tongue weight of the drag was so immense, that there was very little weight left on Huey's front truck tires, and even under good road conditions, it took a "Houdini" to control it. I watched in my review mirror, and uttered many "Oooh"s, as Huey struggled to stay on the road. Even though I **was** a little reckless as a young man, I was very concerned for him, and wishing that I had never started this endeavor.

Astonishingly, we made it back! As I unlocked the front gate, back at Fenske Enterprises, Huey stomped up to my truck, about fit to be tied. Huey **asserted**, "What a **memorable** New Year's Eve **this** has been!" I looked at my watch, and noticed that it had just hit 12 midnight, and I stated, "Hey **Huey, Happy New Year**!" As I stated so, I reached up and gave Huey a big ol' kiss on the cheek. Huey just wiped off his cheek, and stomped back toward his truck, grumbling, "If you **ever** try to talk me into **anything** again…!" After we parked the implements, I did buy us a few beers at the VFW hall, just up Wilson from Fenske Enterprises, as we settled our nerves, and attempted to celebrate.

Huey was a very good friend, always will be, and he helped me tremendously. He is really a welder by trade, working mostly on new building construction. He did a lot of welding repair for DFCC and Fenske Enterprises over the years. He even worked for DFCC as an operator (running a 4-wheel drive tractor), and Fenske Enterprises (running a dozer and trash-compactor) for a year or two, when his Union was on strike. Huey is a great welder, and a very good fabricator, which was helpful, because we were always building something. He didn't have much (any) operating experience though, and early on I had some fun with that.

On one occasion, I was stuck with one of my tractors, when Huey came driving by the field I was in. I knew I was stuck badly (the vacuum tank I was pulling was down to the axle), and I knew that I would need a tow to get out. However, when Huey walked out to where I was stuck and asked how bad it was, I told him that I could probably get out, if I could just keep the front of the tractor down. Typically, the front of a tractor will rise up off the ground, when the rear wheels still have traction, but the tractor cannot move whatever it is you are towing. At my coaxing, Huey crawled up on the hood of the tractor, so that his body weight would help keep the front of the tractor down, which unbeknownst to Huey (in this case) was like trying to hold down a Rino, with a rag doll. For several minutes, Huey was in for the "rodeo ride" of his life, stretched out on the tractor hood, flat on his belly, hanging on with all his might, as if he was riding a bull, while I cranked up the throttle, and worked the clutch in and out. When Huey finally turned around and saw me fighting back the tears of laughter, and realized what I was up to, he stated, "Oh, you **dirty rotten**…!"

Huey actually did help **me** ride bulls, and bareback horses, along with "Easy Rider" (and sometimes my cousin Bob), who took turns as my "Chute Men," at the local Grand Rapids area (Sparta and Wyoming) rodeos, which I entered almost every year, up to the mid-eighties. "Chute Men" will "hook" a bull rope, or saddle cinch strap, that you drop down the side of a bull or horse you are preparing to ride, help get you cinched up, seated, and ready, provide support, and try to keep you calm, until it's "time," and you give your "nod" to the gate man.

I joined the PRCA (Professional Rodeo Cowboy's Association), which was the only way to compete in rodeos after college. I am quite certain the "draw" for my "ride" was usually rigged, because the professional rodeo circuit people all know each other, and take care of their own. The "locals" (like myself) always drew the worst "ride," a horse or bull, which was nearly impossible to stay on, or score high enough on to share in the winner's "purse."

With the idea that seeing Huey try to get away from a mad bull would be good entertainment, at the first rodeo in which Huey was my chute man, I tried to convince him that it was the "chute man's" **job**, to run out into the rodeo ring, and fetch the rider's bull rope, after his ride. However, Huey was too hip to my tricks by this time, didn't bite, and after my ride, the rodeo clowns threw my bull rope back over the fence to me, as they always did. I didn't really have much of a chance of making any money, competing against the professional cowboys who rode year round, but it was fun trying, and a good chance for all of my friends and me to get together for a party afterwards.

One year at the Wyoming City Rodeo, I drew a bull named "The Reverend Mister Black," and when I checked the board for my draw, other competitors advised me to give up my entry money, and not to ride. I was told that the "Reverend Mister Black," had never been ridden the full eight seconds to the buzzer, and was **so** "rank" (mean, aggressive), that he had put the last two riders who had tried to ride him, "Out of commission," as a result of injuries. The other contestants warned me that he was famous for attacking a rider after dislodging him, and injuring the rider with his sawed off horns, or stomping on him while running over him. In spite of their warnings, I had too much pride not to give it a try, and I repeated a statement I had heard, "Just like there never was a cowboy who couldn't be 'throwed,' there never was a bull that couldn't be rode." I didn't want to give up my $150.00 entry fee without a try, and I rationalized my decision, by stating to myself, "There's a first time for everything."

I completely psyched myself up before my ride, slapped my bicep intently, and was really "pumped," when I gave the nod to the gateman. The "Reverend" came out of the shoot spinning like a rocket, and for what felt like an eternity, gave me the wildest ride of my life. Inexperienced as I was, I somehow stayed with him, and I clearly heard the disappointed "oohh" of the crowd, when I finally lost my grip at seven seconds, just one second short of the buzzer. Instinctively, as soon as I hit the ground I sprang to my feet, and started running for the nearest fence.

I heard the crowd gasp as I did so, and as my eyes came back into focus (being a little dizzy from all the spins), I realized that I was running **straight at** the Reverend Mister Black! The bull just stood there momentarily, probably a little shocked that I was **charging him**! Once I came to my senses, I did an about face, and ran back toward the gates as fast as I could, with the Reverend hot on my heels. When I reached the shoot gates, with the bull inches behind me, I could "feel" the tension of the crowd. Somehow I reached up, grabbed the top board, and with a healthy boost from the Reverend, I cleared the six-foot gate, without ever placing a foot on it! I didn't have a share in the winner's purse, but at least I walked away uninjured.

I met many good people in the farming/land application business, like Fred and Rog Mason, located on one of the only remaining farms in the Wyoming City limits, and Lynn Flagerty, near the Grand Rapids suburb town Byron Center. Fred and Rog, and Lynn were some of the last sizable dairy farmers in the near Grand Rapids vicinity. They helped me out by giving me a place to go, when other farmers did not want me on their fields (because of wet conditions), and I helped them, by supplying them with good humus fertilizer at no charge, and at times, with some tractor power to help with fieldwork.

Lynn was "behind-the-eight-ball" on getting a large field of corn planted one wet spring, and it was getting near "D-day" for getting seed in the ground (the growing season being so short in Michigan), when Linda and I and a DFCC employee showed up (to his surprise) with three tractors, and helped him get the job done. We all became good friends, occasionally drank a few beers together, and Linda even dated, and had a relationship with Lynn Flagerty's son for a while.

19

Ottawa Company Farms

Ed Hanberk, a large (3000+ acre) farmer located near the small town of Coopersville (twenty miles west of Grand Rapids), owned one of the farms I permitted for land application. As I got to know him, I became fond of Ed, who was a very successful farmer and businessman. Ed raised beef cattle, hogs, turkeys, and dairy cattle, in addition to owning and operating a building business (selling/constructing commercial buildings for farms and businesses). He was a smart farmer, realized the importance of humus in soil, and worked well with me, to our mutual benefit. Because Ed had so much tillable ground, once we got started working together in the late 1970's, I was applying organics on one field or another of his most of the time.

Since the City of Wyoming WWTP hauling contract required year-round removal of sludge (because the WWTP had so little storage), and since we could not inject sludge (as the MDNR required) once the frost reached a foot deep (nearly impossible in most soil types), or once the snow became so deep that we could not traverse the fields, it was my responsibility to provide winter storage. I asked Ed, and another Coopersville area farmer, if they would each provide me with a location in clay soil, to construct a storage lagoon for winter sludge, which they did. I designed, permitted (by the MDNR), and constructed two large storage lagoons, at the two separate locations, which were roughly 100 feet by 300 feet. I also constructed a third, at another location near Wayland.

I constructed the storage lagoons approximately 12 feet in depth, and almost entirely above ground, with compacted clay dykes (as the MDNR required). With a couple feet of freeboard, the lagoons would each hold close to a two-month supply of Wyoming WWTP sludge, and even in a rough winter and wet spring, I calculated they would get us through. I constructed gentle sloping earth ramps for the loaded semi-trucks to back up, and installed eight-inch diameter pipes (with cast-iron gate valves) in the clay dykes, leading to twenty-foot diameter, four foot deep ponds, at the opposite end of each lagoon, from which the land application vehicles could empty the lagoons. The storage lagoons looked very impressive when completed, they worked very well, and I was proud of them.

The lagoon location on Ed's farm was on a piece of property right across the road from Ed's main farm headquarters, less than a quarter mile off the 96 freeway, and only about an 18-20 mile pull for my semi's. I was at the location the morning the drilling company arrived, which I had hired to auger some test holes, and collect core samples for permeability tests (necessary for the storage lagoon permit). I was impressed by the quality of the blue clay at the twenty-foot depth to which I had hired them to drill (the maximum necessary), so out of curiosity, I requested that they keep going down. Since I was paying them by the foot, they were happy to oblige. I was further impressed as I went down to *100 feet,* with the same quality of clay, and no groundwater. It was much more than I needed, but I had ideas, so I had the driller auger a number of additional holes to the same depth, at various locations on the property, with the same results.

The next morning I met Ed for breakfast, and posed the question to him, "Ed, did you ever think of getting into the landfill business?" Ed responded, "No, I didn't Doug. What are you thinking of, you and me (as he symbolically motioned his index finger back and forth between us)?" I stated, "Yes Ed, a partnership, fifty/fifty. You've got the land, and I've got the know-how." I then proceeded to tell Ed of the depth and quality of clay I had encountered. Ed responded, "Well, Doug, there's not much garbage in Coopersville." I responded, "Don't worry about that Ed. This is less than twenty miles from Grand Rapids. When we get this permitted, we'll get the solid waste out here!" I always discussed and shared everything with my parents, and when I had told them what I was planning, prior to making the proposal to Ed, Mother had stated, "**Good**, if you're successful, we won't be so **busy** at our landfill!" Ed was interested, we shook hands, and I went to work on it with my engineers, gathering topographical maps etcetera.

A few weeks later, Ed gave me a call one morning, and told me that a realtor had contacted him. The realtor had a buyer who wanted to purchase the exact parcel of property that I had taken the borings on. The realtor would not disclose who the buyer was, or what the buyer wanted the parcel for, but had offered Ed **twice** the average area land value. I told, Ed, "It's your property, but if it was me, I would demand to know who the buyer was, and what his intentions were, or no sale." Ed followed my suggestion, and after several weeks of playing "gofer," just as I had told Ed I suspected, the buyer turned out to be Ernie Vandole, who was a local (Grand Rapids area) excavation contractor.

I had heard the rumor from my friend Glenn Cass (who worked for Ernie's company, *Riverdale Excavation*) that Ernie was interested in getting into the landfill business. Glenn was a good friend, and I told Glenn much of what I did, maybe more than I should have, but Glenn always freely shared information with me too. I think Ernie Vandole's interest in this particular parcel of property may have come from what Glenn told Ernie, but who knows. It doesn't matter anyway, even if Ernie heard it from Glenn, I don't believe that Glenn told him to cause me problems. Glenn and I had worked together and farmed together, helping each other for years. He was a neighbor and a friend who had worked for my parents when I was still in diapers (probably babysat me). Anyway, for quite some time I had been hearing rumors that Ernie wanted to get into the landfill business, from a number of other sources.

I explained to Ed how much money there was in the landfill business, and that he didn't need to sell, to make a premium on his property. Ed suggested that we partner up with Ernie, but I had dealt with Ernie on a couple of previous occasions, I did not like him much, and I wasn't enthused, although I did agree to meet with him, along with Ed. We met at a local restaurant in Standale, a small suburb city on the NW corner of Grand Rapids, and from my perspective, the meeting didn't go well. Ernie didn't want me involved, and he proposed that each partner, whom included his two engineers, Prime & Newharp, put up $200,000 cash each, as start up capital. Even though I could have raised the money, it would have been the hardest on me, so I stepped out. Ed was a little resistant, and I told Ed privately, "Ed, we don't need these guys, or Ernie, and his arrogance. Let's go it alone, you and I!"

For whatever reason, I think to minimize his investment; Ed opted to go with them. They had convinced Ed that they could save on costs, because Prime & Newharp would do the engineering, and Riverdale would do the excavation. The four of them formed a partnership, and applied for a solid waste landfill permit under the name "Ottawa Company Farms," and more than once over the coming months (and several years after), I was glad that I had stepped out. Ottawa Company Farms eventually obtained a landfill permit (after plenty of opposition), but that's when the real struggles began. Before it was over, an inner company shareholder lawsuit arose, in which three of the partners (Ed, Prime, and Newharp) sued the other partner (Ernie Vandole), claiming that his company (Riverdale), contracted by the partnership to construct the landfill, had unnecessarily driven costs of construction too high.

Ed approached me on several occasions, asking me if I would reconsider a partnership with him, if the two of us bought out the other partners. I told Ed that I was no longer interested, based on the debt they had accumulated, and the pending litigation. Ed eventually bought out the other partners, and through his own business sense (and price discounts), was finally (after considerable effort) able to attract plenty of business, and turn a significant profit. Ed eventually sold out to a public firm out of Canada (Laidlew Waste Services), which eventually sold to another public firm, BEI (Benning Elliot Inc.), and large profitable landfill operations continue on that location today (2010).

20

CRRI

Another endeavor of mine, independent of Fenske Enterprises, was CRRI. I actually only entered into the Hazardous Waste TSD (land-fill) business (CRRI), at the request of the regulatory agency, which followed a request by the Governor's office, to solve a problem.

Because Detroit is so large in the automobile production business, Grand Rapids became very large in automotive support businesses, specifically electroplating. In fact, Grand Rapids is the largest concentration of electro-metal finishers in the world. Electroplating is the process (through electrolysis) of placing a permanent hardened finish on metal car parts (bumpers, door handles, rear-view mirrors, etc.), as well as electro-plated parts for furniture (appliances, etc.), which Grand Rapids is huge in the manufacture of (known as the "furniture city"). Any type of manufacturing process intrinsically creates waste products, which I came to term as "by-products," proposing that by-products are only "waste" if we "**waste**" them. In the electroplating industry, the manufacturing by-product is known as "heavy metal hydroxide sludge" (the spent solution at the bottom of plating baths), containing a mixture with some combination of chrome, nickel, cadmium, copper, zinc, and numerous other heavy metal fines. These spent solutions are treated with lime (before disposal), to adjust the pH of the sludge, and bring the heavy metals out of suspension (floating freely in liquid plating bath solutions).

171

For years, heavy metal sludge had been considered (ruled) a "solid waste," by the regulatory agency, the Waste Management Division of the MDNR, as well as its predecessor, the Michigan Department of Public Health, and had been allowed to be disposed of in conventional solid waste landfills, such as Fenske Enterprises, and the Kent County Solid Waste Landfill (the only two landfills in Kent County). In 1976, the MDNR decided that heavy metal sludge was no longer permissible for disposal in conventional solid waste landfills, and notified us of such. The MDNR reasoned that the acidic conditions in solid waste landfill leachate (liquid at the bottom of landfill cells) could change the pH of the heavy metal sludge, and put the heavy metals back into solution (making them mobile in liquids), thereby generating conditions which could lead to groundwater contamination.

Kent County's landfill had been closed as a result of groundwater contamination, the **second** Kent County landfill permanently closed by the MDNR, for the same reason. The contaminants were specifically heavy metals, found in the Kent County landfill monitoring wells. The heavy metal contamination at the Kent County landfill sites was the **reason** for the new MDNR ruling in Michigan. I maintained that the contamination at the Kent County landfill sites occurred as a result of the porous, highly permeable soils at the Kent County sites, as opposed to the non-porous, low permeability soils at the Fenske Enterprises site, and my new CRRI site (described ahead), however the rule was adopted.

Since the Fenske Enterprises site was the only operating landfill in the Grand Rapids area at the time, all of the heavy metal sludge generated in the Grand Rapids area came to the Fenske Enterprises site. As the MDNR had ruled, Fenske Enterprises stopped accepting heavy metal sludge for disposal, turning truckloads around at the gate, on Oct. 1, 1976, as instructed. Since there were **10,000** jobs on the line, and because the owner of one of the largest plating companies in Grand Rapids was a personal friend of the current Michigan Governor, it didn't take long for the "*sludge to hit the fan,*" so to speak!

Within days, I received a phone call from the appointed "Chief" of the "MDNR, WMD (Waste Management Division)," Fred Keller, requesting, "that I do something." I responded, "Fred, what do you want me to do? I've only done what your employees instructed me to do!" Fred responded, "I know, but if you will apply for a disposal permit for heavy metal sludge at your Cascade site, I can process the permit **right away**! Heavy metal sludge won't attract birds! However, I need your help, **right now**! If you will build a lagoon for '*Temporary*

Storage' of heavy metal sludge at your Fenske Enterprises site, I can issue you a permit for that **instantly**, and then you can transfer the heavy metal sludge to your Cascade site, as soon as that permit is issued."

I took Fred at his word, and with our two Allis-Chalmers HD-21 bulldozers (myself on one), I had a storage area designed, constructed, and ready to receive sludge at Fenske Enterprises in three days, with borings and permeability tests completed, and monitoring wells installed. Our "Temporary Storage Permit" was issued within a couple of days, the heavy metal sludge had a home, and for the time being the problem was solved. I immediately went to work with our engineers, and other consulting firms, and designed our CRRI, Metal Hydroxide Sludge TSD (Treatment, Storage, Disposal) facility. We designed the facility, with a fully equipped laboratory, an office building, and a chemical storage building (for neutralization chemicals). The site design included four disposal trenches, each with a three foot compacted clay base layer (over 300 feet of natural clay), double 40-mil PVC liners, leachate collection systems, and lysimeters for leak detection between the liners, seventeen filtration cells, under-drains, a holding pond, monitoring wells, etcetera. Within a couple of weeks we submitted an application for CRRI to treat, store, and dispose of heavy metal sludge.

The CRRI site was on the opposite side of Grand Rapids, seventeen miles from the Fenske Enterprises site, but still near the metropolitan area. My partner, Lou Vanderstern (a Fenske Enterprises customer) owned a solid waste hauling business on the opposite, SE side of Grand Rapids, with most of his business near his residence. He had been interested in opening a solid waste landfill on his side of town, to avoid the long haul, and traffic. Having no idea how to do so, a couple of years earlier, he had approached Fenske Enterprises, looking for a partner. My parents, who had no interest, said I should go ahead if I was interested. Mother was always very resistant to me expanding our business, at the Fenske Enterprises location. Mother would frequently state, "Doug, we're filling up too fast now. Limit the amount of trucks you allow in each day. If we make more money, I'll just have to pay more taxes!"

Fenske Enterprises was open six days per week, ten hours per day, and could barely handle the truck traffic it was receiving, without expanding (adding employees and equipment). I, and our consultant engineers had done studies, and Fenske Enterprises actually had **90 years** of landfill airspace (capacity), at the daily tonnage rate we were receiving waste, without limiting **any** haulers. My parents were the owners however, had the final say (Mother really), and for a time we did limit traffic. My father (who, by this time, I had nicknamed "Pappy") was not resistant to growing the business, and making more money, but he didn't want to go against Mother. The Grand Rapids area *clearly* needed another landfill.

Initially Lou and I had formed a partnership, and submitted an application for a solid waste landfill permit at our Cascade site, which was a 160-acre site (later expanded to 415 acres) that we purchased near the airport, on the SE side of Grand Rapids. I did some geological studies with our engineers, looking at all available data, and our CRRI site had some of the best (highly impervious clay) soils for a landfill in the Grand Rapids area, equally as good as the Fenske Enterprises site. However we started receiving resistance directly. Because Kent County was in the solid waste landfill business, even though (at the time) the County's only landfill had been forcibly closed by the state (as a result of contamination of drinking water wells, adjacent to the County Landfill), the County (which also owned the airport) was planning to open a new landfill, and did not want additional competition.

Before very long, a senator from the Grand Rapids area, Gerald R. Ford (later President Ford, *from whom years earlier Mother had requested my appointment to West Point*), on behalf of Kent County, introduced a Senate Bill, to ban solid waste landfills, within 10,000 feet of a federally funded airport, with the argument that solid waste landfills attract birds (seagulls in particular), which can be a hazard to aircraft. Even though our Cascade site was well south of the airport, and parallel to its only runway (which was East/West), our site was "conveniently" within the 10,000 foot proposed ban. The Senate Bill, in spit of my efforts (delivering speeches to the House, and Senate), eventually passed, and was signed into law (in fact inspired a subsequent similar Federal Law), preventing the state from ever issuing us a solid waste landfill permit.

We now had an opportunity to obtain a permit (the law only banned solid waste landfills). I persuaded my partner to incorporate with the name Cascade (the name of the township) Resource Recovery, Inc. (CRRI), convinced that someday the technology would become available to recover the heavy metals in the plating sludge. Having started life with very little money, like my parents (who had been impacted by the "Depression"), I was very resourceful, and recycle minded (as previously mentioned). It made no sense to me then, as it does not now, to mine chrome or copper from one place on earth, and zinc from another, then landfill them as waste, once they and other heavy metals became commingled in the spent plating sludge, only because it was not yet "*cost effective*" to separate them, another of mankind's "inconvenient truths."

We had chosen the CRRI site specifically because of the abundance of highly impermeable soils (1 x 10 to the minus eight clay), and the absence of groundwater. Water will only migrate through "ten to the minus eight clay," at the rate of approximately four inches per year, *under vacuum* (which did not exist at the site). The first usable aquifer was over 300 feet deep, with predominately heavy clay soils over it. As previously mentioned, a million years ago, during climatic changes on earth, in an era known as "The Ice Age," the entire state of Michigan was covered by glaciers a mile or more thick. My geologists explained that this particular site had a massive "kettle hole" on it, which depicted that it had been the location of one of the last, thickest, and hence heaviest ice glaciers, which had left the heavy clay deposits from it's melt waters, when the Ice Age ended. The site had everything going for it environmentally, and it had location (nearness to the metropolitan area), as well as isolation (absence of residents).

As the weeks went by however, I became increasingly unsettled. The sludge storage pile at Fenske Enterprises was growing, and each time I contacted the MDNR, with the question, "Where's my CRRI disposal permit," all I heard were excuses, and demands for more information. Finally after six weeks had passed, and the "Temporary Storage Pile" at Fenske Enterprises had grown to over 2500 cubic yards, I had heard enough. I placed a call to "WMD Chief" Fred Keller, and told him that I was shutting the trucks off. Fred pleaded with me not to, and promised me a permit by Friday of that week, if I would continue to store the sludge. I agreed.

On that Friday, a few days after I had placed the call, I traveled to Lansing to pick up my permit. When I walked into Fred's office, and approached his desk at the designated time, as promised, he handed me a "(TSD)" permit, to Treat, Store, and Dispose of metal hydroxide sludge at the CRRI site. The term "hazardous waste" had not yet evolved in Michigan, and a TSD permit was the predecessor to a hazardous waste permit. When I looked through the permit everything seemed to be in order, at first glance, however under further inspection, I noticed that the cover page of the two-page permit was stamped "DRAFT" in pale, barely legible, red ink. When I demanded of Fred, **"What's this**?!" Fred anxiously responded, "Oh, I just have to run it through a couple of committees." I spun around on my heels, and headed for his office door with the words, "I'm **shuttin' em off!**" "**No don't**," pleaded Fred, "this is **exactly** what your permit will look like! I just have to run it through, and get the 'OK' of MERB (Michigan Environmental Review Board), and a couple other committees. It'll only take a **minute!**" My only response, as his office door closed behind me was, "**I'm done!**"

I was **done**, and as soon as I got back to Grand Rapids, I shut the trucks off. I'm **so** glad that I did, and had the wisdom I possessed at only twenty-seven years of age, because even though I had a notion that we might be in for some delays, I had no **concept** of the **multitude**, and **magnitude** of the obstacles we would experience. It was a total of fourteen lawsuits (including appeals), *two to the Supreme Court,* and **6 & 1/2 years** before the CRRI permit was issued, and the site was ready to operate.

When I saw resistance mounting, I sensed that obtaining a permit to dispose of this heavy metal sludge could be more difficult than the WMD Chief "Fred" had described. Somehow, in spite of my youth (at the suggestion, and with the assistance of a friend, Jeff Dahlman), I had the foresight to approach a State Representative, and explain that it might be next to impossible to permit a facility to dispose of this type of material anywhere, without ensuing local zoning prohibiting such, and litigation arising, which could delay permitting for years, if not **permanently**. To insure success of a properly permitted facility surviving the court process, zoning, etc., the State Rep. and I sat shoulder to shoulder, and drafted House Bill 4390, which had language preventing local interference with a properly permitted facility.

I wore out a set of tires driving back and forth to the State Capitol in Lansing, as I hand walked, and tracked House Bill 4390 through the legislative process, delivering numerous speeches (on the need for the law), which took a couple of years, but eventually passed through both the House, and Senate, and was signed into law by the Governor, as PA (Public Act) 641 of 1978. The Bill however, became very watered down through the process, with amendments requiring county SWMP's (Solid Waste Management Plans), and local (facility site location) input. Elected officials (State Representatives, Senators, and Governors) are extremely cautious about passing laws that override local authority. As a result, I felt the Act/Law had lost its teeth, and would not insure success of a facility ever becoming permitted for disposal of metal hydroxide sludge, so I went back to the State Representative, and started all over again. I repeated the entire process, wore out another set of tires, and finally, after another year, succeeded with the passage of PA 64 of 1979, known as the first "Hazardous Waste Management Act," in Michigan.

Regardless, the effort didn't prevent lawsuits. Groups like ACWI (Ada/Cascade Watch, Inc.), CRAP, Inc. (Cascade Residents Against Pollution, Inc.), the TRA (Thornapple River Association), and the Township of Cascade itself, all sued us (to prevent operation of CRRI). PA 64 had teeth however, and clearly prevented local interference in the operation of a facility, once an Act 64 permit had been issued. I succeeded in getting myself appointed by the Governor to a 200 member "Rules Committee," which drafted the rules for PA 64, and through numerous heated arguments (regarding the "intent" of the law) during the process, I was successful in keeping the "preemption" language intact, in the rules. As a result, PA 64 **did** insure our success, and the courts **all** ruled in our favor, regarding the "intent of the legislature to prevent local interference." After **six and a half years**, CRRI was finally permitted (had been issued a PA 64 Construction Permit), and was **done** with all litigation and appeals!

I employed the services of numerous attorneys over the years, but the attorney (Richard Quest), who was my first attorney, has remained my most unforgettable attorney. I actually was referred to Richard Quest, by a senior attorney (Pete Tatta), in the law firm (Moonby, Goodwrench, and Tatta) whom Richard had signed on with, when he (recently) had graduated from law school. Moonby, Goodwrench, and Tatta was the law firm hired by the GGRWDA (Greater Grand Rapids Waste Disposal Association), an association of most of the private waste hauling companies in the area, with the exception of the large public firms WNI, and BEI, which "claimed" their "corporate by-laws" prevented them from joining any local associations. The GGR-WDA, which Fenske Enterprises joined at my insistence, had been formed, and the law firm had been hired, to combat "Flow Control" ordinances, which Kent County adopted in the early eighties to force solid waste into the Kent County landfill facilities. *The Flow Control ordinances foretold of plans by Kent County, already in the works, which Fenske Enterprises was to feel the "brunt" of, a few years down the road.*

When Pete Tatta told me that his personal plate was too full to take on any more work, and introduced me to Richard Quest, I remarked, "I don't want him! He's just a **kid**!" Pete replied, "So **what**! So are **you**!" Actually, Richard is a couple of years older than me, but what I was seeking was someone with more experience. A number of times in the coming years, during the various CRRI lawsuits and appeals, Richard leaned over to me (seated right beside him in front of the judge), with the question, "What do I say **now**? What do you **want** me to say (to which I usually had a suggestion)?" Richard did very well though, and won all the CRRI lawsuits, or rather **we** did. We became good personal friends, and celebrated numerous victories together. Richard eventually broke off on his own, to a one-man practice, and even though I employed the services of other attorneys in years to come, when I felt we needed a larger firm, I remain fond of Richard, and will always consider him a friend.

During the PA 64 rules drafting process, I was successful in convincing other members of the committee to adopt a rule requiring a reasonable, (*obtainable*) operating bond (to insure proper operation of a facility, proper closure, funds for potential cleanup costs, etc.). By the time we finally obtained our Act 64 "Construction Permit," the rules had changed however, and the required operating bond was now **two million** dollars per acre! CRRI owned 160 acres, and as I had feared, we were unable to obtain a bond. After all of the work my partner and I had accomplished, through the Public Acts, rules, and lawsuits, we were now unable to obtain a bond necessary to operate! There was not a bonding company in the nation that was interested in bonding CRRI, at the astronomical and unheard of amount of two million dollars per acre, and we soon realized that we needed a sizable partner.

In an attempt to find a good partner, and find out which companies had good reputations, Lou and I booked a flight to visit the US EPA in Washington DC, which (before it was over) I thought might have been our **last**! As we were preparing to land, and circling the airport in Washington DC waiting for clearance, we flew through some storm clouds. As we did, there was what sounded like a huge explosion, the plane shook violently, and the passenger seating area **lit up** inside like the **sun**, then went completely dark, and became dead silent! At first no one said anything, for what seemed like a few minutes, but was probably less. My thoughts ran **wildly**! I started thinking, "**Oh my God**, there was a bomb in the plane cabin, and there is **no cockpit** on this plane! We are going **down**!"

Finally a voice came over the intercom, "Ladies and gentlemen, this is your captain; there is no cause for alarm. We had a **near** lightening strike, and we will be landing in a few minutes." After about twenty minutes of circling we landed (very roughly), and out of my window I saw fire engines, and emergency rescue vehicles zero in on us from several directions. As we were de-boarding, I overheard a member of the ground crew state to a flight attendant, who had just de-boarded, "I heard you were **struck** by **lightening**," which the flight attendant **affirmed**! Undoubtedly, the captain had made the "near strike" announcement, to avoid hysteria. Fortunately, because we were not grounded, other than some rattled nerves, everyone was fine. As far as myself personally, this was one of a number of times that I internally questioned my own sanity for continuing this pursuit, and wondered if I was doing the **right** thing. I am not a quitter however. I squelched my doubts, and marched on.

We met with the US EPA, and found out that one company, which stood out in performance and reputation, was a company named Chem Quality Systems, Inc. (CQSI), of Belvue, Washington (near Seattle). After we returned to Grand Rapids, my partner and I began negotiating a potential operating agreement with CQSI over the phone, and within a few weeks we were on another plane to Washington State. Lloyd Anders, who previously had been a politician, and had lost a race for Governor of Washington, as Lloyd put it, "by a handful of votes, so close they had two re-counts," had been the founder of CQSI.

I took a liking to Lloyd, and I will always remember his explanation of his reason for getting into the hazardous waste disposal business. Lloyd stated, "When I lost my run for Governor, I realized that if you're number two in politics, you aren't squat, but if you're number two in business, you're doing pretty **well**!" Lloyd had quit politics, as soon as he lost the gubernatorial election, and had then started into the hazardous waste business, in which he had heard there was large profit potential. He had gone public early on, and by the time we met, CQSI was a 300 million dollar company, with hazardous waste landfills in several states.

Over a period of months, we hammered out an operating agreement with CQSI, in which CRRI remained owner of all the assets (land, buildings, equipment, and permits), and CQSI became the licensed operator of the CRRI facility. CQSI was bondable, we agreed upon a profit split, and both sides signed the agreement. Through loans CQSI advanced to CRRI, we purchased additional adjacent property, and expanded the original 160-acre CRRI site to 415 acres.

We worked together to finalize the terms of the Operating Permit application. Our (CRRI) PA 64 "Construction Permit" (in essence our hazardous waste license) had been issued to us (CRRI), at the successful conclusion of all the lawsuits and appeals. The Hazardous

Waste Law (PA 64) was two-phase however, and required an Operating Permit, as well as a Construction Permit. Once a Construction Permit has been issued, it is normally automatic for an Operating Permit to be issued; however, it does require an operating bond, and an incredible amount of operation detail in the Operating Permit Application. CQSI was sizable enough to be bondable (even though Michigan had the highest bonding requirements of any state CQSI had encountered), and we worked as a team compiling the **enormous** details of the Operating Permit Application. After months of work we finally submitted the application, totaling, *unbelievably,* **2250 pages**, which I personally helped deliver to the MDNR in **eight boxes, on two hand-carts**!

After several more months of review, and numerous required changes, CRRI was finally issued an Operating Permit, naming CRRI as the licensed owner, and CQSI as the licensed operator. On a beautiful spring day, we held an opening picnic, with a ribbon cutting ceremony, at which the news media was present, along with various State Senators and Representatives. At long last, we were prepared to open for business.

We constructed our "state-of-the-art" facility, which included a sizable brick office building, with a number of rooms, and a fully equipped laboratory, managed by a PhD chemist and assistants. At my insistence, we designed, engineered, and constructed the facility, with separate disposal trenches for different types of heavy metal sludge, so that those high in chrome or copper, would be separate from others high in cadmium, zinc, etc., to enable/assist future separation and recovery operations, as recovery technology evolved. We developed a manifest system, the first of its kind (*now state and federally mandated, as a result*), which was a "cradle to grave tracking system" of hazardous waste. We submitted carbon copies of each load of heavy metal sludge accepted at the CRRI facility, signed by the generator company, hauling company, and disposal company (CRRI), on a weekly basis to the MDNR. The manifests documented the waste generator, chemical characteristics, quantity, hauling company, treatment method, and exact location of disposal (on a grid system), of each and every cubic yard of sludge disposed of on site.

In spite of the fact that we were trying to do something **better** than it had **ever** been done, and to help **solve** a problem, which impacted **10,000 jobs** in Grand Rapids alone, as well as industry in general, potentially on a global level, we had been besieged by all the lawsuits. When you are in the waste business, especially hazardous materials, the *public* deems that you are inherently the "**bad guy**." The general public often loses site of the fact that in our current society, industries are generating these materials, which must be dealt with on a daily basis, not only in our country but worldwide. It has always been my goal to recover (recycle), and "*re-source*" waste, in particular "hazardous materials," which are now being **buried**, and will one day surely come back to haunt future generations.

To add insult to injury, one of the many lawsuits we experienced had been filed by the *MDNR,* **against Fenske Enterprises**, for the heavy metal sludge on storage at the Fenske Enterprises site, which preposterously had been placed there at the **MDNR'S urgent request**! The MDNR had lost sight of the facts. When I responded to the lawsuit, with the explanation that Fenske Enterprises had only stored this waste, at the pleading of Fred Keller (MDNR, WMD Chief), the MDNR claimed (through its attorneys) that since Fred Keller had retired, the MDNR had no responsibility for the agreement, and Fenske Enterprises was left "holding the bag."

Once the CRRI site was finally open, I breathed a sigh of relief. CRRI made money, CQSI made money, and the City of Grand Rapids, *and* the state had a solution to a **huge** problem. Ten thousand local jobs were protected, we were happy, the MDNR was happy, and for eleven months, all seemed well. However, when there is a **lot** of money involved, situations can quickly **change drastically**. One morning, I picked up the *Grand Rapids Press*, and shuddered with **shock** at the headlines, which read "**CQSI Consumed By WNI, Through Unfriendly Stock Takeover!**"

Something had occurred, of which I had no knowledge, or experience. CQSI, governed by Lloyd Anders and his board of directors, in their desire to expand (and raise capital, *to do so*), had gone through a "two-for-one" stock split, twice in one year. CQSI's most fierce competitor, WNI (Waste National, Inc., a public firm), through its hazardous waste division CWNI (Chem Waste National, Inc.), became aware of the fact that CQSI had more stock for sale on the open market, than CQSI controlled (owned), and CWNI quickly purchased all available stock. CWNI was able to purchase more stock than CQSI owned, and **bingo**, through an "unfriendly stock takeover," CQSI became a wholly owned subsidiary of CWNI. It was beyond my **wildest imagination**, that a **$300 million** company could disappear **overnight**! Even though CQSI spent four million dollars in legal fees, in the coming months, trying to stop the takeover, CQSI had been "caught with their pants down" (in the court's own language), and the courts ruled that WNI was now in control of, and owned CQSI. CQSI, on the grounds of anti-trust, exhausted an estimated two million dollars more attempting to win an appeal of the judge's decision, and we held out hope for a few months, but to no avail. The verdict stood.

What happened to us at the CRRI site, as a result of the stock takeover, was **devastating**! Through it's acquisition of CQSI, WNI (CWNI) was now the "licensed operator" of the CRRI site. Since operation of the CRRI site had been very profitable, I naturally expected WNI to operate the CRRI site. However, with the CRRI site closed, it was far more profitable for WNI to truck the vast amount of heavy metal sludge generated in Grand Rapids, to WNI's own hazardous waste landfill in Victory, Ohio (**some 400 miles away**). WNI (*in the hazardous waste trucking business, which paid by the mile*) was able to significantly increase trucking fees and disposal prices (at its own site). This allowed WNI to make a lot **more** money, which it did not have to share with anyone! The "monopoly," which CQSI (in its' arguments to the court) had unsuccessfully posed would occur, was now realized!

Immediately following the *Grand Rapids Press* headlines, the CRRI site was closed, and we were greeted at the CRRI front gates by a Pinkerton guard, who remained there for the next **four and a half years**! The MDNR refused to allow my partner and I, as "**owners**," to operate the CRRI site, even if we could obtain an operating bond, because CQSI was the "licensed operator," so we filed suit against WNI, for "Breach Of Contract." Shortly after filing suit, we had a settlement meeting at WNI's corporate office (on the eleventh floor of a Chicago office building), and what transpired was **nerve racking**! After an hour of heated debate, the WNI "Chairman of The Board of Directors" (and CEO) stood up, stared straight into my eyes, and symbolically ground the base of his right thumb on the top of their mahogany meeting table, as he threateningly uttered the words, "**Go ahead and continue your lawsuit. You might win in court, after ten years of appeals, but I *guarantee* you, that you are going to loose!**"

It is a well-known fact that WNI is purportedly mafia based and controlled. Numerous recent headline stories, and televised news stories (similar to the 1975 Jimmy Hoffa story) had arisen, regarding vehicles exploding when the ignition key was engaged, officials turning up missing (presumably finding a resting place in a landfill), etcetera, following a dispute with WNI. There was *no question* in my mind about the message I was receiving from the WNI-CEO, and the

hair stood up on the back of my neck. I am not one to back down however, and as we gathered up our documents, and started out of the
room, I firmly stated, "Then you better have your attorneys **prepared!**"

We did continue the lawsuit, but as most large lawsuits do, ours
drug on, and I was **extremely** uncomfortable, most of the time. One
early spring morning at the Fenske Enterprises office, when the Grand
River was overflowing its banks, I received a visit from two large,
well-dressed men. They were the type of men (with the physique of
NFL linebackers) who look like they don't belong in suits. As they
requested, I naively followed them out to their vehicle to talk, where I
noticed a large concrete slab, containing a steel eyelet, chain, and
padlock, in their pickup truck box. The men made seemingly small
talk of the fact that the Grand River bordering our property was
flooded, and appeared to be deep. As I was curiously studying the
concrete slab in their truck, the two men informed me that they were
aware of the fact that I had refused to settle the lawsuit against WNI.
They advised me that I would be wise to drop the lawsuit, warning me
(gesturing at the concrete slab) that there could be **severe** conse-
quences if I did not. I **directly** ordered the two men **off** of our property, **threatening** to call the authorities if they did not leave
promptly. **Chills** ran up my spine as I walked back to the office.

I was constantly on guard for the next four and a half years, always
checking my vehicle door-locks, and under my dash and hood for evidence of tampering, before starting my vehicle. It is not a fun way to
live (in a legal dispute with the mob), and I don't care to ever repeat
the experience, invariably aware of people around me, and constantly
looking over my shoulder for anyone following me. I am certain however, that this dispute with WNI had a hand in future events at Fenske
Enterprises (described ahead), in years to come.

In its arguments in court, WNI tried to claim ownership of the
CRRI facility, through improvements CQSI had made, and through
claiming default on the part of CRRI. I believe that WNI knew there
was little or no merit in their lawsuit, but hoped to run us out of
money, and at the very least, keep our site closed as long as possible.
The lawsuit finally ended with no exchange of money, other than
enormous legal fees on both sides (far more difficult for us), but with
us in control (as owners) of CRRI. Under the guise of limiting their
liability (which we fought ferociously), WNI requested that the court
allow them to remove all of the waste on site, which had been disposed of during the time the site had been operated by CQSI (now

WNI's subsidiary company). We lost on this issue, and the court did allow WNI to remove the waste. The reality however, which WNI fully understood, was that once all the waste had been removed, totally destroying the site design intricacies, it would tremendously inhibit our ability to ever reopen the site as a hazardous waste facility.

Nevertheless, we then modified our permit renewal application, and began working toward reopening CRRI. The process was grueling, requiring endless extreme effort and expense, because the MDNR insisted on *perfection* (I would not be at all surprised if "**payoffs**" took place)! The MDNR required that we must achieve "Clean Closure" before the MDNR would reissue the permit, which meant reaching "non-detect" levels, in **any** and **all** soil samples taken. We removed countless truckloads of soil, and disposed of them at the Fenske Enterprises landfill. We did **finally** attain "Clean Closure" however (after several years), and CRRI may be the only previously licensed hazardous waste landfill facility in the nation, ever granted such, with non-detect levels on **all** soils! We then went to work attempting to obtain an operations bond, or find another company (to contract with) that was sizable enough to obtain a bond.

21

Life Changes

Meanwhile, after my brother-in-law Dick had been working at Fenske Enterprises for about eight years (managing the Paper Plant), my sister Karen filed for divorce. I never understood why, but I just worked with Dick, I didn't live with him, and anyway it was their business, so I stayed out of it. Their marriage produced one child, a boy named Casey. After the divorce had finalized however, my sister Karen started putting pressure on my parents to fire Dick. I didn't feel that was fair or necessary, because Dick had worked very hard to help build the business, and because he was a great employee, but by this time, Karen was getting tired of teaching, and she wanted his job. Karen can be very demanding and manipulative, and after a few months of insistence she convinced my parents to give Dick notice.

Karen had been an instructor for Grand Rapids Junior College for a number of years; she was strongly politically connected, and she used that to entice my parents to hire her. Waste disposal is a highly political business. Kent County, the permitting agency (through the Act 641 County Solid Waste Planning process), was and is in the waste disposal business, with a solid waste landfill (and later a solid waste mass-burn incinerator). Kent County **was** therefore in competition with Fenske Enterprises, so political connections **could** be helpful. Even though she knew nothing about the business, Karen wound up with Dick's job.

I tried to convince my parents that we would be fine without Karen's connections. I was serving as an appointed member of the county solid waste, and state hazardous waste management planning committees at the time (as mentioned, *further explained ahead*), and I told my parents that I could handle things politically. I argued unsuccessfully, that we should keep Dick employed. Mother stated, "Well Doug, she is our **daughter**, and she feels uncomfortable with her ex-husband working in the family business." I finally lost the argument (my parents **were** the **owners** of Fenske Enterprises), and soon Karen replaced Dick. If I had even an inkling of what was in store for me, I would have argued more passionately. Karen is very good at turning on the tears at the appropriate time however, and she even had me feeling a little guilty at times, for having argued so strongly to keep Dick on.

Karen's employment put a lot more pressure on me, because not only did she not know anything about the waste disposal or recycling business, she did not have the experience or knowledge to assist in the field. She knew nothing about equipment (balers, trucks, forklifts, etc.); in fact, she rarely left the office. Secondly, shortly after she started working at Fenske Enterprises, Karen began dating one of our landfill customers (a young man named Jeff), and that bothered me. I didn't know him at all, only that he was the son of one of our waste customers, and that he drove truck for his father. What bothered me, was that he was only twenty years old (Karen was thirty-five), they came from different backgrounds, seemed to have very little in common, and I could not see the relationship working. He was so naïve that he didn't even seem to understand that Karen was interested in him as a mate, when she first invited him over to her farm for dinner.

I verbalized my disapproval initially; however, my Uncle Ken Fenske offered words of advice. When Uncle Ken at one point stated to me, "Doug what difference does it make if it doesn't work, if he brings a few years of happiness into her life," I saw the wisdom, and stayed uninvolved. My Uncle Ken and my beautiful Aunt Jo Fenske are wonderful people, who brought a lot of love, and joy into our lives, set a good example for all of us, and I took their counsel seriously.

After a short time of employment (a couple years) Karen started to want more control however, and by the time we had our new MRF (Materials Recovery Facility, *explained ahead*) operating efficiently, she told my parents that she wanted control of the new MRF, as well

Left to right: Dad, Mom, Uncle Bob, Aunt Peg, Aunt Jo, and Uncle Ken.

as the Paper Plant. I argued vehemently against Karen's proposal, reminding my parents, that the MRF would not even **be** there, had it not been for me! When my parents told me they were going to put Karen in charge of the new MRF, regardless, I **quit** on the spot. Within two days, Mother called me, and said that she and my father had changed their minds, and she asked me to come back to work, which I did. This caused Karen to quit, I suspect believing that my parents would concede to her demands, but they did not, and she never returned.

Karen became very vindictive after quitting, and one bitter cold winter night (near zero degrees Fahrenheit), not long after Karen quit, my family and I became the victim of her wrath, waking up to a freezing cold house. I lived adjacent to Karen's property, 1/4 mile east, and the natural gas from one of the oil wells on her farm was connected to my house, providing fuel to my furnace and hot water heater. Many oil wells in Michigan, and elsewhere, produce natural gas (in the process of extracting oil); some of it is used for heat and energy, and much of it is vented to the atmosphere, or burned off as a waste product. When I traipsed around in the dark, I discovered that the gas line connection to my house had been cut off. I had to scramble to come up with alternative heat, before my waterlines froze, let **alone** my family! The following morning, I had an emergency backup propane tank installed. I eventually wound up taking my own sister to court, to get the gas line reconnected, because Karen wouldn't even discuss the issue with me. My home was on an 11.5-acre lot that the original owner of Karen's farm had split off the farm property, and sold as a separate parcel (long before he sold the farm to Karen). The deed to my property clearly contained gas rights to the well on the original farm, the court ruled in my favor, and the gas was forcibly reconnected.

What appeared as further vindictiveness, sometime after she quit, Karen filed a childhood abuse lawsuit against our father. The suit maintained that our father had sexually abused her as a child. She also made other vicious claims against our father that included satanic rituals, contending that she had witnessed our father cut our first pet dog (a cocker spaniel named "Sparky") in half with a chainsaw. Karen claimed that these and other incredible events occurred to her as memories, while in adult therapy. My father denied all charges, and my mother, my sisters, and I have no knowledge or recollection of these, or other preposterous events that Karen claimed she recalled as memories, **and we clearly recall Sparky dying peacefully of old age**!

However, Mother became very concerned about what neighbors would think if the lawsuit went to court. My parent's attorney supposedly explained to them that these are difficult cases to win, expensive to defend, and that it would probably cost them less to settle. My father *really* did **not** want to settle. He was very **hurt** and **angered** that these allegations had been made against him, and he wanted to **fight**, and prove that he had done **nothing**, but (according to Mother) their attorney advised him not to, and my mother did not want it to go to court, so they settled.

My father began to lose his vision, and experience numerous other health problems, within months of Karen's accusations. I have always believed that he may have been healthier for longer, had he been able to stand up for himself, but who knows? Nevertheless, my parents paid Karen a considerable sum of money in settlement (I heard in the $40–50,000 range), with no admission of guilt, and the suit ended. I had been very close to Karen at one time; she is my sister, and I will always love her, but this did not set right with me. I just believe that she got angry and greedy (when she didn't get her way), and she sought revenge.

Karen married the young man she was dating, they expanded their waste hauling business, and soon they got into some recycling, actually in competition with Fenske Enterprises. The business was a small (two open-truck) waste trucking business, when Karen became a part of it. Karen knew a lot of people in power positions however, and it didn't take long before their business expanded in size, with a number of packer trucks, and municipal accounts (which I'm sure Karen was able to pull strings to obtain). Their business seemed to have no problem obtaining permits, and before long they had a small waste processing/recycling permit and building, in the Grand Rapids suburb city of Jenison. Eventually, Karen and Jeff sold their business to one of the two public waste companies in Grand Rapids for a purportedly sizable sum, and started another business of growing organic vegetables on their farm.

In my heart, I strongly believe that Karen had involvement in the problems that Fenske Enterprises faced down the line. Although I have no way of proving so, it was always a question in my mind, how her business flourished, and Fenske Enterprises crumbled, but the truth has a way of surfacing, and one day I believe that it will. Karen has ways of getting what she wants. I will always remember some advice that Karen gave me once, years earlier. When I was going through the struggles of obtaining the CRRI hazardous waste permit in Cascade, and attempting to effectively answer some of the questions regarding the dangers of potential contamination, Karen advised me to, "Tell them what they **want** to hear." The issue was the rate of percolation through the clay at the Cascade site, and Karen advised me to tell my adversaries that liquid will **never** travel through the clay at the site. When I stated back to Karen, "I can't tell them **that**, because it wouldn't be **true**," Karen responded with, "What's the **truth** got to do with it? Do you **want** your permit or **not**!?" Karen's advice didn't *set right* with me, and *told me* something about her that I **never forgot**.

In December 1986 my parents retired, I bought Fenske Enterprises, and soon after incorporated as FEI (Fenske Enterprises, Inc.). By all accounts I should have been happy. I had built a "wonderful life" for myself. I owned a couple of successful businesses. I had a healthy child and beautiful home, with the majestic horse barn, which I had dismantled, moved, and hand pieced back together next to my home,

Mom and Pappy, retirement age.

with the thought that the barn would certainly prove to the world, if not ourselves, that we were a happy family. However, our relationship had fallen apart by this time, and that barn became my refuge in my sad and lonely marriage. The tears I shed in the loft were my prayers, and gave me the strength to try for something better. It had been five years since something inside me had "died," and I was no longer willing to try so hard to make my marriage work. Basically, when I began to take a stand for myself, and no longer allowed myself to be controlled, the relationship ended.

Within a few weeks of having "given up" on the relationship, and deciding to file for divorce (in January 1987), I received a phone call from a couple of former Grandville High School classmates. I was asked to join with a number of others on a reunion committee, to help organize our twenty-year class reunion. I did become a reunion planning committee member, and for several months we met frequently. I began running, working out, and getting myself in shape again, and I became increasingly more excited as the date for the reunion approached. Soon after we began the planning, I started to get a strong feeling that I was going to meet someone at our twenty-year class reunion. There were single women on the reunion committee, but no one that I was romantically interested in, and I went over in my thoughts, whom it might possibly be that I was going to meet, but no one came to mind. Still, I could not get over that **strong** feeling! That same *"voice thought"* that I had experienced in my twenties (which in the past had told me, "I had already **met** who I was **supposed** to be with"), started up again, and was now telling me, "You're going to meet someone at **this reunion!**"

Finally, the date for the reunion (September 19, 1987) arrived. I was **beside** myself! I was **so excited**, I couldn't even **think!** I could not **believe** how **ecstatic** I was! I literally **laughed** at myself! I couldn't even focus enough to decide what to **wear**, and as a result, it took me so long to get ready for the reunion, that instead of being **early** to greet guests (with the other reunion planning committee members), I was **late!** Even though I was thirty-eight years old, I felt like a young boy going to his first school dance, and I was *absolutely certain* that I was going to meet someone!!

There were about three hundred guests (counting spouses), which was a little better than a fifty percent turnout (not bad for a twenty year class reunion). Throughout the social hour (before the meal and dance), I searched in vain for this "someone," whom the "voice thought" inside my head, had me convinced that I was going to meet. However when the social hour ended, and an announcement was made to take our seats for dinner, I was **dumbfounded!** I had not **met anyone** whom I was even **attracted** to, let alone **seen** this "**someone!**" I was *actually* a little **depressed**, and so distracted with these thoughts, that I had a hard time relating to or carrying on any meaningful conversation, with the others seated at the dinner table I had chosen.

☺ Then about halfway through the meal it **happened!** I looked up to see this most **striking, vivacious** blond woman, with short, wild, spiked hair, wearing a hip pink outfit (which revealed her stunning, fit figure), and white boots, come walking into the room, proud and confident (with erect posture), straight across the middle of the dance floor. It was *clear to me* by her appearance, that she was not from Grand Rapids, and my heart was **pounding**! I must have been obviously staring, mouth open, because a (married) former classmate, seated (along with her husband) beside me, bumped me with her elbow, and exclaimed, "You better **eat**!" I finished my meal, to the best of my ability, and I tried to fight off the excitement of **who** this woman **was**, by saying to myself, "She is probably some classmate's wife." However, it was **no use**, because other thoughts came to me stating, "I don't **care**, I **have to** meet her **anyway**!" Something inside told me, that **this** was the **one**, the woman I had been looking for *all of my life*, all through **college**, and **after**! It wasn't a conscious thought, but somehow I *knew*!

When the meal ended, ever-present of my quest, I frustratingly could not shake myself free from one person after another, to go looking for this striking woman in the pink outfit, whom I **direly** wanted to meet before the dance started. Then all at once I heard this self-assured voice, "Hi, remember me?" I turned to my left, and there beside me stood the *striking blond woman!* I looked at her nametag (after twenty years, everyone wore name-tags), which read "Kerri James." The name was not familiar, and I stated, "No, but I'd **like** to!" Kerri James replied, "Oh, well in High School, I went by my first name Patricia, last name Owens."

A **million** thoughts at **once** raced through my mind! Thoughts came like, "Oh, **my God**, this is **who** I was going to **meet**! Flash memories returned, of the age-old "voice-thought," "You already **met** who you're **supposed** to be with!" This was the *first girl* in my *life*, whom I had ever **gone out on a date with** (at 16 years old)! This was the girl whom I had been **so** attracted to, and felt like, "I **knew** from somewhere before," way back in **Junior High**, and now she was standing here right **next** to me, **more** attractive than **ever**!! My heart was pounding **again**, and it took *everything I had* to keep my composure!

Not long into our conversation, Kerri informed me that her residence (since 1978) was Santa Barbara, California, a couple blocks from the beach. I **again** had to fight back signs of extreme excitement! Not only had I just met someone whom I was **very** attracted to and I had "**already met**," but *also*, this was "a **blond woman** who lived on a **beach** in **California**!" Could it **be**! Had I just met the woman that the voice inside my head had always told me, "I was *destined to be with*," **and**, "I had **already met**," **and** she was "a **blond**

woman who lived on a **beach** in **California**!!?" This was almost *too much*!! How I ever fought back the excitement, **and** kept my poise is beyond me!

Kerri was born in Grand Rapids, in the same hospital as I, just a few weeks later. Kerri was born January 21, 1949, and named Patricia Kerri Owens, the second of two children (eighteen months after her sister Susan), to a schizophrenic mother, and a chronically alcoholic father (who divorced when she was two). She and her sister Susie were raised primarily by their maternal grandparents, and lived (along with their mother) in their grandparents home in Grandville, just a couple of miles from our farm.

Kerri adored her grandparents, and the secure and happy childhood she had there. That all changed when her mother Margaret remarried, and insisted that her daughters accompany her in her new life. Though the girls were allowed to visit their Grandparents, Kerri was only eight years old, and *so* devastated by this upheaval in her life, that depression set in. She was deeply saddened, and missed her home and her grandmother so much, that she was unable to adjust. She cried often, and had difficulty focusing or paying attention in school. Her desperation and hopelessness lead her to thoughts of suicide. Finally (at eleven years old), Kerri paid a visit to Grandville's Doctor Holden, which gave her the only remedy she needed, **hope**. Doc. Holden recognized Kerri's fragile condition. The doctor informed her that when she became fourteen years of age, she would have the legal right to choose her **own** home, and he made Kerri promise that she would keep "*Holding On*" that long.

The fall of her thirteenth year (just months before her *awaited* fourteenth birthday), after pleading with her mother (and insisting that she would be leaving in a few months anyway), Kerri was allowed to return to her grandparent's home, and she attended Grandville Junior High. This is where Kerri and I first met. Kerri remembers the first time that she and I made eye contact, and the excitement she felt, whenever she was around me. She recalls on one occasion, at age fifteen, an inexplicable "voice thought" that **she** experienced, when our eyes locked. The message Kerri heard was, "*This boy will never hurt you.*" Kerri was startled by this message, and quickly dismissed it, though it never left her. After we turned sixteen, in the spring of that same school year, Kerri asked me to join her at the "Sadie Hawkins Day" dance, which was the first date for either one of us. After our second date, at a classmate's cottage a few weeks later, Kerri was confused as to why she didn't hear from me for the rest of

Susie (above) and Kerri (below) as young girls.

the summer, and assumed that I must not have been that interested. She met another boy that August who was very persistent, and they started dating just before school started in September. This was the boy Kerri married a few years later.

Were Kerri and I put on this planet, and raised just a couple miles apart, because we were **destined** to one day meet, and be together, or did we **bring** ourselves to that place, so that we could meet **again** one day? Regardless, we both **knew** the instant we looked into one another's eyes that we were **home**! Neither one of us understood it, or knew what to do about it at the tender age of thirteen, but it was a **knowing** that never left either one of us! I believe that *knowing* was the internal "voice thought" that had been with me all of my life.

Kerri had not even **known** of our twenty-year class reunion! She had married in Grand Rapids, for six years (right out of high school), had a girl and a boy, then divorced, moved (with her children), and lived in San Francisco, Oahu, Hawaii, and finally Santa Barbara (single for the past fifteen years).

Brian, Tamara, and Kerri when they moved to CA.

I was so **enthralled** to listen to Kerri's story. She left Grand Rapids (in her mid-twenties) on faith, as a single mother (of two small children, eight and four), with **no** income, and **no** child support. Kerri had committed to take responsibility for the children, with the agreement that her ex-husband would not dispute her leaving the area with them. Kerri, with a friend who had a mutual desire to reach California, headed west in a rented U-Haul truck, towing Kerri's '69 VW microbus behind. They left in 1976, and lived first in San Francisco, for approximately a year. After deciding that it was too cold in San Francisco, and not the "paradise" Kerri was seeking, they traveled to the island of Oahu, Hawaii, and lived there for most of the next year. Kerri decided to leave Hawaii for various reasons, but primarily because of the substandard public school system, and unaffordable private schools. Also, many locals on the islands refer to "mainlanders" as "Howleys," and Kerri's light-haired children did not fair well in the local environment.

I loved hearing the stories of some of their adventures on the islands, such as traveling the perimeter of the Oahu Island in a VW "Thing," planning to make it all the way around the island, and running out of *road,* next to steep **cliffs**, with *no* "turn-around!" The kids were **scarred**, and **protested**, and finally, completely out of road, Kerri was forced to precariously back up for several miles, just to get back to an area wide enough to turn her VW around.

When Kerri decided to move back to the mainland, she focused on Santa Barbara. Kerri had visited Santa Barbara once, in the early years of her sister Susie's move to California. Even though Susie, now married and living with her family in Santa Maria (about seventy miles North of Santa Barbara), welcomed Kerri and her children to stay with them, Kerri never forgot the beauty of Santa Barbara, and how much she had loved it there. After staying with Susie and her family for a period of months, Kerri and her children ventured out, got their own place in Santa Maria, and then by March of 1978, moved to Santa Barbara. Eventually they rented a quaint, "funky," 1920's apartment on Oceano Street, only a block off the beach, where they resided, creating many fond memories, throughout her children's childhood years.

Santa Barbara is rated as one of the "ten most beautiful cities in the world," but it **is** very **expensive**. As a single mother with no child support, Kerri knew that she would need to get creative. At first Kerri worked two jobs simultaneously, trying to make ends meet, but this left her with very little time with her children. Being innovative, Kerri decided to go into business for herself, and started her own singing telegram service. This was a natural for Kerri, who is vivacious, outgoing, and a good singer. In Santa Barbara (being a tourist town), there was a demand. Kerri ran an add, and before long she began delivering balloons, bouquets, and personalized singing messages, for birthdays and other events throughout the city, including bookings such as a hospital visit to a child as the "Easter Bunny." As the business grew, it became necessary for Kerri to hire employees to help with the many and varied telegrams.

Eventually, Kerri was busy full time, running her office, answering calls, scheduling appointments etcetera. This gave Kerri time at home evenings with her children, and gave her the income she needed to be able to live in Santa Barbara. She did well as a single parent, as **any** parent, teaching her children the things in life that I believe really matter, like love, togetherness, and family!

Kerri had little money to spare, so she taught her children to enjoy simple things, which cost very little, like skating on the boardwalk at the beach, on rented skates at first, until she could afford to buy some of their own. I hurt for Kerri, when she told me the story of someone breaking into her car, and stealing her purse, and what little money she

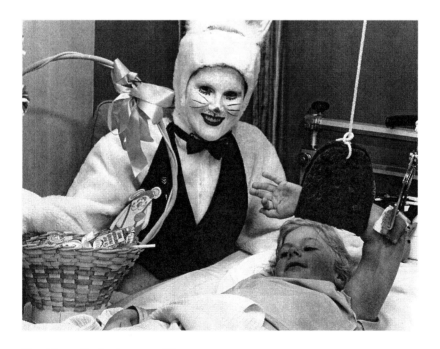

Kerri in an Easter bunny outfit.

had one year (only a few weeks before Christmas), while she and her children were skating late in the afternoon. By the time Kerri and I re-met, her business was flourishing, and one of Kerri's long-term employees ran the business for her, whenever she was out of town.

Kerri had not attended any previous high school class reunions, and since she had left no forwarding address, she had not been con-tacted. Kerri had just traveled to Grand Rapids for a brief visit (one of the few times she had done so, since she left in 1976). She had driven cross-country with her son Brian (sixteen), in his small truck, bring-ing him to Michigan to spend the '87/'88 school year with his father and stepmother, for the first time since they had moved away. Shortly before her scheduled departure (flight) back to California, Kerri ran into a former classmate, who told her of the reunion, and insisted that she stay a few extra days to attend.

After over **twenty years**, Kerri and I were just as attracted to one another, as we had been in Junior High and High School! Our recon-nection was **magical** and *destined!* I think that we must know some

Kerri skating at the beach, late 70's.

Tamara as a teen, skating at the beach.

Brian as a young boy, skating near the beach.

things intrinsically, on a cellular level. How could I **know**, that I had already met who I was supposed to be with, and **know** that I was going to fall in love with a blond who lived on a beach in California, when I had never **met** a blond who lived on a beach in California? I believe that some things only happen in life, when the time is right. A few months after we "re-met" at the reunion, I found a small tin safe, in my childhood bedroom at my parent's farmhouse, in which I kept valuables as a boy. In searching through the contents, having no idea why I saved it, I discovered the map with directions, from our second date (*at 16 years old*), **twenty-two years** prior!

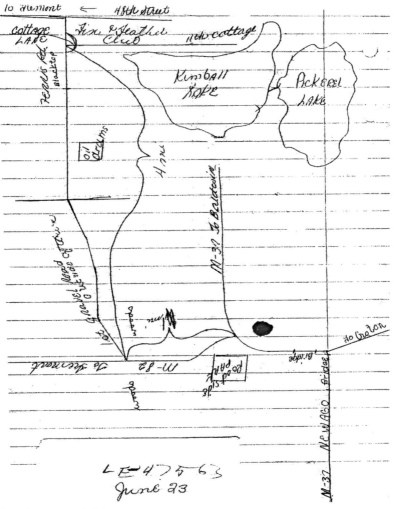

Map of our second date.

Kerri and I had a fantastic time at the reunion, and afterwards we enjoyed a midnight breakfast, laughing, and reminiscing with a group of classmates. We initiated a plan for me to pick Kerri up early the next morning, to take her to the airport. We decided to meet at her ex-husband's house, where Kerri would drop off her son's vehicle, which she had continued to use during her stay in Grand Rapids.

I arrived as scheduled at our destination, a quiet, private cul-de-sac in Jenison, and parked in front of the address Kerri had given me. Within a couple of minutes, there was a young man standing in the front yard, warily observing me. I stepped out of my vehicle, and we walked toward one another. We introduced ourselves, and I explained to Brian, that his mother and I were friends from high school, and that I was meeting her there, so that she could drop off his vehicle, rather than leave it at the airport, as they had previously arranged. When he folded his arms across his chest, turned his glance to a side view, after tentatively shaking my extended hand, I realized that I was being intensely scrutinized. Being my friendly, enthusiastic self, I attempted to win him over. We made some awkward conversation, and within a few minutes, I was relieved to see Kerri approaching in her son's vehicle. I would never have guessed from our initial meeting, that I would eventually develop such a close bond with this young man.

Once Kerri and I drove to the airport, we had a little time to kill, so after we checked her luggage in, I drove Kerri over to see my CRRI site, adjacent to the north side of the airport. While parked on the CRRI property, as I held Kerri's hand (trying to figure out how I was ever going to be able to let her go), I noticed a tear running down her cheek. When questioned, Kerri explained that she thought it might be awhile before we could ever be together. I responded, "Maybe your crystal ball is clearer than mine, but I don't think it will be very long." As it turned out, Kerri's vision was much clearer than mine, and foretold of obstacles ahead (in our struggle to be together), beyond anything I could ever have imagined.

In our discussion, Kerri and I discovered that she had worked at Lear Jet in Grand Rapids, on 52nd Street, only 1/4 mile from CRRI, at a time when she was single (divorced), and I was single (and looking for a compatible mate). I actually had always been looking for "*that someone whom I had already met, and I was supposed to be with,*" although I didn't share my "voice-thought" with Kerri until some time later, when I felt secure enough in our relationship to do so. Some months later, when I did eventually admit to the "voice-thought," which had been with me throughout my adult life, Kerri shared with me, how a psychic had once told her that her future held a "blue-eyed man," with eyes similar to hers, with whom she had "a deep connection" (who may even have been her "twin in another life"), and with whom she would want to spend all of her time.

We had undoubtedly passed one another numerous times on 52nd street (which dead-ended at CRRI), only a few feet apart, without knowing it. We discovered that we each had frequented some of the same nightclubs (for several years), after Kerri's divorce, and before my marriage, and who knows how many times our paths may have crossed, barely missing one another.

After spending every last moment together that we possibly could, I rushed Kerri back to the airport, and said a nervous, but hopeful goodbye. After her plane taxied away, I jumped into my vehicle, and sped to a point at the West end of the runway, where I could park, and see her plane for the longest amount of time. As I watched the jumbo-jet she left on, fade into a small speck in the western sky, I knew that my life would **never** be the same. I didn't know how to get together with Kerri, living twenty-five hundred miles apart, but I **knew** that I belonged with this woman, and I was ***determined*** to find a way!

We started communicating very soon, almost daily, both on the phone and in letters. My whole day would revolve around my call to Kerri, and I felt **elated**, when Kerri referred to me as her "boyfriend," in one of our early letters. We planned our first meeting place to be a couple of months later (mid-November), in Aspen, Colorado. It was a beautiful and desirable mid-way point, and since my younger sister Linda was living there, I could visit her as well.

When I arrived in Aspen, I initially stayed with Linda, and we enjoyed a week together, visiting, and catching up on one another's lives. Linda shared with me how she had always felt that my marriage was a "mis-match," and she was supportive of my choice to end it. On my first night in Linda's little one-room cabin, in the middle of the night, I heard a significantly audible grinding noise, which kept me awake. First I suspected that Linda had a mouse tenant, however the odd grinding sound continued, even after I made my presence known by snapping my fingers. Upon investigation in the dark, which included leaning my head down just inches from hers, I discovered that my little sister had developed the habit of grinding her teeth in her sleep. Linda (who wasn't even aware that she had developed the habit) and I had a good laugh about it the next morning, and she supplied me with some cotton for my ears, in case it happened again.

We did some deer hunting together, even though by this time in my life, I was really not much into shooting anything. Several years had passed, since Brandon had pleaded with me not to, "Shoot the birdie," and the beauty of the mountains was far more my pleasure than the "hunt." It was terrific seeing Linda again, we spent some quality time together, and I came to realize how much I missed my little sister, who throughout my life, had been my good friend, as well as my business confidant.

I was extremely upbeat, excited about life (and **especially** about getting together with Kerri), and for the first time, I felt that I **knew** exactly where my life was going. I was moving ahead full speed to get there, and I shared with Linda, and friends of hers, many of my plans. A cowgirl whom Linda knew, and introduced me to in a bar one night where Linda and I were celebrating, stated to me, "Douglas, you need to **slow down**, and smell the **roses**." I didn't even know what she was talking about. The cowgirl was actually attracted to me, and tried to convince me to go home with her. I didn't want to hurt her feelings, and I cautiously explained that I had a girlfriend, to which she replied, "So what!" I have had very few "one-night-stands" in my life, because I was always interested in a **relationship** with a woman who would love me, as much as I loved her. Now I felt for the **first time** in my life, that I had found what I was looking for, or at least the *possibility* of that with Kerri, and that is **all** that I wanted!

On one of the mornings, while my sister and I were hunting apart from one another, as I was hiking through an open meadow, I started thinking about all the changes my life was going through. I was overcome with guilt over having given up on my marriage, and I fell to my knees and wept. I was filled with *anguish,* and torn between love for, and duty to my family, and the land that I loved (that had always provided for me), and the *love of my life.* I could not *figure out* how I could be together with Kerri, and keep the business that I had spent my life building, in tact.

It was a cold, gray, completely overcast day, and I was entirely overwhelmed with despair. For several minutes I knelt sobbing, with my face in my hands, then gradually I dropped my hands to my sides in hopelessness, and lifted my face toward the heavens, as tears streamed down my cheeks. Slowly, the clouds **right above** me separated, and a beam of sunlight hit me *clearly* in the face! In the distance, I heard and watched a flock of geese take flight from a small pond in a meadow below me, and I could feel the warmth of God's arms embrace me, as the Universe somehow told me, and I *knew,* that everything was going to be all right! With tear-filled eyes, I **understood**, and from the **bottom** of my heart, I whispered a thank you to God.

The following day, Kerri flew into Aspen from Santa Barbara, and we spent a week together there, getting to know each other, and falling in love. Aspen is such a magnificent place, with superb views and overwhelming beauty, and with a classic history, having started as a mining town. The quality, and the beauty of our surroundings helped bring me back to earth occasionally, as I was truly infatuated with **whom** I was experiencing this reality! We had glorious days, and enchanted evenings, with pure white fluffy snowflakes floating around us, as we held hands, and enjoyed twilight strolls through Aspen.

We had the most difficult time trying to say good-by and part, when Kerri's return flight was scheduled. I drove Kerri to the Aspen airport, but planes were grounded, as a result of a snowstorm. We rode together toward Denver, which (though the opposite direction as Santa Barbara) was the closest major airport, and was on my way back to Grand Rapids. When I intentionally ignored, and drove right by the "Denver Airport" exit on the freeway, and Kerri alarmingly pointed that out to me, I stated that flying back to Santa Barbara out of Omaha, Nebraska, would only take an hour longer. I argued that we would have all the hours of driving time together, and Kerri happily

(Left to right) Linda, Doug, and Kerri in Aspen November, 1987.

went along with the plan, only to have me repeat the stunt (to Kerri's amusement) at Omaha, Des Moines, and at every major city, right back into Grand Rapids. We held hands the entire trip, taking time for a quick kiss every few miles.

We spent one last night together in Grand Rapids, only deciding **last minute** the next morning, that I should accompany Kerri back to see Santa Barbara. I packed a few things hastily, and we rushed to the airport, to catch the flight we had scheduled for Kerri to leave on. The airline could not book a seat for me (on this last-for-the-day, Chicago/LA/Santa Barbara flight), in time before the "last boarding call," and it was essential that Kerri make it home that day, to attend a "James Taylor" concert, for which she had purchased "prime" tickets, months in advance. Kerri explained that she loved me, but she loved James Taylor **too**, and she wasn't **about** to miss this concert. We had to say an abrupt good-by, that didn't *feel* right.

After she left, my determination kicked in, and I ran to another airline. I was able to catch a flight (**barely**), which left shortly after Kerri's, and on which I could connect with her in Chicago, and we could then take the remaining flights to Santa Barbara together. "Dirty Dancing" was a current hit movie, which we had seen together in Aspen, and had both thoroughly enjoyed. When I quietly snuck up, and sat down on a bench behind the chair in O'Hare Airport, on which Kerri was seated (seeming sad and alone), awaiting her connecting flight, I started softly singing the words to the theme song from "Dirty Dancing," "*I had the time of my life—no I **never felt** this way before.*" Kerri jumped up, loudly exclaimed, "***Oh my God, you made it***," and threw her arms around me, to the applause of all seated around us!

We traveled together (holding hands) to her home in Santa Barbara, and arrived just in time to unload our luggage, and walk the few blocks from Kerri's house to attend the "James Taylor" concert, to which Kerri "**happened**" to have an extra ticket (purchased for a girlfriend who had cancelled out.) The concert was at the famous "Santa Barbara County Bowl," nestled serenely in the mountains above Santa Barbara, with a panoramic view of the Pacific Ocean. It was a balmy and **glorious** night, and the first of a week we enjoyed together in Santa Barbara, falling more in love with each other, and myself with Santa Barbara.

I met and became acquainted with Kerri's daughter Tamara (19), who lived with Kerri, in a separate bungalow on the property Kerri was renting. On one of the mornings of my visit, Kerri suggested that

I go out and wake Tamara, to come in and join us for some coffee and breakfast. I returned and explained that there was no one in her room, with only piles of clothes on her bed. Kerri stated, "No, she's **there**! Just look under the clothes." After protesting that there was absolutely no **room** for a body in that bed, I reluctantly returned to her room, where to my **amazement**, I heard a muffled, "*Hmm?*" when I called her name. She **was** sleeping there under that heap of clothes, which I came to understand, as I learned more about teenagers, and came to **know** and love Tamara. Over time I became very close to Tamara, who is a beautiful person, internally and externally.

The day I had been dreading arrived, and Kerri and I had to part, but it was not as sad as it had felt in Aspen. I knew where Kerri lived now, had seen her home, had previously met her son, and now her daughter, and I felt more a part of her life. We drug my departure out to the last minute, and I had to run across the tarmac to catch my plane (Santa Barbara has a small airport with no gateways), but I did make it. I had a good feeling as the plane taxied away, with my face glued to the window, watching Kerri every second that I could. I had no idea how many difficult good-byes the future held for us, but I was **certain** of our connection, and I felt *secure* in our relationship.

Tamara and Brian as young adults.

22

Return to Boxing and Business

I became *inspired* and *excited* about life again upon re-meeting Kerri, and establishing a relationship with her (something I hadn't felt for a long, long time). I started to feel **good** about myself again, the way I had felt back in my college days. I came up with a statement that I used a lot, "I got a horse named Buck, a dog named Buck, a Buck knife, and I used to ride in the rodeo, till I got Bucked off." It was all nearly true, but pointless to repeat, except that it demonstrated my enthusiasm about life again, and my self esteem. In truth, the horse I owned at the time was named Toss (**Buck** would have described him as well), and as I often discovered, he came by his name *honestly!* He was a **hardhead**, and nearly every time I saddled him, it seemed like I had to "break him to saddle" all over again. He hadn't been ridden much in recent years, and I used that excuse to on-lookers often, however no matter how often I rode him, he would frequently gift me with a lesson in "saddle-bronx-man-ship."

On one of my early Saturday morning rides, after having a cup of coffee with my father, Toss decided that he did not want to go for a ride that morning. As I stepped out of the farmhouse, and swung up onto the saddle, Toss took off bucking, straight back to the barn, and Pappy shouted, **"Stay with him son!"** It felt like I was back in my rodeo days, and I was on a **wild** one; Toss could **really** get determined! As we bucked through an open gateway, halfway between the farmhouse and the barn, I lost my seat, and came down flat on my ribcage, squarely on the wooden gate (*made of two by sixes*), which I had constructed myself, several years earlier. As the gate crushed under my weight, and I hit the ground with a hard thud, while catching my breath, I heard Pappy say, "*Oh boy,* now you've got a gate to fix!" Actually he knew that I was okay, because before he had even finished his statement, I was up with doubled fists, stomping toward the barn after Toss muttering, "You miserable son-of-a…"!

I missed Kerri very much when we were apart, but I did have Brandon for company every other weekend. Brandon and I became closer than ever. I purchased an extra-long horse trailer, and sometimes we loaded my small flat-bottom aluminum boat and motor into the trailer behind the horses, packed a tent, and enjoyed a weekend of camping, fishing, and horseback riding. On warm summer nights, at remote locations, which we both loved (away from everybody), we sat and told stories around the campfire, roasting hotdogs and marsh mellows, and we went skinny dipping under the moonlight. Whenever Kerri was in town, she was always very sweet to Brandon, when he was with us for weekend visits. The two of them enjoyed many ventures together, when I was busy and could not join them. Kerri even took Brandon shopping, so that he could pick out a Mother's Day gift for his mom. Brandon grew to love Kerri, and all the attention she gave him, and they became close. Brandon visited Kerri and I, and Tamara in Santa Barbara one summer, and enjoyed many activities including ocean fishing, boogie boarding, beach skating, and he celebrated his July birthday with us.

It hurt me for Brandon, that even as time progressed my ex-wife refused to accept the divorce, to accept Kerri into my or Brandon's life, and to get on with her own life. It broke my heart when little six year old Brandon asked Kerri if she would kiss him good-by before we got to his house, as we neared his driveway (bringing him home) one evening. Brandon explained that when his mother had seen Kerri give him a hug and kiss good-by, the previous time that Kerri had been with us, his mother had deprived him of television and video games for a week. On another occasion, as I came to pick Brandon up for the weekend, my ex-wife refused to let Brandon out of the house, when she spotted Kerri in my vehicle. After pounding on a locked front door, I was forced to leave, hearing the cries from my little boy, "Let me **go**," in the background, which **tore** me **apart**!

Brandon on camping/fishing/horseback riding trip with Doug, summer, 1988.

Before I left, I had provided a buffer for Brandon from his mother's harshness, rigidity, and control, and at first Brandon was resistant to his mother. Early on, my ex-wife once complained to me that Brandon had pulled a knife on her, asking me, "What should I do about it, if he does it again!" Since it was a butter knife, and Brandon was only six, I said, "Take it away!" I advised her however, that she should ask Brandon why he was so angry with her.

Eventually Brandon became close to his mother, which I knew was important, *and necessary,* because he lived with her, and she had the control. It angered me, that my ex-wife confided *adult issues* with such a young child, and that his mother would not take at least some responsibility for why our marriage had failed. She instead played the "**victim**," and burdened this young boy with responsibility for her unhappiness, by venting her anger and hostility toward me, on him. I saw how much this was impacting him, and it bothered me, but I did not know what to do about it.

On Brandon's visits with me, he would frequently grill me with questions about why I left his mother, voicing her opinions about that. It hurt me for him that she would confide such personal information to a child, too young to be asked to comprehend. I felt **powerless** to help him! I refused to discuss with Brandon why we divorced, and told him that those were adult issues, that he need not be concerned with. Brandon seemed relieved when I assured him that I loved him, that he didn't need to worry about such matters, and that we should enjoy our time together. In my opinion, it doesn't matter anyway. It doesn't make any difference who is "**at fault**," when a marriage fails. **Nobody** is! There are no "*good guys,*" or "*bad guys.*" When it isn't right, it doesn't work, and that's just the way it is!

I had hoped that things would improve as time passed, but they did not, and it always remained a struggle with my ex-wife. She would repeatedly show up and interfere, at a ball game Brandon was playing in on his weekend with me, or a swim meet, or school event. She always appeared at Fenske softball games, or team parties, even routinely at Fenske family parties, often creating a scene, embarrassing me, Brandon, and everyone else who was forced to witness it. Finally (at a future date), after years of struggle, of trying to have a relationship with Brandon without my ex-wife's interference, and the embarrassment and pain that it caused Brandon, when he was about twelve, I made a decision to just let go of my end of the rope. I wrote him numerous letters (which he probably never saw) trying to explain, and I do not have a relationship with Brandon anymore. I **love** my son Brandon with **all my heart**, and I *always* will! I hope someday Brandon will understand, that the reason I stopped the tug of war, was to spare him any more pain, and I hope that I can eventually have a relationship with him again, but that is up to him. *As of this final edit (12/ 10) Brandon is 29, now married with a beautiful wife (and three beautiful children) whom I have never met, whose pictures I view every day, on our refrigerator door.*

Boxing

Ever since I had retired from boxing at twenty-six years of age (as required), I felt that I had something **more**, something left *undone*. Not long after re-meeting Kerri at our class reunion, I ran into an old friend from boxing, and heard that the USABF (USA Boxing Federation) had lifted the twenty-six year age restriction to unlimited. Being "**inspired**," I decided to stage a comeback. When I talked to Pappy about my plan, he cautioned against it stating, "People will say, what's that old man doing in there?" Nevertheless, I looked up my old trainer Morey, who was in his mid-seventies, and still training fighters. The first night I walked into the gym, and told him of my desire, after not having seen him for a decade, Morey stated, "Where've you been? I always **wondered** when you'd walk through that door!"

I trained with "a *fever,* and *zeal!*" I had a "**new lease** on life!" "Road-work" is a very important part of boxing, and I pounded out the miles, running three miles every morning, sometimes (actually many times) because of Michigan's climate, in rain, sleet, or snow. Michigan's weather (and focus on health and fitness) is very different than Southern California, and I rarely ever saw other runners on the roads, as are continually present on the West Coast. While running in a light sleet, early one cold fall morning, I heard a loud speaker instruct me to, "Hold it right there," as a police cruiser pulled up behind me. The two officers ordered me into the back seat, where they demanded my ID, and inquired, "What am I running from?" After I explained that I was simply working on my conditioning for boxing, and after detaining me long enough to feel confident that no one was chasing me, with looks of disbelief, reluctantly, they finally let me go.

To help me deal with our times apart, Kerri hired a photographer in Santa Barbara, a former professional model, who assisted Kerri in developing a calendar, with each month featuring a photograph of Kerri, in a different pose and setting. Kerri gave me that beautiful calendar (which I will forever cherish) for my birthday, just a couple weeks before Christmas. This gave me an idea, so I dug out my old MSU boxing robe from my parent's attic, and had my picture taken (hand-wraps and all); I had it framed, and mailed it to Kerri as a Christmas gift.

My sparing partner was a Super-heavyweight, "Kevin Whitcomp," who also had graduated from Grandville High, but a decade after me. I knew of Kevin, had watched him in numerous Grandville football games, and had a lot of respect for him. Kevin came from a very athletic family, was big (250 labs), very strong, and he became State Champion. We met in the ring, gained a good respect and fondness for each other, pounding out the rounds night after night, and building a friendship that I knew would last.

It was a good thing that I felt "inspired," because my "comeback" in boxing had plenty of hurdles. One of my first times back in the ring (sparing), I shattered the index knuckle of my hand, throwing a left hook. I was determined however, did my roadwork in near blizzard

Doug in boxing robe.

conditions (on occasion), and healed in time to compete in the (winter) 1988 Golden Gloves tournament, less than six weeks later. Unfortunately however, 1988 was an Olympic year, and for the USA to compete in Olympic boxing, the USA Boxing Federation imposed the thirty-seven year maximum age limitation, allowed by International rules at the time. As a result, a couple of months after I had decided to stage a comeback and started training, I was told that because I was over the maximum age limit (I had turned thirty-nine that December), I would not be allowed to compete in the 1988 Golden Gloves tournament. I was infuriated! I was advised that age discrimination is illegal in the United States, so I sued the USABF. I won a TRO (Temporary Restraining Order), which forced the USABF to allow me to compete.

I wasn't very successful that first year back in the Golden Gloves, nor in the Olympic trials the following spring. I would love to blame my unimpressive performance on the broken knuckle I had suffered, although I am certain that it had more to do with rust, from the thirteen years that had passed, since I had retired from boxing. Nevertheless I continued training.

I was always in training, and I walked around with a black eye most of the time. So much of the time in fact, that during one of our rendezvous, Kerri jokingly remarked (after someone questioned my black eye), "**Black eye**! I thought that was a **birthmark**!" We vacationed for a week together in Florida that first winter, visiting my parents at their winter home in Bonita Springs (near Naples), where my Aunt Louise has a winter home as well. While in Florida, to stay in condition for the 1988 Olympic trials that spring (to keep my wind up), I ran every day. I wasn't getting in any sparing though, so I convinced Kerri to just throw some punches at me, for me to block.

I squared off a garden hose in my parent's side yard, to mark the ring boundaries, and Kerri and I each put on some gloves. I blocked everything that Kerri threw at me, and at first it worked out well, but midway through the first round, one of Kerri's own boxing gloves bounced back, and hit her in the nose, after I had blocked a punch she threw at me. Kerri responded with a loud "*Ooouch*," cupping her gloves to her face, and whimpering. I felt **terrible**, and I reached out with both arms to hug her, apologizing as I did so. I no sooner got out the words, "I'm **so sorry**, when **bam**, I felt the sting of a straight right, directly to my *nose,* as I was reaching around her. Kerri responded, "**Don't** do that **again**, that really **hurt**!" We laughed about it (me mostly), and I was **much** more cautious after that (for my own sake).

Fortunately, my cousin Bob, with his wife Laurie and family came down to visit the second week we were there. Bob had boxed in the Golden Gloves in High School (as had Easy Ridder), he was about my weight, slightly taller with more reach, and he always stayed in pretty good shape. Bob was a good boxer, he was fast, hit hard, and gave me some good sparing for a few rounds every day. Bob also ran with me every day, and helped me get prepared for the spring Olympic trials. Bob and Laurie, and Kerri and I got along very well, and enjoyed many fun days and evenings together, both in Florida, and later in California (in Lake Tahoe), where we vacationed together the following year.

Kerri and Doug (Doug with black eye).

The relationship between Kerri and I blossomed, and we took turns visiting one another. Many friends warned us that long distance relationships don't work, and twenty-five hundred miles **certainly** qualified as long distance. Each time we spent two weeks together, it was **fantastic**, and we fell more deeply in love. Even so, it was very *difficult* to say good-by, each time we faced the average two-month separation between visits, and we experienced the pain that accompanies long distance relationships. Regardless, our love grew stronger and we endured, "Holding On."

Doug and Kerri in Bonita Springs, Florida, 1988.

Doug and Kerri in Florida, winter 1988.

Kerri and Doug at airport, winter 1988.

Business

FEI was growing very well, and I combined the businesses. CRRI (which I was now sole owner of, having bought out my partner), and DFCC were converted to wholly owned subsidiaries of FEI. Kerri and I had become reacquainted with a couple of classmates at our class reunion, Tom and Sally Moyers, who had been personal friends to each of us in high school. Tom and Sally got together in high school, and never broke up. They were married after college, and had three children, two boys and a girl, and they were in the motor-home sales/ service business, at the time of our twenty-year high school class reunion. Their business got into financial trouble shortly after our reunion however, and they lost it.

I needed management help, and I talked Tom into coming to work for FEI, which worked out well. Tom has a good business head (having majored in accounting in college), and we got along terrifically well. Tom learned the business quickly, and soon his two sons, Todd and Chad came to work for FEI (DFCC) as well. Previous to hiring Tom, I had hired a manager Bill Slate, who is a great guy, but FEI had more work than Bill and I could handle, and he and Tom got along well.

Neither Tom nor Bill knew much about landfills, machinery, horses or cattle, but it didn't take long for them to be exposed. One particular day we had some cattle break through a fence, and I got each of them into a saddle to help me round them up. We had an average of four hundred trucks per day coming through the FEI front gates, it could

Sally with grandbaby, Tom Moyers, and Doug.

be nerve racking, and it did them both good to get out of the office from time to time. Tom roared in tears of laughter (does to this day, whenever we recall the incident), when we returned from the all-afternoon roundup, and Bill dropped his drawers, and requested us to inspect his bottom for blisters. Tom indignantly exclaimed, "Bill, **get out of here**. We're not lookin' at your **ass**!"

On another occasion, in the middle of one of Michigan's many drenching spring rains, as we were trying to install a manhole (under the most impossible conditions), in the mud, under a deadline, I saw a side of Bill that I love. When Bill and I both simultaneously, slipped and fell to our knees in the clay mud, exhausted, Bill looked over to me, and noticing my frustration with the futility of what we were trying to accomplish, Bill started to sing lyrics from a popular hit tune at the time, "Don't worry, be happy," and I cracked up. Bill had a way about him, of making light of intense moments, and of not taking life too seriously, which in **our business**, really helped.

I often make the statement (which I believe to be true) that everything happens for a reason (happens as it should). When I had broken my knuckle my first time back in the ring, I became acquainted, and friends with my doctor's receptionist/secretary (Jill), who later came to work for FEI as a very proficient bookkeeper. Bill and Jill hit it off right away, soon were married, and are happy raising a family together to this day. I'm not proposing that their relationship was one of the reasons I broke my knuckle, but I do believe that things happen for a reason, sometimes many interconnected reasons, and often later in our lives, many of those pieces fit together and make sense.

I worked shoulder to shoulder with both of Tom's sons, who are hard workers, good-natured young men, and I became friends with them both. Often in the spring, after FEI closed for the day, Tom would swing by a cornfield, which I was helping to prepare for planting, flag down the tractor I was in, and hand me a cold beer. What a **welcome** sight that was, and a nice break in a long evening I still had ahead of me. Whenever Kerri was in town visiting, we got together with Tom and Sally, and the four of us went out to dinner, and did things together (golfing, fishing, etc.). We had many wonderful times together, in and out of the business, and created countless fabulous memories.

Because I had inspired the original House Bills in the early 1980's (discussed earlier), I was appointed by the Governor (re-appointed by a subsequent Governor), and served five years on the State of Michigan "Hazardous Waste Management Planning Committee," coordinating with other committee members to develop and implement the first state "Hazardous Waste Management Plan" (required by Act 64). Similarly, I was appointed by the Kent County Board of Commissioners, and served six years on the "Kent County Solid Waste Management Planning Committee," helping to develop, write, and implement the first "Kent County Solid Waste Management Plan" (required by Act 641). While drafting language in the original House Bill, and in the numerous speeches I delivered to the House, the Senate, and the "Act 641 Rules Committee," I had made certain that the Act contained language, which required counties to include properly licensed "existing facilities" in county plans.

Kent County (like other counties/municipalities in the state) was in the solid waste disposal business (competing with private enterprise), and would benefit greatly, by putting private companies (like FEI) out of business, and that could not be trusted. In fact, by the mid-eighties, Kent County installed a $100 million "Mass-Burn" solid waste incinerator, only five miles from the FEI site, and when the county's $45/ton tipping fee (gate disposal rate), necessary to pay off the huge debt, would not attract enough waste to fuel the incinerator, (FEI's tipping fee was $26/ton), Kent County **needed** FEI out of business. Kent County's **goal** was to **burn** everything FEI was recycling, even though mass-burn incineration had already been proven not to be a "viable waste disposal solution." Mass burn incinerators had already been banned in many parts of the United States, and throughout the world, because they are known to release harmful contaminants into the atmosphere, which damage the ozone layer, as well as all life breathing the air. With the knowledge of global warming today, it is unlikely that the Kent County mass-burn incinerator would ever have been permitted.

In 1988, following the purchase of the stock of my CRRI partner, through an idea suggested by my friend Jeff Dahlman, we (FEI) began to develop plans to convert CRRI from a Type I (Hazardous Waste) TSD facility, to a "Hazardous Materials (By-Product) Recovery Park." Jeff has been active in the "waste-field" throughout his career, but technically (initially) on the opposite side of the fence as me. He had an executive position with the West Michigan Environmental Action Council when we first met in the early seventies, and we were positioned as potential adversaries. However, in a very short time we came to know, and respect one another, became hard fast friends, and remain so today.

Jeff was always very politically aware, had his finger on the pulse of the waste industry, and has helped me many times, by steering me in the right direction. Jeff is also a very good journalist, well respected by all sides in the waste industry community, and in 1980

(Left to right) Jeff Dahlman, Doug Dane, and Dan Weaver.

he started a biweekly publication known as the "Michigan Waste Report." The Michigan Waste Report (later, *currently,* Waste Information Management Systems, *WIMS*) is known as "The Source" of waste information throughout Michigan (and several surrounding states), and with the assistance of his beautiful wife Lyn (also an excellent journalist, *and friend*), it continues today.

The "Park" we planned would house tenant companies from around the world, to recycle and reclaim many of the same types of hazardous waste, which CRRI had previously been treating, storing, and disposing (land-filling), along with numerous other types of hazardous waste. The Park would include an Energy Center, designed to incinerate any non-recyclable materials, and generate energy (steam, heat, and electricity), for use by Park Tenants, with any excess electricity sold into the power grid. CRRI had plenty of room (415 acres), and was in a prime location for such a park, adjacent to Kent County International Airport, near the Grand Rapids metropolitan area, and mid-way between Chicago, and Detroit (both large hazardous waste generating cities).

All of the staff, and most of the workforce at FEI (by this time 60–70 employees strong) were very excited about the prospect, as were Kerri and I. During 1989 and 1990, we held meetings with the County and Township, with positive results regarding our plan, and we held a press conference/news release (*aired on a couple of local major networks*), announcing our intentions. The *Grand Rapids Press* ran an article on the park, which made the headlines. I met and became friends with a dynamic local businessman, who was developing a 300

April 20, 1990, *Grand Rapids Press* **headline on CRRI Park.**

acre business/industrial park, adjacent to the CRRI property, and whom was helpful and supportive in regard to our project (which could in turn supply energy to tenants of his park).

Kerri and I (and the others at FEI) believed that our plan was sound. Through research, we discovered that recycling technology had evolved immensely, and in other countries, many of the lacquers, thinners, heavy metal sludge, and other types of "hazardous waste" were being recycled, and not disposed of in a landfill, as they were here in the United States. No one had ever done anything of this nature before, and existing by-product recovery companies (from around the globe), which we contacted as possible future tenants, were enthusiastic about our concept of integrating by-product recovery, and unifying the permitting process.

We envisioned and planned to develop similar "By-Product Recovery Parks" throughout the world, and (in that light) changed our company name from Fenske Enterprises Inc, to FEI International Ltd. I soon began taking steps (meeting with county/city officials, realtors, landowners, etc.) in Santa Barbara County, to develop a second By-Product Recovery Park, and we developed a "Prospectus" describing the concept, and the first two parks.

Kerri and I, together with staff, developed an FEI International "Corporate Mission:"

"FEI International's mission is to draw together the collective intelligence of mankind to create a safer, healthier environment on this planet.

Our mission is to effect the environment physically, and to help expand the conscious awareness of humanity.

The company will revolutionize how materials and energy are recovered from by-products through a worldwide network of by-product research and recovery operations.

The company will also revolutionize food production through the introduction of biodynamic farming and chemical-free meat, fish and poultry."

I began the process of switching DFCC farming operations from traditional "commercial fertilizer" farming, to "biodynamic farming" (no traditional NPK fertilizer, *nitrogen, phosphorus, potassium,* pesticides, herbicides, etc. utilized), a transformation that takes several years, because our soils and plants are "addicted." I learned through reading books like "Secrets of the Soil" by Peter Thompkins, and other research, that there are as many microorganisms in a hand-full of "healthy" soil, as there are people on this planet, and that our use of commercial fertilizer (a derivative of the petroleum industry), *a multi-billion dollar business*, is depleting our soil of natural microorganisms. Without their necessary "life," our soils are not able to release the minerals, and nutrients that plants need, and most of the fruits, grains, vegetables, and other food that we eat (including beef, pork, poultry, eggs, dairy products, and commercially raised fish) is nutrient deficient, leaving humans nutrient deficient, and more susceptible to disease. I remembered the wonderful taste of a tomato, cucumber, or watermelon, fresh off the vine in our garden as a boy (with only manure for fertilizer), and I wanted that back.

By 1989 the FEI home base solid waste business was booming. With the knowledge that every reality is first a vision, we constructed a site master plan, and a three-D model of the 262-acre FEI property, depicting all existing and future buildings, and structures, including a waterfront hotel and marina, as well as an eighteen-hole golf course (over some of the land-filled acreage). We continued to win various state and local recycling, and environmental awards (with our focus on recycling), and FEI was in the process of purchasing its largest customer (ABME), a local solid waste hauling company, with 120 employees ($15 million/year gross revenue).

ABME (A Better Managed Environment) was initiated in the 1960's, as a one open "stake-truck" waste hauling business by Bill Stark, one of Fenske Enterprises first customers. Bill was a hard worker, with a good business head, and grew his business well over the years, eventually taking on a couple of partners. Without a contract with a landfill however, as the largest privately owned waste trucking company in Grand Rapids, Bill and his partners felt very vulnerable.

They became very worried, when the national aggressive public companies, Waste National Inc. (WNI), and Benning Elliot Inc. (BEI), moved into the Grand Rapids area, and before long, through purchases and political maneuvering, both of these public companies got into the landfill business. When I made them a fair offer to purchase ABME, and included a discounted disposal rate, and transfer of FEI waste hauling accounts over to ABME during the purchase, they accepted, and we entered into an agreement. We started the transfer of hauling accounts, and the discounted disposal rate immediately. This acquisition would bring our total FEI work force to approximately 200, and our annual gross income to around $25 million (which we felt was pretty respectable).

FEI International CEO Doug Fenske displays the Master Plan for the company's updated World Headquarters in Grand Rapids, Michigan. Fenske managed the company for 15 years prior to purchasing it in 1986. He is recognized as one of today's innovators in by-product research and recovery.

Doug with FEI site Master Plan, 1989.

Our business future looked *very* promising, with *$950 million* in landfill airspace, on the 262 acre FEI site (with 140 adjacent acres under option). The airspace would last FEI eighty to ninety years, at the 1000–1500 TPD (Tons Per Day) volume of solid waste, which FEI averaged, even if FEI saved **no** airspace through recycling, *and* FEI was recycling more than **ever**! We had recently completed construction of a new 62,000 sq. ft. MRF (Materials Recovery Facility) building, housing a new waste recyclables baler (the **largest** on the

3-D model of FEI, 1989.

market), crushers, shredders, sorting mezzanines, and conveyors. The
new MRF, in addition to our existing 23,000 sq. ft. MRF, now made
the FEI business, the largest "all in-door" solid waste recycling operation in West Michigan.

In the early-1980's, I had been contacted by a large aggregate company in Grand Haven (thirty miles west of Grand Rapids), with a partnership proposition, if I would assist the company in obtaining
permits to start a solid waste landfill. Even though their offer was
very attractive, I had turned the offer down, because of the geology
(high groundwater table) at their chosen site. While touring their site
however, I noticed a large building sitting vacant. The building had
been constructed and used for only a short time, to store excavated
clay soils (out of the wet Michigan weather), which were then super-
heated to produce lightweight, decorative stone landscape material.
When the fuel crunch hit in the late 1970's however, the aggregate
company had abandoned the fuel intensive operation, and the virtually new building sat idle for a number of years, until I discovered it.

I purchased the building for Fenske Enterprises, and with some of
our own men and equipment, and two builders (Rog and Ray), who
were good friends of mine, and were actually by then working full-
time for FEI (since we were always building, and expanding), we dismantled, and moved the building thirty miles to our site. We then con-

tracted with a steel erection company (Valley Steel, Inc.), owned by my acquaintance Denny (the company which reconstructed the barn at my former residence). Valley Steel, with assistance from FEI men and equipment, reconstructed the building on the FEI property.

When complete, the massive new MRF building was 200 feet wide, and 310 feet long, with *fifty feet* of headroom (floor to roof beams clearance), and all new steel siding. The building's excellent floor to ceiling clearance was necessary for raising forty-five yard roll-offs to full height, for off-loading. It was also wide open for moving trucks and machinery around, with only one row of support beams down the center, giving it 100 feet of clear span on either side, for the entire length of the building. We constructed massive concrete pillars (four feet square, and twelve feet high) around the center support beams, to protect them, and a four-foot high concrete wall around the entire building perimeter. Our construction included four indoor truck bays, each housing two floor-level, side-by-side forty-five foot trailers (to receive recycled materials), as well as eight enormous sliding doors, four at either end, for truck traffic.

When it was poured, we embedded the entire concrete building floor, with tons of iron ore additives, for abrasive resistance. Though

The outside of MRF, in construction.

this project took several years to complete, the new MRF looked very impressive (was superior to any I had seen), and this "state-of-the-art" recycling system operated impeccably. The MRF included four sorting lines, (fed by two large conveyors) with drop-shoots (for sorted materials), which fed cross conveyors, leading to other crushers, shredders, tumblers, balers etc., for further processing. Truckloads of waste material entering FEI, (which appeared to contain at least fifty per cent salvageable material), were diverted to the MRF for sorting/processing. We worked cooperatively with several municipal agencies, in employing numerous agency assisted individuals for sorting, which worked out very well for the employees, and for FEI. FEI averaged forty percent recovery, on waste materials processed through its MRF's, and averaged several hundred tons per day of recycled glass, cardboard, paper, plastic, wood and metal, sorted from mixed loads of waste material.

Our baler in action. This powerful machine can bale everything from mixed refuse to heavy grade cardboard. Shown here is a pile of corrugated almost 30 feet tall, which will emerge neatly baled in under an hour.

Baler inside MRF with corrugated.

Our MRF system is a network of conveyors which carry commingled materials to areas where the waste is sorted and separated. Shown here are incoming waste conveyors which allow sorting of glass, corrugated, plastic, metal and wood into bins housed underneath. In these bins, materials wait to be baled, compacted, crushed, densified or granulated.

Sorting lines inside MRF.

FEI continued to purchase "source-separated materials," such as corrugated, high-grade paper, plastic, glass and metal. FEI collected most of the source-separated recyclables such as corrugated and news-blank, with its fleet of semi-trailers. FEI collected other materials in roll-off trucks, including various plastics, high-grade paper (computer printout, etc.), glass, and metal. Much of this material was co-mingled with other types of waste, and delivered to the FEI site for sorting and processing, along with co-mingled waste materials from many other hauling companies. Prior to our 62,000 sq. ft. MRF, we had been processing co-mingled waste materials in our front (23,000 sq. ft.) "Paper Plant," but the new MRF was much larger, and we were able to significantly increase our recycled tonnages. Cardboard, newspaper, and high-grade paper were cleaned, sorted, and baled into 2000 pound, mill-ready bales, metals sorted, ground into containers, or shredded and baled, glass sorted, and crushed into cullet, and all materials were shipped in FEI trucks to various recycling mills and foundries, in and out of the state.

Glass enters our MRF by the case, and rides special glass conveyors for sorting into various color categories. Remaining cardboard cases move to the corrugated processing area, while each type of glass drops into the bins shown here.

Glass bins inside MRF (green, brown, and clear).

By 1989, the relationship between Kerri and I was also booming, and on June 4, 1989, we were married in Santa Barbara. Not long after we were married, Kerri's brother-in-law Nick (Susie's husband) had a massive stroke. After a couple of weeks in intensive care, Nick passed away almost immediately, upon transport to a rehabilitation facility. Nick was only fifty-nine at the time, worked a very physical job as a carpet layer, seemed to be in good shape, and it came as a total shock to all of us. I had only met Nick a few times, but I really liked him, and I was looking forward to developing a relationship with my new brother-in-law. Susie and Nick were very close, had been married twenty years, and Nick's untimely illness and death devastated Susie and her daughter. Kerri and I kind of took Susie and Nicole, who was nineteen and their only child together, under our wing (*Nick had adult children from a previous marriage*). Susie (and sometimes Nicole) would accompany us on vacations. I became very close to both of them, we had many laughs and fun times together, as well as deep spiritual discussions, and I remain close to both of them today. *As of this writing, many years have passed since Nick's death, and Susie is now happily re-married, as is Nicole (now with three children), both to loving husbands, Barry and Paul.*

Kerri and I bought a home in Santa Barbara, and a home in Grand Rapids (suburb Cascade), and in the early years of our marriage we continued to live a good deal of the time apart, with one of us staying in each home. Kerri's life, since 1978, had been in Santa Barbara, and even though by 1989 Kerri had sold her business to a long-term employee, and had lived with me in Grand Rapids for a number of months, she missed Santa Barbara, and her friends and family tremendously. When she left Grand Rapids, I just went back to planning my day around my call to Kerri, which was always the most important part of both of our days. Kerri stayed (lived) at our Santa Barbara home, with our daughter Tamara, who touched me deeply, when within a short time (not having had a good relationship with her biological father) she started to call me Dad, and legally changed her last name to mine.

Tamara's name changed again a few years later when she married, and though her marriage to John (a wonderful young man) didn't last, they remain friends, he became a part of our family, and we still consider him that today. Tamara and John brought a beautiful spirit into this world (our grandson), named Sebastian, who was *born* wise, full of love, and whom **everyone** loves. I became very close to Seb, especially whenever the two of us spent time together alone.

On one of my stays in Santa Barbara, when he was only four, Seb and I packed a tent, and went camping and fishing together on Lake Cachuma, twenty miles north of Santa Barbara. After a day of fishing, a campfire dinner, an evening roasting marshmallows, watching stars, and telling stories, Seb asked me, as we crawled into our sleeping bags on our first night, "Grandpa, there aren't any bears out here are there?" Seb was obviously quite concerned about bears, because he had posed similar questions to me previous times, throughout the day and evening. After I unheedingly responded that there might be a few bears, but that they live higher up in the mountains, Seb countered with, "They can't get into our tent though, can they?" I assured him that he had nothing to worry about, because even if one did, "Grandpa

Above: Sebastian with Tamara and Kerri.
Below: Seb and Grandpa Doug camping.

would chase him out of our tent with the hatchet, placed right next to my sleeping bag." Seb seemed comforted by this, and as he relaxed more deeply into his sleeping bag, before drifting off to sleep, Seb quietly stated, "Grandpa, this is the **best** day of my **life!**"

I had so much going on at FEI that I could never be away for very long, so most of the time I lived at our home in Cascade. Our (Kerri's) son Brian (17 years old) had lived with his mother, ever since Kerri and her two children left Michigan in 1976. Since 1987 (as previously mentioned), for the first time since their divorce, Brian was living with his biological father in Grand Rapids (suburb city Jenison), and he was in his senior year in high school. Brian was having some difficulty living with his father, and through a mutual decision, Brian moved in with me. Brian and I hit it off very well, before long we bonded, and Brian started calling me Dad. He was soon working part-time (later full-time) for FEI, and DFCC. My son Brandon (by then eight years old) visited, and stayed with us every other weekend, and he and Brian became friends, as did Brian, Todd and Chad (Tom and Sally's boys).

Boxing/Business Connections

Shortly after my first year back in the "Gloves," Morey lost the lease on his boxing building, so we converted a vacant building at FEI into a boxing gym, and opened the "FENSKE BOXING CLUB." We made some improvements, and the gym had a full size ring, heavy bags, speed bags, a fully mirrored shadow boxing room, a weight lifting room, and a shower/dressing room, with a sauna, scales etc. Unfortunately Morey had a stroke, shortly after the first season, and didn't live to enjoy the gym for very long.

I met and became friends with a guy named Bill Spanora, who was very "media savvy," and I nicknamed him "Visa-Bill" (short for "Visibility Bill"). Bill had been around the boxing profession for years, in fact he had been associated with Mohammed Ali some years earlier. Visa-Bill came to the gym many nights, and watched myself and others train. He promoted the gym, as well as FEI (gave us "visibility) whenever he could, and Bill soon became a good friend. In the type of business we were in, some positive media "Visibility" is always helpful.

On a future occasion in Walker, we applied for a landfill expansion permit from the MDNR, which required a zoning change from Walker City. The zoning change from "Agricultural" to "Heavy Industrial" seemed unlikely, when a neighboring township supervisor (completely as a surprise to me) stood up at a scheduled hearing, and started talking against FEI, and our expansion, making various **false accusations**, such as "FEI was contaminating the Grand River." Just when I thought that we were not going to be successful, the Walker Chairman (also Mayor of Walker) dropped his gavel, told the neighboring supervisor he was totally out of order, reminded him that he did not even **live** in Walker, and called for a vote, which passed *unanimously!* Just like *that,* the Zoning Board granted FEI zoning for an expansion, which gave us an additional **fifty million dollars** worth of landfill airspace! The Zoning Board Chairman met with me after the meeting, told me that he had read a little about my "comeback" in boxing, and the "Fenske Boxing Club" (thanks to "Visa-Bill"), and stated that he admired what we were trying to do. He went on to say that his next-door neighbor (whom he had informed) had a son who trained at our gym, and that it had really helped him.

Brian and I trained nightly at the Fenske Boxing Club (often sparring one another), as did some FEI employees (including Tom, Todd, and Chad) and occasionally Brandon (on his weekends with me) accompanied us as well. On an average night, twenty-five to thirty interested local youths were trained at the gym, by a professional boxer/trainer (Curtis Issah), free of charge, which was one of our ways of giving something back to the community. Curtis (from Kalamazoo, Michigan) was a good trainer, and a good friend, who gave boxing his all, sparing with myself and several other competitive boxers, most every night we were open, then giving us a vigorous rub-down after training.

Boxing often has an appeal to "mis-fits," who do not fit the "mold," or fit into "clicks," or team sports in school. Many times I would witness insecure teens drag their feet, "round shouldered," into the gym on their first night, and then later see them march out "square shouldered," proud and erect, after a few weeks of training. More than once, I had a parent express how their son's grades, attitude, and attendance in school had improved significantly, after starting boxing, and finding a place where they did "fit in."

In 1989, Brian fought in a Golden Gloves toe-to-toe battle, which drew a standing ovation, and was tagged in the *Grand Rapids Press*, as "**The-Fight-of-The-Night**," and made me **so** proud of him that I still brag about him, and that fight today. Brian gave boxing **everything** he had, as he does everything he tackles in life, and he deserved every echo of the applause following his bout, with not a fan in the Civic Auditorium left seated. Brian's performance in his bout inspired me in my own, which I fought and won a short time later that same night. Under Curtis Issah's training, Fenske Boxing Club had two Golden Gloves State Champions that year, who went on to win a first, and a fourth in the nation. I personally won the 1989 West Michigan Golden Gloves Championship, and runner-up State Championship.

A business associate, and good friend of mine named Dan Weaver (who worked closely with, and for Jeff Dahlman) became inspired by my return to the ring, and even though he had very little boxing experience, he decided to take up the sport. Dan is fifteen years younger than I am, but very wise, and a hard charger. As a teenager, Dan had been in a serious car accident, which took a brothers' life (a brother whom Dan was very close to), and *nearly* took Dan's. In fact, Dan had a *"near death experience,"* and the paramedic's were only able to revive him after an extreme effort, actually giving up for a short time. His experience matured him far beyond his years, and in spite of the excessive injuries he had suffered, Dan persevered in most every physical challenge he placed before himself. Kevin Whitcomp retired after a couple of state championships, and even though smaller, and far less experienced than I, Dan became my sparing partner, pounding out the rounds with me night after night. Although he was green to the sport, Dan was a quick study, a hard puncher, and despite giving up experience and some size to me, he gave me everything I was looking for (*and then some*). Dan helped prepare me for the Gloves, and to improve a great deal, and in those years we became very close friends.

Ever since I had started my comeback in boxing, I had the idea in my head, that I could win the West Michigan "Golden Glove Award" again. Many others told me to forget it, stating, "No one in history has ever won the 'Golden Glove Award' *twice.*" I was told by many that, "This would be like winning the 'Heisman Trophy' *twice,*" and that, "It just wasn't **possible**, had *never* been done!" Still, I could not get over the idea, and I trained, and boxed my **heart out**, envisioning receiving the "Golden Glove Award." On the last day of the 1989 Golden Gloves tournament, when I heard my name announced over the loudspeaker, requesting that I report ringside, I *knew* why!

At forty years of age, I became the only man in history to win the "Golden Glove Award" *twice!* I was **thrilled!** After I was presented the award, while still in the ring, I asked for the microphone, then verbally, and symbolically, dedicated the award back to the crowd, stating (to a standing ovation) that those present were the **true** spirit of the Golden Gloves. On numerous future occasions, when I was presented with the fact that this was the only time in history, that anyone had ever won the "Golden Glove Award" **twice**, I would laughingly respond, "It had been so long (*21 years*) between awards, that they probably **forgot** they gave it to me the first time!"

Soon after the Golden Glove Award, with a desire to learn from the best, I traveled to Miami Beach, Florida, and trained under Angelo Dundee, who had previously trained (most notably) boxers like Mohammed Ali, Sugar Ray Leonard, and George Foreman. After I explained to Angelo that I desired to win the "Golden Gloves National Championship," and requested his assistance, Angelo questioned my age. "How old are ya kid?" I replied, "I'm *forty*. Does my *age* scare you?" I will never forget Angelo's response, "I'm **sixty-nine**! Does mine scare **you**? Get into the ring with Bruno here, and we'll see what you got!"

The boxer he pointed to looked like a buffed NFL lineman, and *shocked* I replied, "Crawl into the ring with that **gorilla**? I'm a light heavyweight! He must weight **250 pounds**!" Angelo came back with, "260 actually, but you should be faster than him 'Chuck,' at least for your sake, I **hope** you are!" When I reminded him that my name was Doug, Angelo just replied, "Yeah." I crawled into the ring, and as

Doug with Angelo Dundee, 1988.

Doug with Angelo Dundee, in boxing gym.

Angelo laced up my gloves, I asked him if there was anything he could tell me about the guy I was about to face, that would help me. He responded, "**Yeah**, he hits harder than **hell**! Stay away from him, and don't get **hit**!"

I *thanked* him for his **advice**, actively punching, dodging and weaving for several rounds, trying to stay in one piece. Angelo finally stated, "That's enough. Come on over here, and I'll take your gloves off." As he did, trying to get a read on his impression, I asked, "Well, what'd ya think?" Angelo's only response was, "It's a *damn* good thing you were *busy!*" He dropped the gloves on a table, and headed for the door, *leaving the gym,* with out saying another **word**! As I was puffing to catch my breath, I shouted out, "**Well**, are you going to train me or **not**?" Barely audible, as he rounded the corner out the door, Angelo uttered, "Gym opens at *eight AM,* Chuck. Don't be *late!*" I hollered, "**You won't be sorry**," as I realized I had shown enough potential, to attract the interest of one of the **best trainers** in the world! I trained daily for the next few weeks with Angelo, and again, on another occasion. I have not **yet** won the National Championship, but I learned some very important things, and I made a good association, with one whom I will always consider a friend.

Once I "officially" moved to California in 1990, even though still spending most of my time in Michigan, California became my state of residence, and I continued to pursue my boxing in California. I began my training, at Primo Boxing Club, in Santa Barbara, operated/managed by Joe and Jean Pommier, where I still train today. I have made many good friends at Primo, and have been fortunate enough to have some good sparing competition, such as with ex-middle weight state champion George Calderone, then for years to follow, and currently Rudy Lopez, along with trainers Joe Pommier, and Mark Lee. Since there is no Golden Gloves tournament in Santa Barbara, I have traveled to Los Angles (the nearest major city) each year to compete.

Unfortunately the California USABF (now USA Boxing) would not honor the TRO that I had been issued in Michigan, in 1988. I went back to court, and obtained a California TRO, which forced USA Boxing to allow me to compete in California. LA Times interviewed me, shortly after picking up the story in the "CA Legal News," and asked me, "Didn't I feel that it was a disadvantage to be in the ring, with boxers more than twenty years younger than me?" When I responded, "Yeah, it probably is, but how **else** are they going to learn," the reporter responded, "Oh, you think that it is a disadvantage for **them**?" to which I responded, "**Yeah**, don't **you**?" Even though I knew what the reporter meant, I do believe that much of age is a *state of mind.*

The *Santa Barbara News Press* ran an article on me the following spring, which made the headlines "Still In The Ring At Forty-Something." I have won the Southern California Golden Gloves Championship several times, and runner-up in state, but with much resistance. It seems that I must overwhelmingly dominate my opponent, and stop him, or knock him out, in order to win. There are people who believe that I am too old to compete, and some of the officials may be angry, and take it *personally,* that I sued USA Boxing.

I have had numerous fights stopped by (USA Boxing referees), and given to my opponent (most often with the crowd booing the decision to stop the fight), which I am confident I could have won, had I been

Santa Barbara Ne

136th Y

.nty Edition   Santa Barbara, California, Saturday, April 27, 19

April 27, 1991

STILL IN THE RING AT FORTYSOMETHING

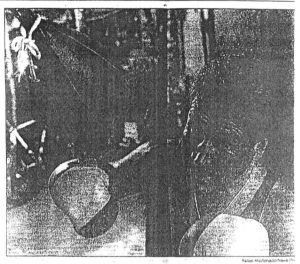

Boxer spars n court, oo

By John Lankford
News-Press Staff Writer

Like any smart boxer, Santa Barbara's Doug Fenske is taking middle age one fight at a time.

Tonight in Los Angeles, there is the fight for the state Golden Gloves title in the cruiserweight division.

Last weekend, there was the fight for the Southern California Golden Gloves championship, which Fenske won, qualifying for tonight's battle.

Before that, there was the fight with the American Amateur Boxing Federation (ABF), which has a rule prohibiting anyone over the age of 37 from competing in its tournaments. Fenske won that one, too, with the help of Lisa Frawley, a Santa Barbara attorney

Doug Fenske of Santa Barbara punches a bag while tuning up for his boxing match in Los Angeles tonight

Rafael Maldonado/News-Press

SB News Press, 04/27/91 headline article: "Still in the Ring at Forty Something."

allowed to continue. The former USA Boxing, CA Golden Gloves Tournament Manager once said to me, "The court tells us that we have to let you box, but it doesn't tell us we have to let you **win**, or **finish**!" Unfortunately, even though that particular party has retired, his attitude continues with some of the USA Boxing officials today. Regardless, with only a couple of exceptions (when I was back in Michigan, at the time the Golden Gloves tournament was held), I have entered the California Golden Gloves tournament every year, since 1990. I have been required to return to court many times to renew expired TRO's. Finally, in 2000 I obtained a permanent restraining order against USA Boxing, which restrains them from *"Preventing the plaintiff from participating, discriminating..., segregating..., or treating the plaintiff differently on the basis of his age."*

When I first sued USA Boxing in California (as part of their defense tactics), a "Masters Division" was formed, which USA Box-

Doug in LA receiving S. CA Trophy in mid-90's.

ing argued is where I belonged. The US District Judge understood, and agreed with my position however, that I was the only competitor in this newly formed division, and forcing me into the "Master's Division" (for all boxers over the age of thirty-five), would leave me fightless. The judge then issued my first TRO in California, which finally became permanent in 2000.

The year 2005 was the first year that I had any serious competition in my weight class (Light-Heavyweight, 178 pounds), in the Master's Division, so I entered the Master's, with hopes that I would get fair treatment. A good friend and trainer, ex-boxer Ron Kinney of Camarillo, CA worked my corner. I met Ron at Sylva Boxing Gym in Ventura, not far from where I worked the previous year, managing a Concrete/Asphalt recycling plant. The gym owner "George Sylva" allowed me to train at his gym, which was convenient, right on my way home from work each night. *The Santa Barbara News Press* ran my picture in the Sports Section of the 4/30/05 addition, with an article

1 | DAVID S. SILBER
ATTORNEY AT LAW
2 | 21 East Canon Perdido #213
Santa Barbara, California 93101
3 | (805) 564-8250

4 | Attorney for Plaintiff

ORIGINAL FILED

DEC 6 4 2000

COUNTY CLERK

5

6

7 | SUPERIOR COURT OF THE STATE OF CALIFORNIA

8 | FOR THE COUNTY OF LOS ANGELES

9 | CENTRAL DISTRICT

10

11 | H. DOUGLAS FENSKE,
                        Plaintiff,
12 | vs.

13 |
UNITED STATES OF AMERICA
14 | AMATEUR BOXING FEDERATION & DOES
1-20 ,
15 |
                        Defendants.
16 |

CASE NO.: BC 227102
JUDGMENT,
ORDER and INJUNCTION

17

18 | On proof made to the court's satisfaction, and good cause appearing:

19 | **IT IS ORDERED** that the above-named defendants, and each of them, and their

20 | officers, agents, employees, representatives, and all persons acting in concert or participating

21 | with them, are enjoined and restrained from engaging in, committing, or performing, directly

22 | or indirectly, by any means whatsoever, any of the following acts:

23 | a) Preventing the plaintiff from participating in any boxing competition:

24 | b) discriminating against the plaintiff based on his age;

25 | c) segregating the plaintiff based on his age or

26 | d) otherwise treating the plaintiff differently on the basis of his age.

1

2 | The court reserves jurisdiction to modify this injunction as the ends of justice may

3 | require. *THE PLAINTIFF IS AWARDED COSTS IN THE*

4 | *AMOUNT OF $191.00 . PLAINTIFF TO GIVE NOTICE*

5 | *THE CLERK IS ORDERED TO ENTER THIS*

6 | *JUDGMENT.*

7 | Dated: __DEC 0 4 2000__   __IRVING S. FEFFER__

8 | Judge of the Superior Court

State of California permanent restraining order.

titled "AN AGELESS WONDER." My competition was only thirty-six years old, but over the thirty-five year maximum age limit for the Open Division, and thereby forced into the Master's. USA Boxing "rules" only allow five years of age differential between competitors in the Master's Division, and my opponent was twenty years my junior. However, since I have a "Permanent Restraining Order" and the right to compete in the Open Division (with boxers 30 years and more younger than me), the officials agreed to waive the five-year rule.

Though I felt that I had done very well, and the officials did let me finish the bout, the decision went against me. The crowd obviously felt differently, and loudly protested the decision, which made me feel good. Dennis Heffner, who manages the "Rock Boxing Gym" in the Torrance/Carson, CA area helped Ron (who was still recovering from a serious leg fracture) work my corner. Dennis had worked my corner the previous year, when no one from my gym had showed up, and he and Ron both thought that the decision was controversial. As Primo

"I do think he's crazy, and I love it. Doug (Fenske) has so much energy, enthusiasm and spirit. He scares me."

4/30/05   **Kerri Fenske,** wife of 56-year-old boxer Doug Fenske

STEVE MALONE / NEWS-PRESS

Doug Fenske says that he has fought in over 500 fights during his 16-year career and has never been knocked out.

AN AGELESS WONDER

FENSKE, 56, IS BY FAR THE OLDEST BOXER AT TODAY'S GOLDEN GLOVES IN L.A.

SB News Press—"An Ageless Wonder."

Boxing trainer Mark Lee put it, "The people **knew** who **won!**" Maybe it will not be any different in the Master's Division, but I went right back to training. As I put it to Joe and Jean Pommier, "I'll out last them! I'll just keep coming back until I wear them out!" Regardless, the training keeps me fit, and I love the thrill of the competition (and if I am honest, the spotlight attention as well).

As a total surprise to me (brought to my attention by a neighbor), my picture in the *Santa Barbara News Press*, Spring 2005, made a special section in the January 1, 2006 SBNP, titled "2005 THE YEAR IN PHOTOGRAPHS," and was in color, centered, and the largest picture (14 x 14 inches) on a two page spread of pictures, titled 'KOCK-OUT IMAGES." The picture/publicity inspired me to give it another try, although honestly, I never really gave up on the idea, or stopped training. Maybe there is some truth to the lyrics in the 1970's Simon and Garfunkel song titled "The Boxer," *"In the shadows stands a boxer, and a fighter by his trade, who carries the reminder, of every glove that struck him down, or cut him, till he cried out, in his anger and his pain, I am leaving, I am leaving, but the fighter still remains."* Maybe I'm just a "die-hard," or maybe boxing is addicting; who knows. I do have plenty of "reminders" (from 500 plus fights), including a six-times broken nose, broken (crushed) knuckles, broken fingers, broken ear drums, cracked ribs, etc., but in addition to my

SB News Press **pic and article "2005 the Year in Photographs."**

appreciation for the condition the training keeps me in, the pain of the sport helps me (*in some bizarre way*), to deal with the pain of what has happened to my life's work, and my plans (to be explained).

When the 2006 six tournament was only weeks away, just as I was about to call him, to see if he would work my corner again, Ron Kinney gave me a call. I was a couple pounds over the Light-heavyweight, 178-pound limit, at the Golden Gloves tournament sign-up/ weigh-in, which USA Boxing held one week before the tournament start, so I opted to enter the "Cruiserweight," 201-pound class. There were no Master's Division opponents in the upper weight classes, so I entered the "Open Division." I received bye's into the Southern California finals, where I met Paul Statzer, a "buffed," fit, twenty-eight year old from San Diego.

In the later part of the first round, the referee gave me a "standing-eight-count," which is standard procedure, when one of the fighters is hurt, and it costs the injured fighter some points. I had been caught by a punch, but I was not affected, and I protested to the referee, to no avail. In the second round, I landed a solid left hook, which staggered my opponent, and knocked **him** back into the ropes, where I went after him. The referee stepped in and stopped the bout, giving **me** another "standing-eight-count," to the crowd's roar of objection! I threw up my hands in protest, and both Ron and Dennis Heffner (who was helping Ron again) shouted at the referee, "You're giving the **eight-count** to the **wrong** fighter!"

Not long after that, the referee stopped the bout, and amidst our protests, as well as disapproval from the crowd, gave the fight to my opponent. I may not have won the contest, but my opponent seemed to be tiring, I was not, and I would like to have had the chance to find out. It appears the resentment over my restraining order continues.

I went right back into training for the 2007 season, running three miles a day, working the bags, and sparing at the gym most every night. Unfortunately, about two weeks before the Golden Gloves tournament was scheduled to start (March 2007), I got a little too aggressive in a sparing match, and chased my opponent into the corner. I threw a right designed to drop him, he ducked, and I hit the boxing-ring steel corner-post. Primo's trainer/manager Joe hollered, "Man Doug, why'd you swing so **hard**!" Rubbing my hand, and wincing from the pain I replied, "Cause he made me **mad**!" Joe came back with, "Well if you'd a hit **em**, you'd a **killed** em! Ya hit the corner post so hard, ya cracked the **welds**!" I said, "Oh, that's probably been cracked loose for a long time." Joe replied, "The *hell* it has. Look at those cracks, they're *fresh!*" I assured Joe that the corner-post was okay for the time being, and when my hand felt better, I would repair it, but as it turned out my hand was broken, and my competition in the 2007 Golden Gloves tournament was over. After a couple of months, my hand healed just fine, and I went right back to training, full well knowing that I hadn't yet **peaked**!

23

FEI under the Gun

The waste "Flow Control" ordinances that Kent County had adopted in the early eighties, to force solid waste into the "designated" Kent County solid waste disposal facility (previously its landfills), by the late eighties, required delivery to the "Kent County Mass-Burn Incinerator." The ordinances (signed with various municipalities/townships within Kent County) required delivery of solid waste (by all licensed haulers) to Kent County's mass-burn incinerator, enough to meet its needs. The ordinances were absolutely necessary (required), in order for Kent County to secure the funds, through sale of bonds, for construction of the County's **one hundred million dollar** mass-burn incinerator, which was *outdated* by the time it was constructed.

On many occasions, we saw county employees parked outside FEI's front gate, watching and counting trucks entering FEI, in an attempt to catch FEI accepting "flow-controlled" waste. The solid waste disposal rate at the Kent County incinerator was $45/ton (which was necessary to pay off the huge capitol investment), as opposed to $26/ton at FEI, and (although 15–20 miles from Grand Rapids) even lower at both the WNI, and BEI landfills. Because the disposal rate was so much higher, Kent County *needed* to **force** solid waste into its incinerator! However, "Waste Flow Control" was later (May 1994) declared "unconstitutional" by the Federal Supreme Court, in a landmark case, titled "Carbone vs. Clarkston."

Even though they operated their own landfills, long before the Federal Supreme Court ruling, oddly, both WNI, and BEI started cooperatively delivering enough solid waste to the Kent County incinerator to meet its needs, and continued to do so, even after "Flow Control" was declared "unconstitutional." Both companies are huge public companies (a couple of the largest waste companies in the world), with annual sales in the multi-billion dollar range, and both are purportedly mafia based, and controlled. WNI was purportedly started, and is purportedly controlled by the Dutch mafia in Chicago; BEI was purportedly started, and is purportedly controlled by the Italian mafia in New Jersey, and something did not seem right.

The mass-burn incinerator was designed to incinerate up to 650 tons/day. The solid waste generated within the county at the time was around 2500 tons/day, and even though the incinerator seldom operated at capacity, keeping the incinerator fed was a huge commitment. WNI's and BEI's actions made no *sense* to *me,* or to *anyone else* in the waste industry, because both companies were doing all they could to attract more waste to **their own** landfills, (through lowering disposal rates, monthly large tonnage discounts, etc.). Secondly, both companies had expended vast sums of capital, and effort (for years) fighting "flow-control" on a national level, as well as locally, through contributions to the Greater Grand Rapids Waste Disposal Association. When WNI, and BEI were questioned about their "unforced" delivery of waste to the incinerator, both companies gave the same explanation, that it made sense economically, for them to deliver light (partial) truck-loads to the incinerator, as opposed to the 30–40 mile round trip to their own landfills. Both companies however, for many years prior, had been FEI customers, and the rate at FEI (even more convenient than the County Incinerator) was **$19/ton less**! When questioned why not then just deliver the "light (partial) truck-loads" to FEI, as they always had in the past, both companies had, "*no comment.*"

Both of these public companies had been *major* financial contributors to the Greater Grand Rapids Waste Disposal Association, to cover legal fees in the former "flow-control" lawsuit, filed by the GGRWDA. The lawsuit challenged the legality of the waste "Flow Control Ordinances" that Kent County had adopted (in its attempt to force waste into its landfills, *now the County Mass-Burn incinerator*), and had been filed prior to the federal "Carbone vs. Clarkston" decision, declaring waste flow control "nationally unconstitutional." There were 35–40 private waste hauling companies in the Grand Rapids area, and with few exceptions, all were members of the GGRWDA, and all were FEI customers, delivering a large portion (many the majority) of their solid waste to FEI. It was **obvious** that WNI, BEI, and Kent County, had reached *some* type of agreement!

In 1990, things at FEI changed. During a routine groundwater sampling, the MDNR detected low levels (in the parts-per-billion range) of some contaminants, in a couple of the FEI monitoring wells, in a shallow "perched" water table (located on the banks of the Grand River). In spite of our explanation to the MDNR regulatory agency, that the parameters (contaminants) were substances which were not even present in the FEI leachate (liquid in landfill cells), and our arguments that monitoring wells placed between the edge of our landfill and the contaminated samples (in the direction of groundwater flow), were *non-detect* (**clean**), the MDNR would **not** renew our permit!

We presented the argument to the MDNR, that the FEI landfill cells were constructed in such highly impermeable clay, that it would take several hundred years for liquid to travel (under vacuum *which does not exist,*) vertically down through the seventy plus feet of clay, to the first aquifer. Our geologist explained, *also,* that the aquifer was under *high artesian pressure upward* (**to, and above** landfill cell bottom elevation), which meant that even if there ever was a crack in the eighty-mil PVC (poly-vinyl chloride) cell liner, through the two foot (ten to the minus seven) constructed clay liner (compacted to 95%), and through the seventy plus feet of natural (ten to the minus seven) clay, all the way down to the groundwater table, the landfill cell would experience groundwater *entering the cell,* not leachate or contaminates **escaping** the cell! Additionally, we pointed out that natural water samples taken from the Grand River, one-quarter mile *upstream* from the FEI landfill, had *higher levels* of the *same contaminants!*

Our further efforts at proving that our landfill was not the source of contamination (through the introduction of tracer dye into the landfill cells) were fruitless. Even though our monitoring wells, located *directly* on the downstream edge of our landfill cells, picked up **no** contaminants, and **no** tracer dye, proving beyond a **shadow of a doubt**, that our landfill cells were **not** leaking, and **proving** that our landfill was **not** the source of contamination, the MDNR would *not* budge! The **obvious source** of the contamination was the Grand River, and even though separate individual employees of the MDNR would admit so to us, and the MDNR's main geologist even stated (as we discovered years later), in a memo to her superior, "The (FEI) landfill is **obviously not** the source of the contamination," the MDNR was static in it's position.

The MDNR used excuses for dismissing our evidence, such as "the level of tracer dye in the landfill cells was not high enough," even though we (FEI) had injected *four times* the amount of tracer dye that the "*MDNR approved*" tracer dye plan required. Over the twenty-four years that Fenske Enterprises had been in business, we had always worked cooperatively with the MDNR, and I did not understand their rigid position.

On November 4, 1990, the MDNR issued a "Cease and Desist Order" to FEI, which closed our gates, stopped our cash flow, and put FEI in a desperate situation. No matter **what** solutions we presented, the MDNR was **determined** to keep FEI closed. I had to ask myself **why**! I believe there is a strong possibility that the two public companies (WNI, and BEI), my sister Karen (and her waste company), Kent County, and several politicians were all involved. With Kent County at the lead, all in the waste business certainly had plenty of financial reason to want FEI out of business.

As well as benefiting by the increased revenue at their own landfill, with FEI closed, WNI had an axe to grind with me personally, over WNI's failed attempt years earlier, to gain control of my CRRI (hazardous waste) site, and my reaction of filing a lawsuit against them. BEI, with the next closest landfill to Grand Rapids, enormously benefited (financially), with FEI closed. Kent County had more than a good reason to want FEI closed; it had a **need**. Kent County's $100 million mass-burn incinerator, without "flow control," was a financial "White Elephant," and the political "**heat**" was **immense**. Also **exceedingly curious**, was the fact that my sister Karen, with her *strong political ties* to the County Chairperson (who's brainchild had been the mass burn incinerator), sold her waste hauling business to one of the aforementioned public companies (for a purportedly *exorbitant* amount), shortly after FEI was forcibly closed.

My sister Karen never got over her anger that my parents would not acquiesce to her demands to control more of the family business, and for years after she quit working for FEI, she remained bitter, and cut all ties with the Fenske family. When my parents sold the business to me not long after she quit, I believe this further infuriated Karen, which prompted the gas to my house being shut off, fueled the lawsuit against my parents (the accusations against my father), and may have prompted her to take actions, which promoted the highly profitable sale of her waste business, as well as instigated the actions of the

MDNR, and it's determination to close FEI. I had no way at the time of proving my suspicions however, and the unreasonable stance of the MDNR, drove a viable business (without income) into bankruptcy, within one year.

I owned one hundred percent of the FEI stock, had signed guarantees on some of the huge loans for FEI recycling equipment, and this put not only my business, but also myself personally, and my family, in an ominous financial position. I could not **believe** or **understand** what was *happening,* after all of the environmentally **responsible** and **exceptional** work that FEI had done, and all of our plans to create By-Product Recovery Parks, and help the environment, as well as decrease our world's dependency on landfills and incinerators! This caught me *totally* off guard, and floored me like the *best* knockout punch ever delivered!

There is a lot of money in the waste business however, and it is **very** political. FEI competitors, the County of Kent, Waste National Inc, Benning Elliot Inc, and my sister Karen, were all highly politically connected. WNI, BEI, and Kent County, all with their own landfills (thirty to forty-mile round trips from Grand Rapids), and Kent County with its 100 million dollar incinerator, could not (financially) compete with FEI (with our strategic location, and technology), if FEI continued to exist.

Within a few months, repercussions of our immediate, nearly complete loss of cash flow began. We lost the new 62,000 sq. ft. MRF in a fire, six months after the "Cease and Desist Order." Without income, we had been unable to keep insurance premiums current, and our "State Of The Art" recycling center (MRF) was a total loss. My father lost his eyesight from a stroke, and eventually his life (from a second stroke), a few years later, I believe partially brought on by a broken heart, over what had happened to his life's work. This was too much for him to bear, after the pain, embarrassment, and anger, brought on by the sexual abuse lawsuit filed by my sister Karen (which was when his health really began to rapidly decline).

After the MRF fire, Kerri and I decided we should sell FEI. My first contacts were my friends, Stan and Linda Wasewska, who owned a private waste hauling company (White-Lake Landka), and their own solid waste landfill near the small town of White Lake, sixty miles North of Grand Rapids. Stan and Linda had a number of waste hauling accounts in the Grand Rapids area, and as I suspected, they were very interested. Their landfill was not near a large metropolis like FEI, and their own trucks hauled in the majority of the solid waste

Mother and Pappy, not long before Pappy died.

The smoke is intense as firefighters from several area communities battle the huge blaze which ravaged the Fenske Enterprises recycling facility in Walker.

Blaze still smoldering at ruined Fenske operation

GR Press Article—"Blaze Still Smoldering at Ruined Fenske Operation" received at their landfill. We were good friends, we got along well, negotiations went well, and had the sale progressed, I believe it would have been a good thing for all of us.

However, it was not to be. Stan's younger brother, who was very involved, and had a large part in running their company, lost his life as our negotiations were proceeding. He crawled down a (leachate line) manhole (on the edge of their landfill), to make some repairs early one morning. He was young (late thirties) and strong, and he and others had done this very same thing, on numerous previous occasions with no problem, but this time he was overcome by methane gas (commonly generated in landfills), which had traveled down the leachate drain line. Once he was discovered, several employees had to struggle to keep Stan from crawling down the manhole after his brother, until a rescue team arrived. Understandably, the tragedy sent Stan and Linda into a tailspin, and they had to back out. Kerri and I then found a business-sales realtor to sell FEI, and we signed an agreement.

The bank, which carried the debt on the CRRI property, very quickly put our note up for sale. My old friend Ed Handberk was a shrewd businessman, and kept his nose close to the ground on legal proceedings, like bank foreclosures, from which he could make a quick profit. When I found out that Ed had purchased the bank note on the CRRI property, I immediately called his office. I stated to him, "Ed, I understand you purchased the note on my property. I hope you know that I'm not going to let you walk off with eight million dollars worth of real estate, for a 1.2 million dollar note!" By Michigan law, I had twelve months to redeem the note. Ed responded, "Well Doug, I *assumed* that, but I thought we could work out a deal to develop the property as partners. Let's get together, and see if we can hash out an agreement."

A few days later, Ed and I met, and shook hands on a deal in which I would not redeem the note, Ed would carry the debt on the property, I would continue to own 115 acres to develop the "CRRI By-Product Recovery Park," and we would jointly develop the remaining 300 acres, and split the profit 50–50. The large industrial development of several hundred acres, called "Medowbrook," right across the road from the CRRI property, was already selling lots, the entire airport area was growing industrially, and the idea seemed quite feasible. We agreed to put our agreement in writing for signatures in the near future, but as we both verbalized, our deal was "set," and we shook hands on it.

A few months earlier, in July 1990, when everything was rolling smoothly with FEI, Kerri and I had been interested in purchasing a 2500-acre cattle ranch in Santa Barbara County, about forty miles north of Santa Barbara, near the small town of Los Alamos. Kerri and I both **loved** the ranch, and wanted to live there. We intended to keep our home in Santa Barbara, for weekends, etc., but we planned to spend most of our free time at the ranch. I was not cut out for "town-life," and Kerri loves the out-of-doors just as much as me. This was the first I had lived in town since college days, and even when in college, I was home on the farm, hearing the cattle "lowing" most every weekend. Whenever I am away from rural country, I miss the open space, and the comforting sounds of cattle *immensely.*

A Santa Barbara county realtor, whom we had searching for a ranch for us, attended church with the ranch owners (the Tatricks), and even though the ranch had not been on the market, our realtor knew that it could be purchased. Our realtor introduced us to the Tatricks, who seemed anxious to sell, and invited us to spend a weekend on the ranch with them. The price they were asking seemed reasonable, and we really thought that it was going to happen. The Tatricks "wined, and dined" us, seemingly interested in developing a friendship with us. Steve Tatrick invited me on a fishing/camping trip with he and some of his friends, and I also accompanied him in a two-man "dune buggy," on a grueling 500-mile cross-country race, through some incredibly wild, rugged country, in Baja California.

Kerri and I actually had very little in common with the Tatricks; however, there were things about Steve Tatrick that I enjoyed. When FEI received the "Cease and Desist Order," Kerri and I realized that we were no longer in a position to purchase a ranch, and we didn't want to leave the Tatricks hanging, so I stopped by to see Steve Tatrick, at his business office (United Funds Corporation) in the little town of Santa Ynez. I explained what had happened to our business, and that we were not going to be able to purchase their ranch, unless a business realtor we had signed an agreement with in Michigan, quickly found a buyer for FEI. Steve Tatrick told me that he was in the finance business, and that business sales were his specialty. He asked if there was any way out of the agreement we had with the business realtor. I informed him that we had a cancellation clause in our agreement, and he went on to offer that he could represent us in the sale of our business, and we could then proceed with the purchase of his ranch, with the closing on the ranch sale contingent upon a sale of FEI.

Steve Tatrick stated that he knew of a national waste disposal firm based in New York that would be interested in FEI. It sounded reasonable to Kerri and I, so we cancelled out on the agreement we had with the realtor in Michigan, and entered into an agreement with the Tatrick's, granting them a sizeable commission on the sale of FEI, as well as agreeing to close on the purchase of the ranch, when FEI sold. We put a $50,000 deposit (in escrow), on the ranch purchase, and went to work.

Steve Tatrick and I flew back to Michigan. I introduced him to key individuals at the County, the MDNR, the waste disposal industry, etc., and we worked together for weeks. Gradually however, Steve Tatrick began to seek more control, and became very resistant to my involvement, stating that he could do much better without my interference. When he soon came up with some very interested buyers (the company in New York), whom he introduced to me on a conference call, I began to have more faith in him, and I stopped insisting on my participation in every step.

After several months Steve Tatrick put together a seemingly good "Sales Agreement," which we signed, with the public firm "United Refuse Systems" (URS), of New York. The Sales Agreement specified that Kerri and I would receive approximately $43,000,000 (with all royalties), over a number of years, and the Tatrick's would receive an $8.5 million commission. Over the coming months, during which Steve Tatrick worked on putting the deal together with United Refuse Systems, I continually questioned him how he was progressing with putting the deal in writing, which Ed Handberk and I had shook hands on, regarding the CRRI property. Steve Tatrick continually stalled me off, with excuses of being too busy on the FEI/URS deal. **Finally**, when I threatened to come into Grand Rapids to put the deal with Ed Handberk together myself, Steve Tatrick told me, "Ed Handberk **won't** do a deal, and it won't do you **any** good to come into Grand Rapids; he's **out of town**." The amount of time I had left to redeem the note was waning, and even though I still had a few months, I started to smell a **Rat**!

I knew Ed Handberk pretty well, he was not the kind of person who would back out on a handshake agreement, and something seemed **amiss**. I got busy on the phone immediately. The "out of town runaround," that Ed's office staff-person (his cousin Glenn Handberk) gave me, did not work on me, and I was able to find out where Ed was staying, attending a convention in Cincinnati. When I finally got an answer in Ed's hotel room, at eleven PM that same night, I stated, "Ed,

why are you refusing to enter into the agreement we **shook hands on**?" Ed stated, "Whoa Doug, slow down a minute. Didn't you grant Steve Tatrick the redemption rights on your Cascade property?" I responded, "**No** Ed! Why would I hand over the rights to six and a half million dollars of equity to a **realtor**?" Ed came back with, "Well I *wondered* about that, but Steve Tatrick produced a document in which you granted him the redemption rights, so I already sold the property to Steve Tatrick, and a business associate of his named Doug Nagen."

Doug Nagen was a Grand Rapids businessman, who had been interested in my Cascade property for development purposes for some time, and had contacted me previously, unsuccessfully trying to purchase my property. He had a widespread reputation for being dishonest (I had refused to deal with him), so I guess it is no surprise that he and Ta*trick*, connected. **Stunned**, I shouted into the phone, "**Ed, you can't sell** you something that you don't **own**!" Ed claimed to have a check for $1.5 million ($300 thousand more than he had spent on the bank note), which Steve Tatrick and his business associate had paid him for the **$8 million** property. Ed claimed to have agreed not to cash the check for several months, until after my redemption rights expired, and he was then legally the owner of the property. Ed stated to me that Steve Tatrick had convinced him that he himself (Steve Tatrick) would redeem the note, unless Ed sold them the property, and that it was necessary to handle it this way for tax purposes. When I stated, "**This is going to court**," Ed, exclaimed, "**No**, *I don't want any lawsuit!*" Ed then agreed to meet me in Grand Rapids a few days later.

I flew into Grand Rapids three days later, upon Ed's return from Cincinnati. When Ed and I met, Ed produced the document Tatrick had presented to him titled, "ASSIGNMENT OF REDEMPTION RIGHTS (Absolute Assignment/Not For Security)," purportedly between Cascade Resource Recovery (me), and United Funds Corporation (Tatrick). After I reviewed the document, I stated to Ed, "There are two problems with this document Ed. Number one, **I've never seen it before in my life**, and number two, it's **unsigned**!" Ed replied, "Well that always **bothered** me, but Steve Tatrick told me that he had a signed copy back at the office." I exclaimed, "Well it should have *bothered* you Ed, because he **doesn't**!" I told Ed, "Either you enter into the agreement we shook hands on, **right here and now**, or this is going to **court**!"

Ed would not enter into a written agreement, even though I am certain Ed *knew* that I was being truthful. I had known Ed for over fifteen years by this time, and we did business with a lot of the same people. I had initiated with Ed, what eventually became the Ottawa Company Farms Landfill (which made Ed **millions**), and Ed **knew** me to be a straight-up guy. However, I believe that the 1.5 million dollar check from Tatrick and Nagen (with $300 thousand profit *to ED*) was burning a hole in his pocket. I also think Ed believed (because of my financial condition) that I did not have the ability to follow through on my threat.

A few weeks later, Kerri and I filed a lawsuit against all three parties, Tatrick, Nagen, and Handberk. We retained a law firm with a good reputation in Santa Barbara, which worked with another firm in Michigan. Handberk settled out early on, by paying a nominal fee. Although Ed Handberk had refused to return the check to Tatrick and Nagen, and follow through on the deal he had with me, I did not really believe that Ed had much guilt in what had transpired (just greed), and I needed the cash for attorney fees. United Refuse Systems became suspicious before very long, when they became aware of the fact that the owner of FEI had sued the realtor who had structured the URS/FEI purchase agreement, and URS backed out of our "Sales Agreement," refusing to close. They were *too incredulous* to continue.

I tried my utmost to clarify to the principles at URS what had transpired, and why I had filed the lawsuit, with no success. I explained that the lawsuit was in regard to Tatrick's actions on a separate parcel of property; it had nothing to do with FEI, or FEI's value, and would not effect our agreement in any way, but they were static. I later found out that one of the principles of URS had a previous relationship with Steve Tatrick, and as I had learned through my own experience, Steve Tatrick could be extremely manipulative and convincing. No matter how hard I tried, I could not put the deal back together with URS. They would not even discuss it with me. Fortunately for my friends however, a resulting sale of Stan and Linda Wasewska's company to URS did go through, and close.

Stan and Linda had been kind of rattled ever since Stan's brother died, and they were going through a lot of struggles with WNI in their own business. WNI can be ruthless in their pursuit of control, and had been hiring truck drivers right out from under Stan and Linda, by offering higher wages, start-up bonuses, whatever it took. As fast as Stan and Linda could put a new driver on, WNI would hire the new driver away from them. Stan and Linda were scared, and really wanted to sell and get out of the waste business. When I had first started negotiating with URS, and sold FEI to URS, I had lined up an introduction of the URS principals to them, and Stan and Linda did the same, selling their company to URS.

Stan and Linda were at first **furious** with Kerri and I, when we filed the lawsuit against Tatrick and Nagen, afraid that it might screw up their sale to URS, but they had only heard Tatrick's side of the story. When I explained why I had filed suit however, and showed them the fictitious document Tatrick had forged, in his attempt to steal the $8 million Cascade property from us, they understood. Kerri and I are happy for them that their sale was unaffected, and closed on schedule.

Similarly, I had introduced Steve Tatrick/URS to Bill Stark, and his partners. Bill and his partners were also shaken by what had happened to FEI, and very concerned over what the future held for them. Fortunately a favorable sale of ABME to URS was structured before we filed suit against Tatrick, and that sale was also unaffected, and closed.

After the FEI business had been closed for a few months, some FEI creditors (as well as vandals) began breaking in at FEI, and stealing equipment, which was one of the things that prompted us to file bankruptcy. My parents still lived on the farm property, with a lifetime residency built into the land contract (under which I had purchased the property), and what was happening was scaring and upsetting them. The lawsuit proceeded very slowly, and growing short of capital for attorney fees, with no end in sight, after about nine months I approached Steve Tatrick, to see if he was interested in a settlement.

I felt that he would have a better chance of putting the deal back together with URS than me, and he had a lot to gain. I *could not* understand why someone would risk losing an $8.5 million commission, to try to steal some property in the **first place**, but then I don't think like Tatrick. I have no idea what Tatrick's deal was with Nagen (on the CRRI property), and he could have been entitled to a sizeable portion, potentially several million dollars. My reason for trying to settle with Tatrick was this; even though what had transpired had cost us $6.5 million (equity on the CRRI property), if Tatrick's relationship with the principals at URS, allowed him to put the FEI property sale back together with URS, we would be better off then we would with continuing the lawsuit. We were out of cash, we had property taxes coming due, and if the lawsuit drug on too long, it could cost us everything. Unfortunately with our legal system, it is quite often the party with the most money who wins, regardless of who is telling the truth. In any event, we settled.

I have few regrets in life. I have always said, "Most of my regrets are the things I *didn't do,* not the things I *did.*" Not continuing this lawsuit is one of my regrets. I had hoped and believed that Tatrick could put the URS sale back together, and I guess that I was just scarred of losing everything. Tatrick and Nagen's settlement demands, including indemnity from future litigation were high, and we gave up rights to all but forty acres of the CRRI property. Since our CRRI permit was tied to the forty acres we retained, believing that it had the most value, I settled with them, holding them both harmless. I just accepted that I would have to downsize our planned "By-Product Recovery Park," from 115 acres, to forty acres. Neither Kerri nor my attorneys wanted to settle, but *regrettably,* I convinced them to.

A short time later, Kent County International Airport contacted us, wanting to purchase the forty-acre parcel we still owned at the CRRI site for a new North/South runway. The County purchased 180 acres of the 375 acre property, which Tatrick/Nagen received out of the settlement (at a significant premium over the price Tatrick/Nagen paid for it), and *of course,* Tatrick and Nagen had undoubtedly known *all along,* that this (runway) was coming. We refused to sell our forty acres to the County, for the "*average real estate value*" the County offered us, contesting that we owned an extremely valuable Type I TSD permit, and that we had plans to construct a "By-Product Recovery Park." I expressed that we would abandon our plans, and sell to the County, if the County would increase their offer significantly.

The County would not pay us any more than average real estate values, and sued us to force a sale. Kerri and I retained a Grand Rapids area attorney, and the case drug on for many months, accumulating debt. We requested a jury trial, not trusting any "County appointed judges," however we lost the case on the issue of "Eminent Domain" (the rights of the public, *the County Airport,* supercede private rights). Even though I tried to explain (when I was on the stand) how a "By-Product Recovery Park" would be of significant *value* to the public, it was no use. The jury awarded us a higher per acre fee than the County had been willing to pay, but nothing close to the value of a "By-Product Recovery Park," or even the true value of the property, and nowhere near what we had invested. When the trial concluded, we received just barely enough for the forty acres to cover attorney fees. The County eventually built its North/South runway, and 747's are now landing on the CRRI property, on which we had planned to build our "By-Product Recovery Park."

The settlement with Tatrick and Nagen was pointless, because Tatrick could *not* put the URS/FEI sale back together. URS apparently no longer trusted Tatrick either. To complicate things further, the bankruptcy court was now involved, and Tatrick was right back to his same old dishonest behavior. Working with the bankruptcy "Trustee," Tatrick attempted to force us into an unfavorable sale of FEI, which he and the Trustee had structured with BEI. The bankruptcy court was unable to force us to cooperate however, because I had purchased the land from my parents personally, and I had not personally filed for bankruptcy. Even though FEI was bankrupt, the court ruled *correctly,* that the landfill permit stayed with the land, and the land belonged to me personally. I had already *known* that Tatrick could not be trusted, but I had acted in *fear,* instead of *faith* when I settled. It has been a very hard and painful lesson for me.

For years we fought against the forced closure of FEI, like David, with his small stone against Goliath, until all of our savings were exhausted. We were fighting against an ever growing metropolis, and the unscrupulous actions of a county government (with the assistance of the state), so threatened by private enterprise, that it needed to squash its competition, to guarantee success. We had a farm auction on site (which broke my heart so badly, I couldn't watch), and we sold off all the cattle and farm equipment, in an effort to raise money to pay bills. I had only purchased the FEI business from my parents a few years earlier, and it was demoralizing to watch what it did to them, seeing a business deteriorate, which they (and I) had spent a lifetime building.

Kerri and I lost our home in Michigan, and we were barely able, through borrowed money and refinancing (to pay off FEI debt), to save our home in California. More than once, our home was slated to be up for sale on the steps of the Santa Barbara County Courthouse, and we redeemed it at the last minute. We struggled for eight years, trying to prove our case and reopen FEI, forcing Kerri and I into painful separations again. I stayed with my parents or other family members or friends, each time I came back to Grand Rapids (often for six-eight month lengths of time per stay). I spent much of the off-time that I had, with my friends Tom and Sally Moyers. After he left FEI, Tom took a job (managing used car sales) at a Grand Rapids dealership. He was able to line up transportation for me (free of charge) each time I was in Grand Rapids, and I repaid Tom and Sally in ways that I could.

On evenings and weekends, I helped Tom build a deck on their home, on a private lake south of Grand Rapids, and the three of us enjoyed many weekends together, bass-fishing, and playing golf, and I think of them often. They are good friends, and they helped fill up my idle time, but I missed Kerri terribly whenever I wasn't occupied. I was right back to my whole day revolving around my call to Kerri. Throughout that time we kept "Holding On" to the hope that we could turn things around, reopen FEI, and get our lives back on track.

I was unable to keep up child support payments to my ex-wife, which (in my divorce) had been set by the court at the highest legal rate, because of my income level at the time of my divorce. I had been extremely generous in my divorce, and I had willingly left my ex-wife very comfortable. Maybe I had some feelings of guilt (for giving up on a relationship that wasn't working), but I wanted my son Brandon to be comfortable, and I had left my ex-wife our home and property, our best vehicle, and all of our cash investments, and savings (which were substantial). My ex-wife was bitter over the fact that I had divorced her, but she was well taken care of, and she did not need the child support payments to live **well**.

Regardless however, in the state of Michigan, a "Bench Warrant" for arrest is automatically issued, once child support arrears reach a certain level. During a return visit to California, I discovered that a "Bench Warrant" had been issued for my arrest, and I knew that there was a warrant for me to deal with, when I returned to Michigan. My attorney (working on contingency, *since I was broke*) was able to convince the court to issue a "Quash Order" on the warrant, so that I could return to Michigan, and do the work necessary to sell FEI, and then bring my child support and other debt current, once the sale was complete.

Finally in 1998, with the assistance of the Governor's office, I was able to reveal evidence, which I had gleaned from the MDEQ files (*Michigan Department of Environmental Quality*, split off from MDNR, for waste regulation), through use of "FOIA" (the Freedom of Information Act). After I discovered the documents, I rang the Governor's phone off the wall, demanding to be heard. I presented the information at a meeting in the State Capitol, arranged (at my *insistence*), and chaired by the Governor's staff. The evidence (documents) **irrefutably** proved that the MDEQ was **well** aware that the FEI landfill "was *not* the source of the contamination," eleven months prior to the Cease and Desist Order, in written statements by the MDEQ's **own** experts, *advising* MDEQ "principals" to **reissue** (renew) the FEI permit, and allow FEI to **reopen**. The result of the meeting was a signed statement by the MDEQ (**ordered by the Governor's office**), dated October 14, 1998, admitting that the FEI landfill *"was not known to be causing groundwater contamination at the time of the Cease and Desist Order,"* and stating that the FEI landfill *"could be re-licensed,"* provided it was *"consistent with the County Solid Waste Plan."*

This became our "Catch 22." Kent County, FEI's **most vulnerable** competitor (with the $100 million debt, on the "Kent County Mass-Burn Incinerator"), had removed the FEI site from the "Kent County Solid Waste Plan." Kent County took this action, even though state law clearly **requires** counties to include "existing facilities" in county solid waste plans (which language I had previously been instrumental in having included). I had been **insistent** to the 200 member Act 641 "Rules Committee" (which I had also been a "Governor appointed" member of), that this type of language was "the *intent* of the Act, was *in the Act*, and was *essential,* or counties in the state like *Kent,* which were competing with private enterprise, would use 'County Plans' to eliminate competition." In spite of the language in the **State Law** (Act 641), Kent County removed the FEI site from the Kent County Solid Waste Plan!

Shortly after receiving the 10/14/98 letter, I met with Kent County Solid Waste Director "Curt Kempen," and explained to him (reading sections of the **law**) that it was *illegal* for Kent County to remove the FEI site from the County Solid Waste Plan. Curt Kempen stated to me that a plan-update process was currently under way, and that he would put me on the agenda, and I could address the "Solid Waste Planning Committee" at the next meeting, the following Thursday night.

I knew that I would need capital to get FEI up and running again, once it was "consistent" with the county plan and re-licensed, so I brought an interested investor, Larry Harmen (and his attorney), along with me to the meeting. Larry, whom I had known for many years, owned a local, sizable, private solid waste hauling company, and he had some landfill experience (having previously owned and operated a small solid waste landfill himself). We were a little early for the meeting, so we sat in Larry's car visiting, and preparing for the meeting. Within minutes of having pulled into the Kent County Public Works Building parking lot, I noticed two men approaching our car. One was an armed, uniformed police officer, and as soon as they reached our vehicle, they asked if one of us was Doug Fenske. When I affirmed that I was, the officer asked me to step out of the vehicle.

As soon as I did, the officer read me my rights, and proceeded to arrest me. I asked if I could get into my brief case, and present a "Quash Order" to the "Bench Warrant" I was being arrested under. When I did, the officer reviewed the "Quash Order," then presented a **new** "Bench Warrant" which had just been issued in the last few days, with no "Quash Order." Larry and his attorney sat speechless, as I was handcuffed, and hauled off to the Kent County Jail. It became **clear** to me, that the County had **no** intention of allowing me to make a presentation to the "County Act 641 Solid Waste Planning Committee," and expose the *illegal action* the County had taken, in removing the FEI site from the "County Solid Waste Plan." The Planning Committee would have had no legal recourse, but to reinstate the FEI site into the County Plan, which would have allowed the FEI facility to reopen. There is no *doubt in my mind* that Curt Kempen (with his superiors), had made the necessary phone calls, and had arranged for the **new** "Bench Warrant," and arresting officer to be waiting for me.

I spent the first night of my life in jail, and at a hearing the next day, my attorney was **unsuccessful** in convincing the judge to issue a second Quash Order. My attorney argued that I *needed* to be present to reopen my business, that the state had given FEI a "*green light*" to reopen, and that once I reopened my business, I could keep my child support current, as well as pay *all arrearages*. It was obvious by the ("**County**") Judge's demeanor, that someone had given him "*instructions!*" The once reasonable judge, who just weeks earlier had seen the "Quash Order," as a means of getting the child support arrears paid, was now taking an unreasonable stance. The judge issued a "Pay-or-Stay" (balance due in full) order, and sentenced me to the longest *45 days* of my life! There was absolutely nothing that I could do. There was no bail allotted, I had no way to raise the $40,000 total amount due (with all court fines, penalties, and interest), and I was forced to serve the full 45-day sentence (the maximum allowed by law). I was locked in a small eight-by-ten foot cell, with a single flat steel bed (no springs), small single steel sink, and stainless steel toilet, with no toilet seat (to avoid removal, and use as a weapon). I was issued one small face towel (which I used as a pillow), and one single thin blanket, under which I shivered on a bare thin mattress all night (the temperature is maintained at 55 degrees F. to keep inmates sedate), every night.

Inmates are only allowed to leave the cell for thirty minutes twice per day (at five AM, and five PM), to eat in the cafeteria. I quickly discovered that those last in the food line, frequently were not given time to eat anything, because most of the allotted thirty minutes were used up in line. Often the "Return to Cells" buzzer sounded, just as an inmate (near the end of the line) received his food plate, and he was required to scrape his untouched meal into the trash barrel, as he immediately exited the cafeteria. After listening to my stomach growl all night several times, I learned to be standing at my cell door, at five AM, and five PM, waiting for the auto-lock release sound. We were not given much to eat, (just enough to keep hunger pains at bay), which I learned to live with okay, but I really missed my morning coffee! The jail officials do not allow any coffee, even decaf, because coffee is a "stimulant," and "supposedly" could create fights, riots, and etcetera.

My arrest, and the hundreds of hours that I was confined, only *strengthened* my conviction that the County was very **threatened** by me, and was doing *all* that it could to stop me. It caused me to have grave doubts about our legal system, as well as exhausted the little remaining faith I had in politics in general. During my confinement, I verbalized what I had experienced, my opinions of county and state politics, and how those interacted with our legal system, to all open ears on my floor of the county jail. I gained the nickname "Governor," and was denominated, and referred to as such by fellow "inmates" (many whose faces I never saw), housed in cells in either direction, adjoining the cell in which I was locked. Often I received loud vocalized requests from sleepless inmates, as much three doors down the hall, "*Governor, tell us some more about **crooked politics**!*" Because it helped me to relieve some of my built up frustration, as well as pass the time, having the "floor to myself," I was more than happy to accommodate my "captive" audience, delivering numerous hourslong discourses, on into the night.

Since I was incarcerated, and "conveniently" unable to make my presentation to the Solid Waste Planning Committee, which would have assuredly (**based on law**) reinstated the FEI site, the County Solid Waste Plan update was completed, without the FEI site included. The MDEQ *of course,* would then not reissue an operating license to FEI, because FEI was "inconsistent" with the "County Solid Waste Plan." The "Catch 22" was complete!

What was done to FEI, and Kerri and me *personally* (**contrary to the letter of the law**) is such an "*injustice!*" I am confident that we could have legally challenged the County's action and won, however it seemed that no *local* attorneys were willing to file suit against the *County,* in which they practiced law, and had a vested political interest. Though we did talk to numerous non-local attorneys, Kerri and I were unable to convince an attorney to take the case on a contingency, especially since the case would be heard in a "County" court (ruled on by a "County" judge), and we were out of cash. We continued the struggle to reopen FEI for a couple more years, but by this time (having exhausted all savings), we were in the survival mode, "Holding On."

24

The Aftermath

By 1999, unable to pay taxes, and faced with a creditor (Derkstra Excavation) who foreclosed upon, and attempted to gain ownership of the FEI property, including the homestead where my parents still resided, we were forced to enter into a sales agreement on the FEI property. The sales agreement, which was on the largest, most valuable portion of the FEI property, was with a development company (Lane & Company), owned/operated by a neighbor, Paul Lane and his two sons-in-law in Grandville, whom although interested, knew nothing about the landfill business.

Paul Lane, who owns most of Lane & Company, had been an employee of my parents as a young man, trucking sand and topsoil. Paul had purchased, or inherited a trailer park in Grandville from his parents, built on the farm property he grew up on (right across the river from our farm), along with a hotel on the property (Lane's Inn), which Paul had convinced his parents to invest in. Being a good businessman, Paul (Lane & Co.) now owns numerous apartment complexes throughout the Grand Rapids area, as well as other places in Michigan.

Lane & Company experiences a sizable ongoing monthly landfill expense, from waste generated by their apartment complexes. Knowing the landfill business to be profitable, and the FEI real estate to be valuable, Paul had approached us, knocking on my parent's farmhouse door one afternoon. I had known Paul all of my life, and had previous favorable interactions with his two sons-in-law. One had been a town board member, in a Grand Rapids suburb town (Byron Center), a few years earlier, when DFCC had applied for land application permits (and he had ruled in my favor). Believing them to be trustworthy, Kerri and I entered into an agreement with them.

The "Purchase Agreement" (with lifetime residency to my parents, if they chose) included a profit share plan, if we were successful in reopening the site as a waste facility, and established a new property owner company, New Era (*Environmental Recovery Associates*) LLC, a name which Kerri came up with. The Purchase Agreement also included a development profits share plan, if we were unsuccessful in reopening the site as a waste recycling/landfill facility, and instead developed or sold the property for other purposes. Naturally Paul Lane (Lane & Company) was interested in developing the property with a large apartment complex (which was his initial reason for approaching us), and the Purchase Agreement included a profits share of rental income, if that became the case.

Paul and his sons-in-law put in some effort to reopen the FEI site (New Era) as a waste facility initially, by attending a couple of meetings (along with me) with the MDEQ in Lansing (which I arranged). They gave up on the idea relatively quickly however, when they saw resistance mounting, and realized the complications involved in amending the "County Solid Waste Plan," to re-include the FEI (New Era) facility. They then approached Walker City (numerous times), and encountered strong resistance to rezoning from Heavy Industrial, to Multi-family Residential (necessary for an apartment complex), and use of the property has been on hold.

Lane & Company, now aware of the vulnerable position that Kerri and I are in, refuses to honor the terms of our Purchase Agreement. Lane & Company has taken possession of the property (and claims ownership) through foreclosure, which took place *only* with our agreement. One creditor (Derkstra Excavation), which had performed physical work on the property (and as a result, had a "Mechanic's Lien" on the property) really wanted to own the property, and refused to accept a payoff.

Lane and Company offered that if Kerri and I would allow them to foreclose, this would give them a position over Derkstra Excavation, would force a settlement, and they assured us that they would then honor the terms of our Purchase Agreement. We accepted their offer, agreed to allow them to foreclose, and the plan worked well. However, Paul and his sons-in-law now claim to have no memory of our agreement, and they have no explanation of how they were able to foreclose with no resistance from us.

Lane and Company is aware that we are out of cash, and that we do not have the ability to force them to honor their commitments, or challenge them legally. My mother informed us, that the local newspaper soon ran an article explaining that Lane & Company even sold some acreage (five acres) on the property to an industrial user. A large FEI creditor, which was not paid off (by Lane & Company), as the Purchase Agreement required, attacked Kerri and I personally, and attempted to force a sale of our home in California. Our only option was to re-finance, and pay off the creditor, by attaching the debt to our mortgage. We now owe far more on our home, than when we purchased it in 1989, and we struggle each month to make the payments, "Holding On" to the one thing we still own.

Not long after we sold the property in Michigan, I moved the only remaining horse on the farm "Onyx" out to California. Onyx is a Quarter-horse/Arab cross, who was supposedly an eight year old (although he seemed too immature), when Kerri and I purchased him for Brandon's eighth birthday. We kept Onyx at the farm, however Brandon is not a horse lover like me, and whenever I was in California, Onyx didn't get much exercise, so after a number of years, we purchased Onyx from Brandon, and had him delivered to a stable just south of Santa Barbara, near Summerland. Though Onyx was not a young horse when we moved him to California, he was in great shape, and he has one of the best dispositions of any horse I have ever been around, so we decided he was worth the investment. While boarding Onyx at the stable near Summerland, I met an individual named Perry, who has become a very dear friend to both Kerri and I. He has helped us in our struggle, in any way that he has been able to, even helping draft letters, but most importantly by lending an empathetic ear. Unfortunately Perry's line of work keeps him out of town, and we don't get to see him often, but we hope that in the future, that will change.

After a couple of years, I moved Onyx to a stable on a large ranch up in the mountains, about forty miles north of Santa Barbara, near the small town of Buellton. I don't get up to ride as often as I would like, but I *love* it, whenever I do! There is a lot of "outdoorsman" in me, and this location provides some rugged mountain terrain for me to ride in. Many times I have taken Onyx up into mountainous country, with little more than deer trails to follow. It's very wild country, and I normally try to get back to some main trails before dark, how-

ever coming out at dusk one evening (a little later than usual), I spotted a mountain lion, crouching on a ridge about two hundred yards
above me.

I wasn't too concerned (being unarmed), because I was on horseback, and even if this was a rare mountain lion, that did not fear the
scent of man, we could most likely out-run or out-distance him if he
did attack. When I saw him come to his feet, shortly after we had
passed him however, with his tail nervously twitching, I became very
concerned. I noticed that he was looking at something behind me, and
when I turned around to see what he was looking at, there was **JT**, my
Jack Russell terrier! JT, who usually stays right behind us, had fallen
about a hundred yards behind Onyx and I. I spun Onyx around on a
dime, and galloped back for JT as fast as I could, shouting his name
as I did so! JT (who had no idea why I was so concerned) accompanies me every time I go for a horseback ride (JT and Onyx get along
great), and he loves to go along.

When I reached JT, I stretched down and grabbed him with one
hand, without even stopping or dismounting, and placed him cross-
ways between the saddle horn and myself, where he often rides

JT on Onyx.

(whenever his short legs become exhausted). I looked up and saw the cat (which had already started down the ridge), put on the brakes and crouch, as soon as I spun Onyx around to look up at him. It was clear that I had foiled the cat's plan for a Jack Russell sandwich! I rode the rest of the way back to the ranch, with JT **on** the saddle! From that day on, whenever it gets near dusk, I make sure JT is up on the saddle with me, and I keep a wary eye open for mountain lions!

We battled valiantly for over ten years, and tried many different approaches to right the wrongs we had suffered. We wrote letters to "Prime Time Live," "Dateline," "Twenty-Twenty," "MSNBC," "Oprah," "John Walsh," and numerous others, trying to spark an interest in our story. Although I was raised in a traditional "religion" (Lutheran), and attended conventional "Catechism" classes studying the Bible, I am not "religious;" however I do consider myself very "spiritual." I tried desperately to understand why we were experiencing all these struggles in our lives, and what I may have done to cause them. Over and over I have prayed and asked God why this has happened, and for a sign of what to do, or a direction, and though none has yet appeared clearly, I have faith that one will. I have always believed that everything we experience, everything that happens in life, happens for a reason.

In the early nineties, Kerri and I began attending "A Course In Miracles" lectures in Santa Barbara. "A Course In Miracles" is an approximately 1800-page book, transcribed (authored) by an individual (Neale Donald Walsch), who according to his writings had internal conversations with Jesus. The same author later (similarly) transcribed (authored) a second book titled "Conversations With God," and I have no doubt in my mind, based on the content, that the books are genuine. I *intently* studied both books, for years, filling notebooks with hundreds of pages of quotes, trying to grow, and understand what it was we were supposed to learn from all we were experiencing.

By the late nineties, Kerri and I started to read and study "The Power Of Now" (an incredible spiritual book) by Eckhart Toole. We have re-read The Power Of Now numerous times, and we continue to do so today, in our effort to improve our lives, and our understanding of life, along with another more recently published book titled "The Secret" by Rhonda Byrne. The Secret, featured on "Oprah," has helped me significantly, to understand and accept what we have experienced. The Secret, contains a statement "Mediocrity always attacks excellence or greatness," which I have found to be true, and this fact

often impedes progress for humanity. Not that there is anything special, or great about myself or Kerri, but what FEI was doing, and trying to do, was "Excellent," and was "Great," and would have
benefited mankind immensely.

I had planned for many years to make our story into a feature film,
including our rekindled relationship, and my return to boxing. I just
had no idea that our lives would take the twists they did, when I first
conceptualized doing so. Kerri and I both have always had an interest
in acting. I took some acting at Michigan State University, Kerri took
acting at Santa Barbara City College, and early on in our relationship
we took private acting classes together in Hollywood, planning to ful-
fill portions of our roles in our own film. For the last three years I have
taken private acting classes here in Santa Barbara, most recently
taught by a very talented professional actor/director Rich Crater, and
sponsored by a wonderful spirit, Tamara Root (a former professional
actress), who will always have a special place in my heart.

Tamara is aware of our financial situation, and having enough
faith in my abilities and me, has held most of my fees in abeyance.
I landed a part in a feature film "Notes From The New World," an
independent film (produced/directed by Vitaly Sumin), being shot
now, scheduled for release, 2011. My part is an interesting charac-
ter named "Homeless," who is an ex-boxer (go figure), and though
not a large role, is a very significant and interesting role. There is a
website regarding the film ("www.notesthemovie.com"), where one
can click on my picture and name (Doug Dane) on the coverpage,
and bring up my blog. *Update: Last scene filmed 4/30/09—"Wrap
Party" held 5/10/09—Final edit 2010*

I have developed a number of good relationships through acting. In
2007 I met and became friends with actor Spike McQueen (Fred
Spiker). Spike is from Detroit, and like his father (actor Steve
McQueen, *now deceased*), Spike migrated to Southern California as
an adult. Having both come from Michigan, Spike and I have similar
backgrounds, and interests. We are both interested in engines (Detroit
being the "Motor City"), and Spike (more adept than me) is good at
rebuilding them. In fact Spike recently purchased the rights to the
Hall Scott Motor Car Truck & Engine Co. I have helped him a little
(working on an engine), but I rely on Spike's experience, and mostly I
just twist the wrench where Spike tells me. Spike has an interest in
rebuilding old fire-engines, and we plan to make a trip back to Michigan together to visit our mothers (close to the same age), who both

reside there, and check out a late forties/early fifties model fire-engine that I have stored in a pole barn on the farm.

Finally, by July 2001, at Kerri's pleading, I agreed to drop the struggle to reopen FEI, and/or force Lane & Company to honor the Purchase Agreement, to get jobs, and to get on with our lives. I had to make a choice between yesterday, and tomorrow, and I chose tomorrow. Kerri obtained a "secure position," at a local college, just prior to 9/11/01. I did not, and I have tried continually, for the last nine plus years, to find a permanent position. I have worked temporary jobs as a tow truck driver, heavy equipment operator, dude ranch wrangler, and manual laborer, trying to sustain us. We have scrimped, and gotten by on **so** little, for **so** long, just barely making enough to make ends meet, and save our home. Finally, I decided that maybe the thing to do is to write a book, and tell our story. I started writing this, after work, on nights and weekends, and at times that I wasn't employed, with editing assistance from Kerri, whenever she could.

My father was a good man, who had worked hard all of his life. People loved my dad, and he had many friends, partially because he was never too busy to lend a helping hand. He died of a stroke in 2002, and although he had Alzheimer's, which had been progressing over the last few years of his life, he would have moments of clarity, even near the end. He knew that something wasn't right, and sometimes he would tap the sides of his head in frustration, and complain, "I just can't get my brain to *work* right!"

I was strolling around the perimeter of the farmhouse with Pappy, once in the later years of his life, when I noticed tears rolling down his cheeks. I questioned, "What's wrong Pappy?" My father responded, as he stared straight into my eyes, "I **remember you**! We used to work **so hard** together!" I said, "I know," and hugged him, as he briefly wept. The moment of clarity that he experienced that day did not last very long, but it was a **gift** to me, that I shall forever cherish! Life can deal out some cruel blows at times. I believe my father's deteriorating health, his Alzheimer's, and his death, were all brought on by the loss of his life's work (as well as the pain he suffered, from the lawsuit by my sister Karen). I had **so earnestly** wanted to be able to turn things around, and reopen and/or sell the business as an operating entity, while he was still alive. Maybe I was just "Holding On" to some impossible hope that his health would improve if I did so, but I wanted him to know (on some level) that we had *won* the battle, before he died.

Patty (kneeling) with Janice (sitting).

My younger sister Janice passed away in March 2005 of breast
cancer. Jan had a MS degree in Fisheries Management, and had
worked for the MDNR (Fisheries Division, *separate from the MDEQ*)
for 27 years. She was happily married to Kelley Smith (a fellow
MDNR Fisheries Division employee), who is well loved by all who
know him, and whom eventually became, and now is, MDNR Fisheries Division Director. Jan was also very well loved by all who knew
her, had received numerous awards for her accomplishments in her
work, and she was highly respected in her profession. Jan's breast
cancer had started out with one small tumor, which was discovered
early, but the tumor was inadvertently cut into during a biopsy; the
cancer got into her blood stream, and rapidly spread throughout her
body. Despite months of various treatments, the cancer spread to
other vital organs. Jan fought fervidly and courageously for a couple
of years, but finally succumbed. I loved Jan dearly, and I feel very bad
that I could not be there to help her. I had also wanted Jan to be able
to see things turn around in the family business, if for no other reason
than for the sake of my mother, to whom Jan was so close.

I am not sure exactly what to do next. Even though Kerri (who I
nicknamed "Sugarbabe") and I are struggling to get by, we have managed to keep our home, and though it is much in need of repair, we
still feel fortunate. We have our health, and each other; we have a

beautiful family, and we live a few blocks off the beach in one of the most beautiful cities in the world. At times, we can hear the waves roll in at night, and listen to the seals as they talk to one another.

Our lives are not yet where we would like them to be. We miss our dear grandson Sebastian so much since he and his father have moved away from Santa Barbara, and we deeply want to renew our relationship with him, but we accept that life happens on its own terms, and in its own time. We are no longer fighting to "right the wrong" we feel we have been dealt, but we are not defeated. Politics and big business appear to have won, however it was not the size of his stone, but the strength of his will, that brought David victory over Goliath. I am a very determined individual, and often in my life, I have repeated the statement, "It ain't over till it's over." In our hearts we know, it is the journey, not the end result that makes life, and to paraphrase Tom Hanks, in one of our favorite movies "Castaway," "Just wake up another day, and keep breathing, you never know what the tide will bring in." In the mean time, we will continue to work hard, maintain our conditioning, keep boxing, training, running, skating, teaching aerobics, enjoying our lives, and **"Holding On,"** to our *hopes*, our *dreams*, and our *enthusiasm!*

Kerri and Sebastian in Santa Barbara.

February 3, 2010

Bethany Burns/Channels

Student Sandy Badone, left, Instructor Kerri James-Fenske and Student Maria Napoli work out in the "Total Workout" class at the continuing education's Wake Center on Thursday.

Kerri teaching aerobics for SBCC, February 3, 2010.
(From article in Santa Barbara "Channels" newspaper.)

"I am grateful that Doug wrote this book, because I am now included in all the minutes of his life that I missed."

—Kerri James, 5/07/10

Afterwords

In 2007, I began communicating with, and developed a relationship with an individual in Southern California, Vern W. Woolf, PhD (now relocated to Cottonwood, Az) regarding an extremely effective process (known as Super-Plazma Arc), which generates energy (to be captured, and utilized), and converts non-recyclable waste materials (hazardous, and non-hazardous) into a state that will not harm the environment. The carbon ash residue from the process can then be utilized in a type of battery (known as an energy cell), which will power vehicles far more effectively than the type of batteries (lead/acid) currently in use. Kerri and I intend to develop a By-Product Recovery Park (re-named Remediation Park), including a Plazma-Arc Energy Center, at the former FEI site, and elsewhere throughout the world. I have been in contact with Lane & Company, and they will sell their interest in the property (now deeded to New Era) back to us. Our efforts continue, as this goes to publication.

In addition, through a mutual interest in boxing, I have become good friends with an attorney (William Poulis), who is assisting Kerri and I on a contingency basis. Bill Poulis put me in contact with a second group of individuals of Westlake Village, CA, who own a company named Remediation Earth Inc. (REI), which owns US rights to a process (pyrolysis, developed in Japan), which converts waste products into a liquid fuel, which can be utilized in conventional combustion engines. They are interested in our site in Grand Rapids; we have discussed REI potentially becoming a "tenant" in a "Remediation Park" at the FEI site (as well as elsewhere), and negotiations are underway.

SANTA BARBARA NEWS-PRESS   **SPORTS**   FRIDAY, MARCH 7, 2008

RECREATION ROUNDUP

'Sundance Dane' answers the bell

SBVC teams win tourney titles over weekend

ASSOCIATED PRESS

Santa Barbara boxer Doug Dane-Fenske is making a comeback — at age 59. The veteran Golden Gloves competitor says he'll square off against a 19-year-old in the L.A. Open Division finals on Saturday night.

Since his college days at Michigan State he's fought under the moniker "Sundance Dane," and his father, Howard Dane-Fenske, was a former pro heavyweight. Last year he broke his hand a week before Golden Gloves competition started, but says "this year I'm looking good at 59."

"One of the officials at the weigh-in last Saturday told me that he already had three calls," Dane-Fenske said. "'Is that old guy coming back?' I said, 'What old guy? They can't be talking about me!'"

FISHING

Local experts will share their knowledge on fishing for trout, bass, crappie and bluegill, as well as give pointers on saltwater fishing, casting, knot tying, fly fishing and Cachuma Lake at a workshop for adults presented by Neal Taylor at the Cachuma Lake Nature Center on March 29.

Pre-registration is recommended, as the workshop is limited to 50 participants. Check-in for the workshop is at 8:45 a.m. with presentations from 9 a.m. to 12:45 p.m. A fee of $5 for the workshop will be charged plus a park fee of $8 per car due at the entrance gate.

To reserve a spot, a $5 check should be mailed to the Cachuma Lake Nature Center, 2265 Highway 154, Santa Barbara, 93105.

Speakers at the workshop will include Bruce Vanderhoof, Mike Moropoulos, Dave and Barb Hale, Harry DeWitt, Judy and Kirby Duncan, and Melissa Kelly.

Assisting them will be Van Barr, Mike Buck, Dick and Lois Cofiell, Peter Dullea, Brenda and Lonnie Box, Sandi and Jerry Witcher, Patricia Martin, Susan Ham, and Linda Taylor.

A free registration (worth $30) to the Cachuma Lake Nature Center's 13th annual Trout Derby on April 19-20 will be raffled off.

The Santa Barbara Fish and Game Commission is underwriting the cost of this event, covering token bags of tackle for each participant. No equipment is needed to participate.

For additional information call 693-0691.

CYCLING

Echelon Santa Barbara members competed in last Sunday's Piru 20K Time Trial and came away with a few high finishes in tough conditions, including headwinds of 30-35 mph.

Dan Wesolowski was first in the Eddy Merckx category (for those not using standard, aerodynamic time trial bikes or aerodynamic helmets); Dylan Schuyler took second in the boys junior field; and Anna Roberts was 8th and Anne Chen was 9th in a very competitive women's field.

SKATING

The city of Santa Barbara's Parks and Recreation Commission is seeking applicants for the following Skaters Point Advisory Committee positions: youth skater (13-17 years of age), adult skater and community member.

The Advisory Committee is responsible for providing guidance to the Parks and Recreation Department on the operations of Skaters Point Skate Park. The committee meets every third Tuesday of the month at Casa Las Palmas, 323 East Cabrillo Blvd., from 6-8 p.m. Special meetings may also be scheduled. City employees are not eligible to serve on the Advisory Committee.

Applications outlining experience and/or education, background information, and interest in serving on the committee should be submitted to the city's Parks and Recreation Department. Applications are available at the Parks and Recreation offices at 620 Laguna Street, the Cabrillo Pavilion Arts Center, 1118 East Cabrillo Blvd., and online at www.SantaBarbaraCA.gov/home.htm. Call Judith Cook for more information at 897-1982.

Applications must be received by May 9, 2008.

FENCING

The Presidio Fencing Club fielded two teams at the Division I Southern California qualifiers in Pasadena last Sunday, and both won silver medals, qualifying them to the National Championships to be held in Portland, Ore., in April.

Chris Noyes, Tom Pingel, and Tim Robinson competed on the men's foil team, and Pingel and Robinson also fenced on the men's epee team, along with team-member Hank Lin.

VOLLEYBALL

Last weekend was a good one for the Santa Barbara Volleyball Club, with five teams winning tournaments. Four of the club's teams—the 18-Elite, 16-Elite, 15-Elite and 14-1s — are now competing in Division 1 of their age groups.

On Sunday, the 18-Elite team went 3-0 in the last of its qualifying rounds in Anaheim, beating Channel Islands, Long Beach 18-2 and Nevada Jrs.

"We got solid all-around play from Kristen Dealy," said coach Jason Donnelly. "Jane Hinkle seems to always give us a spark when needed. Her defensive energy was great all day."

Teams 17-1 and 18-1 also both went 3-0, and both will start the season in Division 5.

Team 14-1 moved up to Division 1 by winning six matches in San Diego, sweeping three matches in pool play before going 3-0 in the playoffs to win the tournament.

"The team practiced solid for three weeks with the goal in sight of getting into division one and it paid off," said coach KC Collins.

Team 15-2 moves up to Division 6 after finishing 3-0 in pool play.

Team 14-2 finished 1-2 to finish third and remains in Division 4. Team 13-1 placed second with a 2-1 record and also remains in Division 4. Team 15-1 remains in Division 3 after going 1-2 in pool play and 2-1 in playoffs.

SBNP article —"'Sundance Dane' answers the bell"

March 7, 2008, the *Santa Barbara News Press* ran an article on me that made the Sports Pages, "RECREATION ROUNDUP" headline, with the title "'Sundance Dane' answers the bell." March 9, 2008, I was awarded the S. CA Golden Gloves, Open Division, Cruiserweight, Runner-up Title. I suffered a shoulder injury and missed the 2009/2010 Golden Gloves tournaments, but I have healed, and I am back in training.

("You never know what the tide will bring in.")

Son Brian and his beautiful wife, Tricia. Married Oct. '09, now expecting their first child, due Nov. 2011.

CPSIA information can be obtained at www.ICGtesting.com
Printed in the USA
BVOW010339120911

270949BV00002B/4/P